THE NATIONAL ARCHIVES
OF THE UNITED STATES

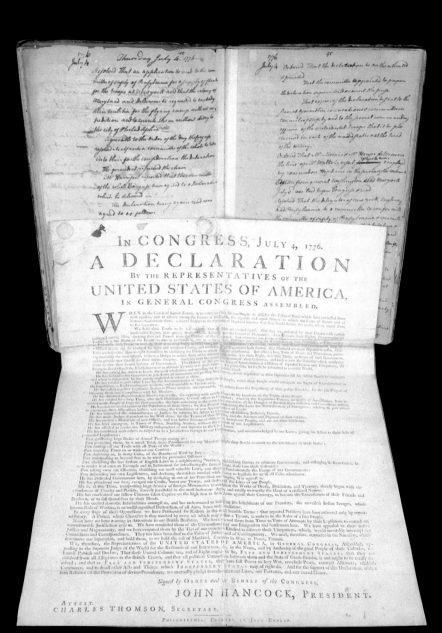

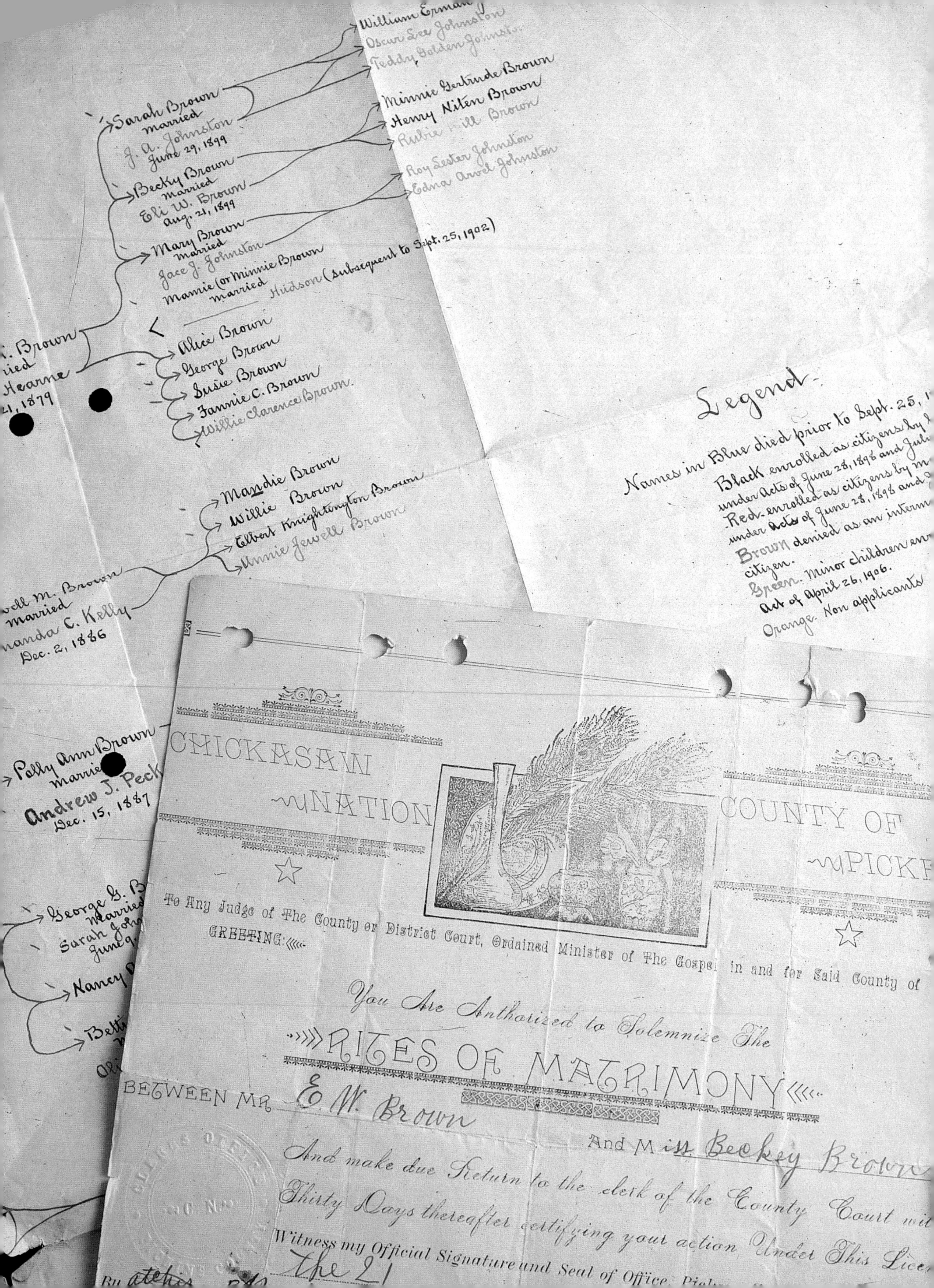

William Erman J.
Oscar Lee Johnston
Teddy Golden Johnston

Minnie Gertrude Brown
Henry Niten Brown
Rubie Hill Brown

Roy Lester Johnston
Edna Arvel Johnston

Sarah Brown
married
J. A. Johnston
June 29, 1899

Becky Brown
married
Eli W. Brown
Aug. 21, 1899

Mary Brown
married
Jace J. Johnston

Mamie (or Minnie Brown)
married
Hudson (subsequent to Sept. 25, 1902)

T. Brown
ried
Hearne
1, 1879

Alice Brown
George Brown
Susie Brown
Fannie C. Brown
Willie Clarence Brown

Maudie Brown
Willie Brown
Elbert Knightington Brown
Minnie Jewell Brown

well M. Brown
married
nanda C. Kelly
Dec. 2, 1886

Polly Ann Brown
married
Andrew J. Peck
Dec. 15, 1887

George G. B
Married
Sarah John
June

Nancy D

Betti

Oli

Legend.

Names in Blue died prior to Sept. 25, 1

Black enrolled as citizens by
under Acts of June 28, 1898 and Jul
Red enrolled as citizens by m
under Acts of June 28, 1898 and
Brown denied as an interm
citizen.
Green Minor children enr
Act of April 26, 1906.
Orange. Non applicants

CHICKASAW
NATION

COUNTY OF
PICK

To Any Judge of The County or District Court, Ordained Minister of The Gospel in and for Said County of

GREETING:

You Are Authorized to Solemnize The

RITES OF MATRIMONY

BETWEEN MR.   E. W. Brown
And Miss Beckey Brown

And make due Return to the clerk of the County Court wit

Thirty Days thereafter certifying your action Under This Lice

Witness my Official Signature and Seal of Office, Pick

the 21

By

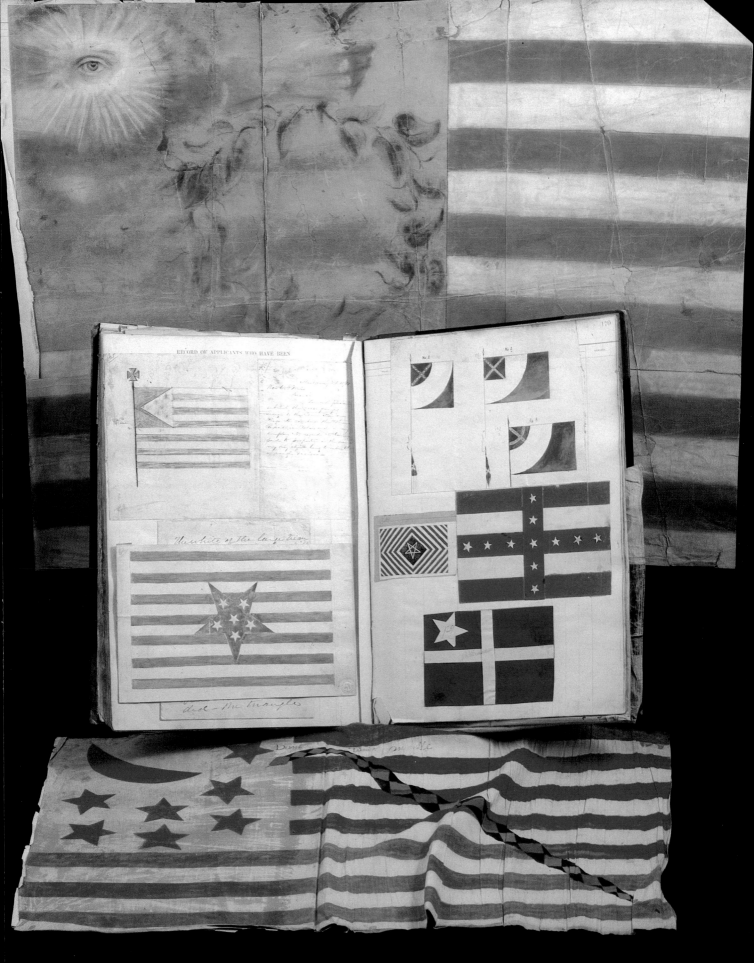

PASSENGER'S INSTRUMENT BOARD

PILOT'S INSTRUMENT BOARD

FIRE WALL

GAS TANK

U.S. MAIL - K

PASSENGER'S FORWARD BULKHEAD

PILOT W. C. HOPSON
AIR MAIL SERVICE
WINTER FLYING CLOTHES

MICHIGAN

ELKHART LAGRANGE STEUBEN

KIUSKO NOBLE DEKALB

Scale 7 miles

one inch

WILLIAMS FULTON

MACOUPIN DEFIANCE

JERSEY

WOOD

BOWLING GREEN

Mee-ne-doh-gee-fogh

Pee-wan-she-me-nogh

Wey-me-gwas

Gob-mo-a-tick

Che-go-nickska
(an Ottawa from Sandusky)

Sho-pe-ne-bu

Nau-ac (for himself
and brother Che-me-thet)

Ne-nan-se-ka

Ree-fass (or Sun)

Ka-ba-ma-saw
(or himself & brother
Chi-sau-gan)

Sug-ga-nunk

Wass-me-me
(or little pigeon)

Wa-che-ness (for himself
and brother Pendargof) Shok

Wab-she-caw-naw

La-Chasse

Chipawa's

Ottawa

Pottawatamies of the River Saint Joseph.

Ottawa's

Ne-gee-laugh-au.

Hah-goo-fee-kaw.
(or Captain Reed.)

Au-goosh-away.

Ree-no-sha-meek

La Molice.

Ma-chi-we-tah.

Tho-wo-na-wa.

Se-baw.

Mash-i-pi-nash-i-wish
(or bad bird)

Nau-sho-ga-she.
(on Lake Superior)

Ka-tha-wa-sung

Ma-fass

Ne-me-kass.
(a little Thunder)

Se-shaw-kay.
(or young ox)

Nan-guey.

Ottawas

Chipawas

nogh for
Wa-wa-Sek

go-maw.

win-

go-maw

nogh

nogh quoh

THE NATIONAL ARCHIVES OF THE UNITED STATES

HERMAN J. VIOLA

Original photographs
JONATHAN WALLEN

Foreword
ROBERT M. WARNER

Introduction
DAVID McCULLOUGH

HARRY N. ABRAMS, INC., PUBLISHERS, NEW YORK

Reprint 1987

Editor: Edith M. Pavese
Designer: Patrick Cunningham

Library of Congress Cataloging in Publication Data

Viola, Herman J.
   The National Archives of the United States.

   Bibliography: p.
   Includes index.
   1. United States. National Archives.
I. Title.
CD3023.V56   1984   027.573   84-2889
ISBN 0-8109-1367-4

Printed and bound in Japan

CONTENTS

INTRODUCTION

The building is colossal, imposing, even by the standards of monumental Washington. From Constitution Avenue a sweep of granite steps leads to a huge Corinthian portico, over which rises a massive stone attic. There are no windows to be seen, not a glimpse inside, only the main entrance with its tremendous, sliding bronze doors.

The architect was John Russell Pope, who designed the National Gallery of Art and the Jefferson Memorial, and his intention, plainly enough, was to convey feelings of permanence and grandeur. Yet the effect is more than a little forbidding. It might be the temple of some august secret order. Only those privy to the mysteries and privileges of Scholarship need enter here, you might conclude, and that would be mistaken and a shame. For the great collection of the National Archives is one of the wonders of our country, the richest, most enthralling documentation we have as a nation of who we are, what we have achieved, our adventures, and what we stand for. Everything within is about us, all of us, all the way back for more than two hundred years, in good times and bad. It is a momentous, inexhaustible story, on paper— no one knows how much paper—and on microfilm and electromagnetic tape, in big leather-bound ledgers and albums, in maps, drawings, and something over 5,000,000 photographs.

The three incomparable founding documents are the best known treasures. The Declaration of Independence, the Constitution, and the Bill of Rights are enshrined here, in heavy display cases in the marble rotunda inside the main entrance, and they remain, year after year, among Washington's principal tourist attractions. But here, too, is housed the Louisiana Purchase Treaty of 1803, that piece of paper by which, with a stroke of a pen, Napoleon Bonaparte signed over a territory larger than that of all the original thirteen colonies. Lincoln's Emancipation Proclamation is here. So is the Homestead Act. So is the instrument of surrender of the forces of Japan signed on board the battleship *Missouri* in 1945.

There is an old amnesty oath bearing the signature of R.E. Lee. There are the long, slim, pale blue ballots from the impeachment trial of President Andrew Johnson. There are the Nixon tapes.

Eli Whitney's cotton gin, Samuel Colt's revolver, Elisha Otis's elevator, Edison's light bulb are all to be found among the collection of original patent drawings. In a photograph from the Records of the Post Office Department, young Charles A. Lindbergh is seen loading cargo just before take off for the first air mail flight from St. Louis to Chicago in 1925.

Officially, the Archives is the storehouse for those federal papers and records judged to be of permanent value. With few exceptions there is no treaty or proclamation, no ordinance, act of Congress or amendment to the Constitution, no government document of importance that is not here. And to hold one of them in your own hands can be an experience you never forget.

I once made a special visit to the Archives, to the Records of the Department of State, to see the original Hay-Bunau-Varilla Treaty of 1903, the treaty which cleared the way for the building of the Panama Canal and which remained a bone of contention between Panama and the United States for another seventy-five years. There was no practical need to see the original—I knew what the treaty said—but I was writing about the peculiar circumstances under which it was signed and it was not until I actually held those neatly typed, very official looking pages, and studied the two signatures, of John Hay, the Secretary of State, and Philippe Bunau-Varilla, the Frenchman who had made himself Panama's envoy, that I felt a direct personal contact with that distant turning point. The sensation is not easy to describe and one that historians and researchers experience often in the Archives.

Such official documents are the landmarks of History with a capital H, history as it is usually understood and taught. Far greater in quantity and, to my mind, of even greater value to our appreciation and enjoyment of the past is the incredible documentary record of everyday affairs and of people who never ever imagined themselves as Historical.

It is in the census records, the ship manifests, the immigration records, land titles, military service records, applications for soldiers' pensions, public health records, tax assessment lists, and citizens' petitions that we touch the human reality of other times and feel the good common ground of the American experience. Conventional history by nature is extremely selective. It leaves out most of humanity. The ordinary almost never qualifies. Not so in the National Archives.

An album of photographs taken of the army's 1916 foray into Mexico to capture Pancho Villa is a rare chronicle of life in the ranks before our entry into the Great War. They are pictures I have pored over by the hour and will again. The Lewis Hine photographs of child labor, in the Records of the Children's Bureau, are among the most powerful historical documents I know.

But I like especially the old ships' passenger lists with all the names, with everybody accounted for—age, gender, occupation, baggage ("1 Bag Clothing" is the touching entry you find so often). Sometimes there are even physical descriptions and to come upon somebody you have been searching for—someone important to a story you are trying to piece together or one of your own kinsmen perhaps—is an enormous thrill and one waiting for anybody who wants to make use of all that is available at the Archives.

The feeling you have when working with this surpassing, national collection is that nothing and no one has been lost, that there is no anonymity. Each new fragment of information leads to something more, almost always, and the personal satisfaction, the education that comes with the search only increases the farther you go. What may have seemed at first a lot of mountainous dusty old paper—deadly stuff from the dead past—becomes vital evidence. You are caught up, carried forward by all the elements of surprise and fascination in detective work. You find things you were not looking for and these trigger new ideas that never would have occurred to you otherwise. It is what is called the serendipity of original research. The driving force is the excitement of

discovery. You feel a bond with those vanished people. They are not just anybody and nobody any more and they never will be for you ever again.

I am told that the majority of those who use the Archives are people doing genealogical research, personal family history. But it might also be said that everybody who comes here, whether briefly to look at the great documents enshrined beneath glass, or to work with the collections, is somebody who feels the kinship in all our history as a people. The collection is of us and it is for us. "This building holds in trust the records of our national life. . ." reads an inscription carved in one wall and it is that feeling of *life* that draws us here. That above all. We can never know enough about those in whose footsteps we follow. We will never tire of their stories. As much as has already been found in the records of our past there is still more to be found, much more.

DAVID MCCULLOUGH

THE TIES THAT BIND THE LIVES OF OUR PEOPLE IN ON
OLUBLE UNION ARE PERPETUATED IN THE ARCHIVES OF OUR
AND TO THEIR CUSTODY THIS BUILDING IS DEDICATE

ARCHIVES OF THE UNITED STATES OF AMERICA

$\mathcal{T}$he Fourth of July is the most American of holidays and in the city of Washington it is celebrated in grand style. At the National Archives there are inevitably long lines of visitors waiting patiently in the usual heavy heat of mid-summer to see a faded piece of parchment that they know instinctively represents what the Fourth is all about—and, for that matter, what this nation is all about. Their wait ends in the great rotunda of the National Archives where the Declaration of Independence is splendidly enshrined along with the Constitution of the United States. To be sure, some of these sweltering visitors are drawn to the Archives by the sound of gunfire from the mock battle between British and American troops waged in front of the building every Fourth of July. Some may be drawn by the sound of an actor's voice as he reads Thomas Jefferson's great words from the steps of the Archives. Others are attracted by the grandeur of one of Washington's most impressive buildings. But most of these Fourth of July celebrants come because of their sense of history and their respect for the documents that created this nation.

In the Archives of the United States are assembled the documents that are the essence, the spirit, and some would even say the soul of America. Here are the records that portray, sometimes tediously and sometimes graphically, the United States of America and its citizens. The Archives' three and a quarter billion documents comprise a unique historical record of a nation. Because it is the record of a democratic society, it touches in some way the lives of nearly every American, the living and the dead, the great and the humble.

Throughout the bulky volumes of the Census of 1790 and its decennial successors are the names of people from every part of the globe, names that represent the rich mosaic of the American people. The millions of military service records, the hundreds of thousands of pension claim files, the comprehensive naturalization and immigration records, also help to form a magnificent and remarkably detailed portrait of the American people.

The great events in our nation's history have left their documentary footprints here. The birth of the nation is recorded in the proceedings of the

Founding Fathers as they charted the course toward independence. Ornamented with fancy seals and protected in elaborate cases, the treaties that recognized our sovereignty, expanded our lands, ended our wars, and helped promote our commerce are preserved in the Archives.

The more routine work of government agencies can also be found in the National Archives, represented in utilitarian volumes or boxes, indexes by the yard, folded and faded correspondence, and efficient-looking carbons. Hidden in these prosaic sheets are the efforts, hopes, and fears of men and women who helped develop and expand the nation, fight its wars, and work for better health, education, and housing. These "ordinary" records too are part of the rich treasure of the nation's history.

Documents written by our chief executives are highlights of the course of American history. These documents, both the formal and informal, provide information on matters of national importance and reveal glimpses of the personal lives of our presidents and their families as well. They are included among the records of government departments in Washington and, for recent presidents, they provide the central focus for the presidential libraries.

The laws and lawmakers of our land have left their imprint on our nation's documentary heritage. The engrossed laws, those beautiful parchment sheets that are the final record of our legislators' work, are in the National Archives along with the reports of the debates that enlivened our ninety-eight Congresses and a rich assortment of the records of Congressional committees. Records of the Supreme Court, the Courts of Appeal, the United States District Courts and other federal courts can be found in the National Archives. In these court records is a rich store of documentation of Revolutionary War prize cases, admiralty disputes, criminal cases, and bankruptcies.

Not all history in the Archives is found in written records. Much of the fascinating story of the United States can be seen in maps that range from the carefully drawn work of the explorers who first saw the face of our western lands to the sophisticated cartographic results of modern technology. Products of America's inventive spirit too can be seen in the thou-

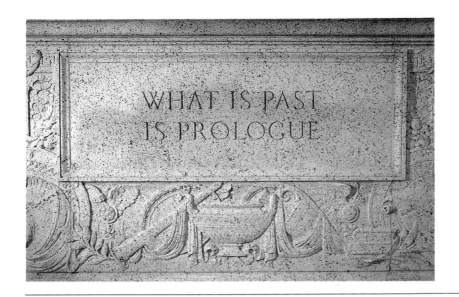

sands of patent drawings that mark great milestones in technological progress as well as catalogue the impractical ideas of obscure and long forgotten dreamers. More than 5 million photographs and 81 million feet of motion picture film in the National Archives give a fascinating visual glimpse of the panoply of events and people who have comprised the American scene from the Civil War through most of the twentieth century. The opening of the west and the crash of the stock market, Sherman and Lee and Lincoln, immigrants on Ellis Island, Depression-era farmers, and teens in bobby socks all continue to live through their images in the National Archives.

This volume is the first fully illustrated treatise to review the Archives and its rich holdings. Dr. Herman Viola has done his work with sensitivity and care. He was assisted in his challenging undertaking by dedicated volunteer docents and the capable staff of the Archives. This volume is a tribute to the knowledge and devotion of Dr. Viola and these associates.

The year 1984 marks the fiftieth anniversary of the National Archives. The scholars and national leaders who proposed and established this institution recognized the importance of a full and accurate record of a nation's government to ensure its people's continued liberty. The National Archives now holds such a record, but also much more. The National Archives of the United States tells the story of the American people and remains a monument to our democracy and its values.

We at the National Archives and Records Service hope that this handsome volume will encourage you to explore the rich historical resources of the Archives yourself, whether in Washington in the familiar grand building on Pennsylvania Avenue, in one of the fifteen records centers, or in one of the seven presidential libraries. In each of these facilities, the records of our nation's life are carefully maintained and protected. We hope you will use them. After all, these records belong to you.

ROBERT M. WARNER
Archivist of the United States

elcome to the National Archives, the nation's memory, where the Archivist of the United States and his staff hold in trust the documentary legacy of our past. To many Americans the National Archives is a place of mystery, difficult to penetrate, even more difficult to comprehend. We hope this book will erase some of the mystique, for the National Archives is a national treasure that belongs to us all.

Opposite: The Articles of Confederation, ratified March 1, 1781, established the first government of the thirteen independent states. The Articles are engrossed on six parchment sheets stitched together to form a scroll.

To begin with, the "National Archives of the United States" is the official title for that body of federal government records that are permanently preserved because they have historical or other research value. The National Archives is a massive neo-classic two-city-block building in Washington, D.C., and it is also a network of Presidential Libraries, Regional Archives Branches, and Federal Records Centers across the country. Its official institutional title is the National Archives and Records Service, and it is administered by the General Services Administration.

The mission of the National Archives is to identify and ensure the preservation of those records of the United States government considered to have continuing historical value so that they are available for use by federal agencies and the public. This may sound simple, but it's not.

The National Archives has undergone a remarkable transformation in the fifty years since its establishment. Before 1934, official records were controlled haphazardly, all too often inaccessible to the government and the public. Today, by contrast, the records of our government are among the most accessible of any nation in the world.

Each year the federal government creates some seven million cubic feet of records, of which only one to three percent are worth preserving. Identifying that historical nucleus is known as "appraising records," and for this process the National Archives relies on its most knowledgeable and senior staff members. From an agency's total accumulation, the appraisers select those records they consider important enough to preserve. Since the alternative is destruction, these decisions are irrevocable.

Most doomed records are not destroyed immediately, however. For legal or administrative reasons, many must be retained for a while. Tax returns,

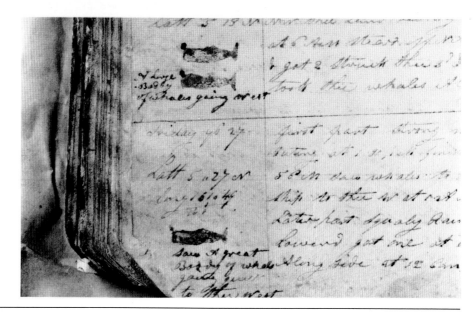

A detail of a ship log recording whale kills, one of hundreds collected by Matthew Fontaine Maury for his oceanographic studies.

Opposite: "Sea Letters," also known as "Mediterranean Passports," issued by the United States in the early years of the republic as a means of protecting its vessels from Barbary pirates, who had been capturing American ships, selling the cargoes, and either enslaving or ransoming the passengers. Thanks to a treaty signed with the Dey of Algiers in 1795, the Algerians agreed to accept sea letters such as these as official U.S. passports. Because of their ornamental engravings and scalloped tops, they were easily distinguished by Algerian ship captains, few of whom could read English.

for example, are kept for seven years. Each year's returns fill the equivalent of ninety railroad box cars. Obviously, all such material cannot be shelved in the Archives Building. It goes instead to a records center, a warehouse-type facility for temporary storage. There are thirteen of these centers around the country. One archivist describes them as a kind of purgatory where records "await their time, after which the good records go to the heavenly archives and the bad ones go to the flames."

The National Archives, through its records disposition program, tries to get rid of at least one million cubic feet of records each year, a goal it first reached in 1977. That year the total volume of federal records decreased from 34.2 million cubic feet to 33 million, the first significant drop in twenty years. Still, archivists are barely able to stay ahead of the on-rushing avalanche of records. The centers now hold about fifteen million cubic feet of records; government agencies hold about twenty-two million more. Unfortunately, the overall trend is still upward.

Information in documents considered to have continuing value, of course, is retained. Each year the quantity of these documents also increases. Since the National Archives Building has space for only about one million cubic feet of records, it became necessary in 1967 to locate some of them in an annex about six miles away. This facility now houses nearly thirty percent of all the records comprising the National Archives. Because still more space was needed to hold archival records, in 1982 the National Archives transferred maps, architectural drawings, and selected audiovisual records to a second annex in nearby Alexandria, Virginia.

The archives branches were established in 1968 for two primary reasons: to house records of continuing value created by regional operations of the federal government which contain information primarily of local and regional interest, and to deposit in these branches microfilm copies of records in the National Archives Building that would be of significant value to researchers residing near them. Records to be found in the branches vary from those created, for example, by the U.S. District Courts, Bureau of Indian Affairs, and U.S. Customs Service to documentation produced by

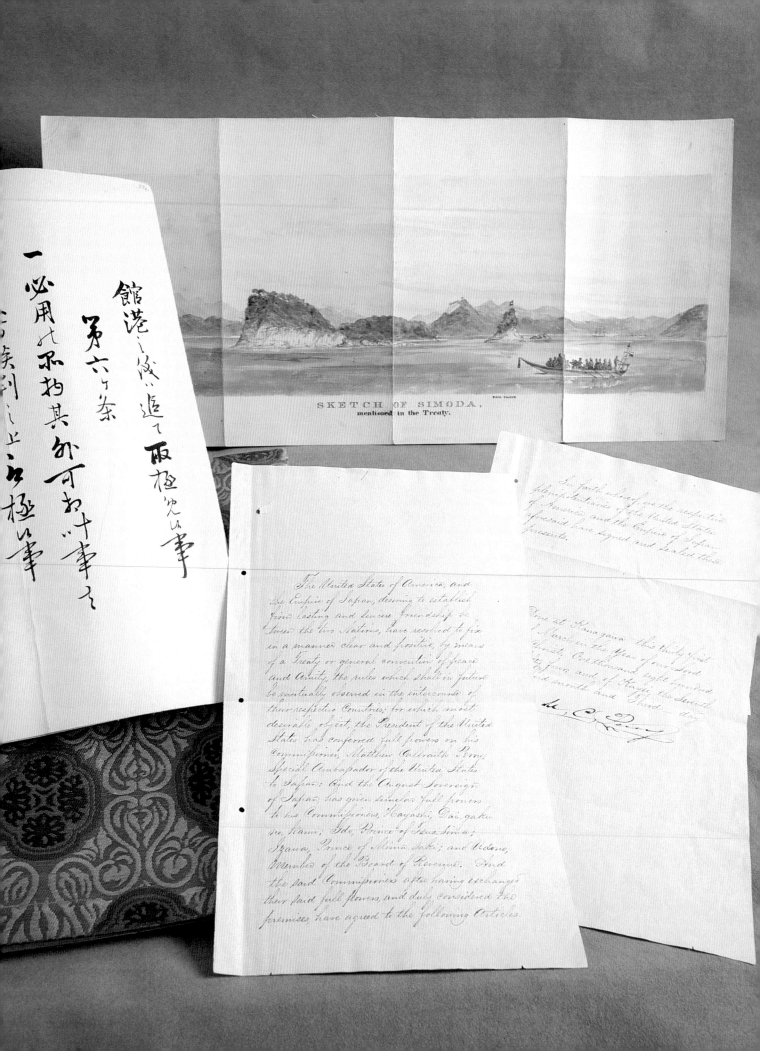

SKETCH OF SIMODA,
mentioned in the Treaty.

一 必用ハ不拘其外可相心事ニ
右実利ハ上ニ至極ハ事

第六ヶ条

館港ニ候追テ取極ハ事

The United States of America, and the Empire of Japan, desiring to establish firm lasting and sincere friendship between the two Nations, have resolved to fix in a manner clear and positive, by means of a Treaty or general convention of peace and Amity, the rules which shall in future be mutually observed in the intercourse of their respective Countries; for which most desirable object, the President of the United States has conferred full powers on his Commissioner, Matthew Calbraith Perry, Special Ambassador of the United States to Japan; And the August Sovereign of Japan, has given similar full powers to his Commissioners, Hayashi, Dai-gaku no Kami; Ido, Prince of Tsus-Sima; Izawa, Prince of Mima-saki; and Udono, Member of the Board of Revenue. And the said Commissioners after having exchanged their said full powers, and duly considered the premises have agreed to the following Articles.

In faith whereof we the respective plenipotentiaries of the United States of America and the Empire of Japan aforesaid have signed and sealed these presents.

Done at Kanagawa this thirty first of March in the Year of our Lord Jesus Christ, One thousand eight hundred and fifty four and of Kusje, the Seventh year, third month, and third day

M. C. Perry

the Bonneville Power Administration, the Tennessee Valley Authority, or the government of Samoa. Although most of these records were already housed in the records centers in which the archives branches share space, some were transferred from the National Archives Building because they related closely to records in those branches. In fact, the regional branches now hold about nineteen percent of all of the government's archives as well as microfilmed copies of such valuable source material as the Papers of the Continental Congress, nineteenth-century diplomatic correspondence, and the census population schedules from 1790 through 1910.

Not all the material the National Archives acquires ("accessions" is the official term) is immediately open to public research. The use of some records might be exempt from release by provisions of the Freedom of Information Act or because they contain national security information. The periods for restricting use vary from situation to situation.

Accessions are not limited to those received from federal agencies. The National Archives accepts some gifts from private citizens and organizations. Through the eight Presidential Libraries, it solicits the personal correspondence of individuals closely associated with a president, like that of Harry Hopkins, the confidant of F.D.R. Accessions also occasionally occur because of chance discoveries of federal records that somehow escaped government custody.

In 1979, members of a Presbyterian congregation in Falls Church, Virginia, found videotapes marked "Office of Equal Opportunity" in the garage of a home they had purchased for their minister. Their inquiry to the National Archives launched an investigation that led to the recovery of two hundred videotapes produced nearly a decade earlier as part of an experimental project titled "Experiment in Democracy." During the Lyndon Johnson administration, the O.E.O. videotaped interviews with residents in six rural communities across the country, who were asked to express their views about food stamps, school lunches, and other anti-poverty programs. It was believed that the airing of extreme positions on videotape could soften the hostility that often developed during face-to-face discussions of these

Opposite: The Japanese and American versions of the Treaty of Kanagawa, signed March 31, 1854. The treaty was negotiated by Commodore Matthew C. Perry, whose celebrated expedition to Japan opened the island empire to the western world. In the background is a watercolor by one of the expedition's artists.

Opposite: Among the thousands of patent drawings from the nineteenth century in the National Archives collection is this amusing one for a convertible bedroom piano.

issues. Since program officers interviewed people from all social levels and ethnic backgrounds, the tapes are virtual time capsules of these rural communities. When the Nixon administration moved to abolish the O.E.O., members of the staff took records home for safekeeping. One of them had owned the house in Falls Church where the first batch of tapes was found.

The tapes were clearly government property, but did they merit saving? In this case the appraiser was film archivist Jane Lange. Her decision was not difficult to make. The project had been innovative; the tapes documented public reaction to government nutrition and poverty policies; and they represented a significant example of the use of an audiovisual medium as a tool of community interaction. By all means, the videotapes deserved preservation.

Their importance established, the tapes still posed serious archival problems. Many were in poor condition, having been stored in a less than ideal environment. Furthermore, the tape stock was obsolete; merely finding a machine to play them had been difficult. For the tapes to be useful to researchers, archivists would have to transfer them to a more standard format, thereby ensuring their preservation. Happily, the staff solved these problems, and today sixty-five videotapes from this unique experiment are in the National Archives and available to researchers.

As the example of the videotapes shows, accessioning records is a considerable commitment. The credo of the National Archives is "here today, and here tomorrow!" There are two basic methods of ensuring the availability of documents to future generations of Americans: one is to transfer the information to another medium, if the material is easy to duplicate or the copy will be more permanent than the original; the other is to coax the longest useful life from the original by retarding its deterioration.

Unfortunately, deterioration can never be completely stopped, merely slowed. The basic threats to the life of paper are light, oxygen, humidity, pollutants, mold, heat, and insects. Archivists try to prevent unnecessary exposure of papers to light, especially to the ultra-violet rays of the sun and to fluorescent light. Stable atmospheric conditions—ideally an aver-

Charles Hess.

2^{52}
N° 56.413.

PATENTED
JUL. 17 1866

Convertible bed room piano.

56,413.—COMBINED PIANO, COUCH, AND BUREAU.—
Charles Hess, Cincinnati, Ohio.
I claim a combination of piano, couch, and bureau, arranged
and operating substantially as represented and set forth.

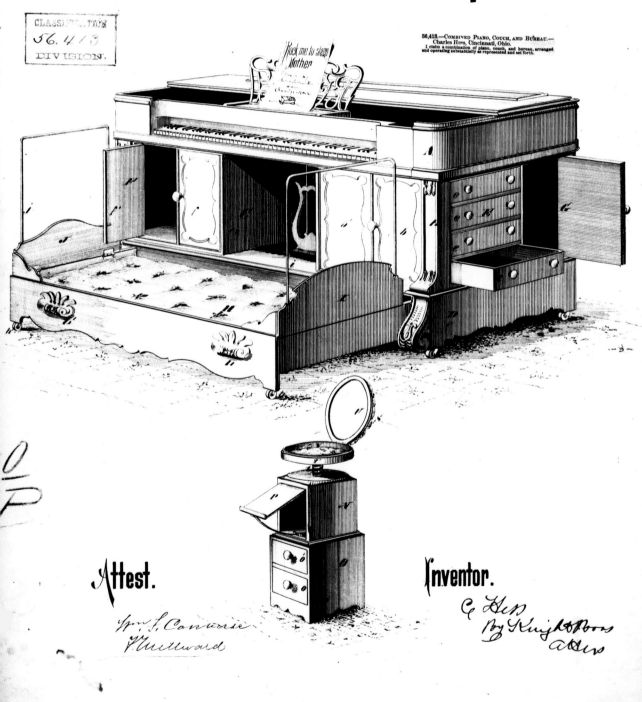

Attest.

Wm. S. Converse
T. Millward

Inventor.

C Hess
By Knight Bros
attys

age temperature of about 68 degrees fahrenheit and a relative humidity of about fifty percent—combat both brittleness and mold or mildew. To kill mold and insects, staff technicians fumigate paper records before shelving them in the Archives Building. Then processors unfold them, to relieve stress on the creases, and place them in acid-free folders and boxes for safe, long-term storage. The acid content of paper is a leading contributor to its deterioration; folders free of acid protect the documents from additional contamination and provide a more neutral environment.

The more important the documents, the more elaborate are the procedures taken to protect them. The documents that have received the greatest attention of conservators are, of course, the Declaration of Independence and the Constitution.

Each type of record—whether tape, film, photograph, or paper—has its own characteristics and requires its own kind of care. Maps, usually oversized and colored, are encapsulated between thin sheets of polyester film and then stored flat in uncrowded drawers. Films, photographs, tapes, and similar materials are often reproduced onto permanent, stable media, an expensive and time-consuming procedure.

Because of sheer bulk (more than three billion separate sheets), paper records pose the greatest preservation headaches for the Archives. Since space is expensive, archivists are presently evaluating the benefits of transferring paper records onto microfiche, microfilm, or another reduction process.

Present practice at the National Archives is to retain the paper record as long as possible. Even modern paper, which has a short life span compared to parchment or eighteenth-century rag, will last many decades if left untouched in a cool environment and acid-free container. Use, however, accelerates deterioration. Some valuable documents could be ''used'' into oblivion if the National Archives did not require researchers to use microfilm copies. This is particularly true of census records and some military service records, which are in great demand by genealogists. After records are once microfilmed, the originals are retired from circulation. Their

Archivists dusting records from the Veterans Administration, 1936.

Opposite: Most of the nineteenth-century records received when the National Archives opened for business were contained in vertical wooden files, the invention of E. W. Woodruff. These Woodruff files proved, however, to be inappropriate as containers for records because the folded documents eventually tear along their creases.

microfilming serves the dual purpose of providing a user copy on a different medium and of saving the originals from excessive wear and tear.

Records, once received and cared for, must be made available to the public. Archivists call this "reference service"; it is a job at which the National Archives excels. To quote Winston Churchill: "Never have so many owed so much to so few!" Each year 450 archivists and archives technicians are called upon to assist more than 200,000 researchers at the main building, the Archives Branches, or the various Presidential Libraries. This same staff, moreover, responds to over 250,000 written inquiries from researchers who do not come in person.

Noted scholars have used the National Archives' resources to write a multitude of well-known historical books and articles. But the scholars are not the major users of our records. All sorts of people use them, people whose research may be of little interest to anyone but themselves—students writing their master's theses, army veterans seeking information about their old units. Most are people who hope to fill out their family trees, and genealogists form by far the most numerous and dedicated clientele of the National Archives.

New users of the research facilities at the National Archives are often puzzled by the absence of subject indexes or card files like those in a library. The reason is simple: an archives is not a library. While a library houses books, which can be classified by subject, an archives houses the raw materials from which books are written. These materials are voluminous and complex, and no catalog scheme would be adequate for the diverse research demands of the future. The intellectual management of the records is instead determined by their origin, in accordance with two archival principles: provenance and respect for the integrity of the files.

Archivists, as far as possible, preserve the original order of records. They believe that to regroup papers—by subject, for example—would destroy their organic character as evidence of the ordinary business of the office and would consequently diminish their value for research.

This system is more demanding of the researcher than the familiar card

William Henry Jackson's photograph of a plank bridge over the Beaver Head River at Point of Rocks, Idaho, 1871.

Opposite: Sitting Bull, the Sioux chief instrumental in the defeat of the Seventh Cavalry at the Battle of the Little Big Horn, later toured with Buffalo Bill's Wild West Show. So many people wanted his autograph that he learned to write his name. Although this letter to President Grover Cleveland was written for Sitting Bull by another member of the troupe, the old chief signed it himself.

September 3, 1983, marked the bicentennial anniversary of the signing of the Treaty of Paris, which officially ended the American Revolution. Before the treaty could be displayed in the Exhibit Hall, however, it required the attention of conservators. For example, the treaty had been reinforced with silk that had become weak and brittle. During the conservation treatment, the personal wax seals of the signers—John Adams, John Jay, Benjamin Franklin, and David Hartley—were consolidated, the weak silk was removed, and the tears mended.

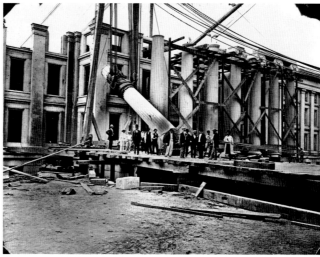

catalogs. In fact, before coming to the National Archives, patrons must do their homework—the background reading and library research that define how the subject may have had contact with the federal government. The archivist can locate records that will be of value to the person who says: "I am working on a biography of General Philip Sheridan, and I am especially interested in his activities as head of the Western Department of the Army following the Civil War. He held that post from 1866 to 1867." The same archivist cannot pinpoint records for the visitor who says: "I have to write a term paper about a famous military figure. What does the National Archives have about cavalry leaders of the nineteenth century?"

The success of archival research often depends on the archivist. The computer has not yet been invented nor the finding aid devised to replace a person who has spent years working with a particular group of documents, arranging material for microfilming, writing inventories, and answering public inquiries. Each sifting of the documents makes the archivist more knowledgeable about what they contain.

What sort of person is an archivist? There is no type. Their ages, personalities, training, and approaches to archival work are diverse, although most of them are historians and most find satisfaction in handling original materials like letters from the pen of Thomas Jefferson or glass-plate negatives from the camera of Mathew Brady. They also share a sense of mission: to keep the documentary legacy of our country safe for future generations of Americans.

The service of these people is exceptional. Without archivists at work caring for our nation's documentary heritage there would be no National Archives. It would be, instead, a warehouse stuffed with paper, useless to both the federal government and the American public.

Two special functions carried out under the aegis of the National Archives do not fit into the activities so far described. The National Historical Publications and Records Commission, created in 1934 along with the National Archives and first staffed in the 1950s, promotes the publication of authoritative texts of papers which, in its estimation, contribute most fully

Above, left: Among the photographs in the National Archives is a series of the Washington Monument under construction. This photograph shows the massive footings required to support the monument, which is 555 feet tall and exerts a pressure of nine tons per square foot on the ground beneath it.

Above, right: Typical of the magnificent construction photographs found among the records of the Public Building Service is this one by Lewis Emory Walker taken in June 1862, which shows workers using a block and tackle to position a stone column in the facade of the U.S. Treasury Building.

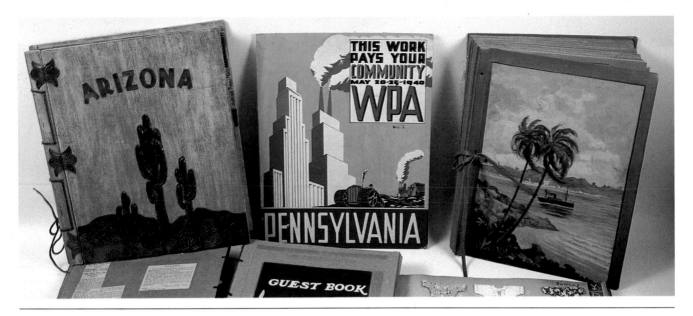

In 1940 the WPA Professional and Women's Project sponsored a nation-wide celebration of the non-construction activities of the Works Project Administration. As documentation, the directors of the Professional and Service divisions in the states were asked to prepare a scrapbook containing copies of press releases, souvenirs, dinner menus, speeches, photographs, and other materials. Many are embellished with elaborate covers and examples of needlework and crafts.

Opposite: The deed of gift for the Statue of Liberty, a Centennial present from France to the American people.

to an understanding of America's history.

Another significant organization within the National Archives is the Office of the Federal Register. In 1934, legal scholar Erwin N. Griswold protested the haphazard way in which the federal government promulgated its administrative rules and regulations. "It seems scarcely adequate to say what we find is chaos," he wrote. "We have recently seen the spectacle of an indictment being brought and an appeal taken by the government to the Supreme Court before it was found that the regulation on which the proceeding was based did not exist."

Griswold expressed the frustration of lawyers, businessmen, and plain citizens at the lack of an orderly system for publishing federal administrative "law." He appealed for the creation of "some regular and systematic scheme of publication."

Broad support for his position paved the way for passage of the Federal Register Act of 1935. A new office in the National Archives was created and began issuing a daily *Federal Register* on March 14, 1936, which has been published ever since for every federal working day. It carries proposed federal rules for comment by the public, as well as final rules and a wide range of official notices of government activities and actions. The Office of the Federal Register also compiles and edits the *Public Papers of the Presidents*, the *United States Government Manual*, the *Code of Federal Regulations*, and other official periodicals. It also receives the state ratifications of Constitutional amendments and, every four years, the Electoral College votes for president.

To place all this in perspective, let's compare the National Archives to the average family. Every family acquires and saves papers which it must find when the need arises—birth certificates, college diplomas, wills, deeds, receipts, insurance policies. Then there are those papers and things kept for sentimental reasons—family photographs, letters, the odds and ends of a lifetime of memories. If yours is a typical family, storage is a problem. A prudent household separates its papers: important documents are placed in a safe-deposit box; papers of temporary value may be kept in a house-

A L'AMITIÉ SÉCULAIRE DE LA FRANCE ET DES ÉTATS-UNIS

L'an mil huit cent quatre vingt-quatre, le quatre Juillet, jour anniversaire de la fête de l'Indépendance des États Unis.

En présence de Monsieur Jules Ferry, Président du Conseil des Ministres, Ministre des Affaires Étrangères, Monsieur le Comte Ferdinand de Lesseps, au nom du Comité de l'Union Franco-Américaine et de la Manifestation nationale dont le Comité a été l'organe, a présenté la statue colossale de "La Liberté éclairant le Monde" œuvre du statuaire A. Bartholdi, à son Excellence Monsieur Morton Ministre plénipotentiaire des États Unis à Paris, en le priant d'être l'interprète des sentiments dont cette œuvre est l'expression.

Monsieur Morton, au nom de ses compatriotes, remercie l'Union Franco-Américaine pour ce témoignage de sympathie du peuple Français; il déclare qu'en vertu des pouvoirs qui lui sont conférés tant par le Président des États Unis que par le Comité de l'œuvre en Amérique représenté par son honorable président, M. William M. Evarts, il accepte la statue et qu'elle sera érigée par le peuple Américain, conformément au vote du Congrès du 22 Février 1877, dans la rade de New-York en souvenir de l'amitié séculaire qui unit les deux nations.

En foi de quoi on a signé :

Au nom de la France.   Au nom des États Unis.

Au nom du Comité
de l'Union Franco Américaine.

UNION FRANCO AMÉRICAINE

1776   1876

WASHINGTON

LAFAYETTE   ROCHAMBEAU

G. Washington

			York	Lawful
1776	By amᵗ broᵗ forward £200		£2676.7.9	
Aug.	By Cash from the Pay:		300	
Oct 9	master Genˡ . 1000 Doll		2976.7.9	
	York Curʳ. redᵈ to Lawfˡ £.50 —	£200 —	150 —	
	Amount of the Money		£3126.7.9	
	recᵈ from the Public			
	in the Years 1775 & 6			
	By Ballᵈ due G. Washington		599.19.11	
	& carrᵈ to accᵗ for 1777 *			
			£3726.7.8	

* This Ballᵈ arises from the Expenditure
of my private purse. — from which (as
doth appear from the dates of the public debits against me) my outfit to
take the Command of the Army at Cam-
bridge — The Expences of the Journey
thither — and disbursements for some
time afterwards, were borne — It being
money which I brought to, and rec
at Philadelphia while there as a De-
legate to Congress, in May & June 177

G. Washington

Left page (partial):

...ed States... ...

	York	Lawful
...ard	£772.18.4	2757.12.4
	.2.11	150 —
...Capᵗ.500		6
...tures		
...20 Doll		
£4.6.0 Pay		3.8.10
.17.2	5.10	
Sundry times		
...ed Messˤ		6
...ch Expen		
...Expences		
...Caryand		
...Octʳ & part		
...ile Capᵗⁿ		
absent with		217.13
...p accⁿ		
725½ Doll 6/		
	£780.19.4	3140.13.4
...redᵈ to Lawful	195.4.10	585.14
...tures of the		£3726.7.0
...s 1775.&6 —		

...Curry, Extended at Lawful £7.11.5

	£4.0.0	4.4.0
		6.10.5
Deduct		£3719.17.3

hold working file; items of sentimental value are kept almost anywhere, in a shoe box, a shirt drawer, perhaps a trunk or attic. From time to time, usually when the family moves, the material is reviewed and sorted. Some things are thrown out, others are kept a while longer.

The United States of America is, in a sense, an extended family comprising some 220 million persons presided over by the federal government. To store the "family" records, the government depended on the shoe box and shirt drawer approach until 1934, when the National Archives was established. The National Archives is our safe-deposit box. In it are kept our vitally important documents. A specially constructed vault protects our birth certificate (the Declaration of Independence) and our coming-of-age papers (the Constitution and the Bill of Rights) as well as the other records that document our "family's" growth and development. Most of the household files are in Records Centers, where those of temporary value are stored for a while and then thrown out; those of permanent value go to the National Archives. As for things in the attic, all components of the National Archives and Records Service have a small share. In the Presidential Libraries, for example, you can find gifts encrusted with jewels from foreign potentates as well as more humble mementos like the Declaration of Independence reproduced in noodles from alphabet soup.

Like many attics, the National Archives Building even has a ghost. Its presence is sworn to by security guards and cleaning personnel who have encountered Thaddeus, as they call him, when on duty in the wee hours of the morning. According to common belief, Thaddeus came into the building long ago, probably with a shipment of records. Somehow or other he got separated from his "possessions" and he has been wandering the building ever since, trying to find his identity. In this respect, Thaddeus is very much like the thousands of Americans who come in daytime hours to search the "family" papers for their own and their nation's history. Perhaps, after reading this book, you will wish to join them.

Opposite: While serving his country during the American Revolution, George Washington refused a salary, but he did permit Congress to reimburse him for his expenses, which he carefully recorded in this account book.

BUILDING THE ARCHIVES

*O*ow the National Archives came to be, how it evolved into an institution that serves the needs of the government, the scholar, and the private citizen, is a story of struggle and determination. The tale begins with the first Continental Congress and Charles Thomson, the patriot-scholar. Since then the archival baton, as in a relay race, has passed from hand to hand.

Opposite: The pediment of the National Archives Building.

Now considered the godfather of American archivists, Thomson in 1774 was a merchant returning to Philadelphia from his honeymoon when his carriage was met on Chestnut Street by a messenger, who told him the Continental Congress requested his presence. Thomson hurried to Carpenter's Hall where the delegates were assembled. "Deep thought and solemn anxiety were observable on their countenances," he recalled. Thomson walked to the podium, bowed before the president, and told him he awaited his pleasure. "Congress desires the favor of you, sir, to take their minutes," came the response. Thus Thomson became Secretary of the Continental Congress and America's first archivist. He served throughout the Revolution, until a permanent Union of the states had been formed. His legacy comprises 518 bound volumes of records and miscellaneous papers, the archives of the United States from 1774 to 1789.

Between 1774 and 1800, during the Revolutionary War and its unsettled aftermath, the federal records moved with the Congress eleven times. With the establishment of the government in the new capital on the Potomac it was expected that the papers would be relocated permanently. But the British advance on Washington during the War of 1812 brought a wild scramble for carts, wagons and river barges to haul the government and its records to safety. The White House and the Capitol were burned, but all of the important documents were saved. Left behind were a few military manuals and copies of a treatise on drum-beating, which the Inspector General considered "of no material consequence."

Although these frequent moves led to some loss of records, they were not a significant source of destruction compared to what occurred later. One government official in 1911 reported finding "thousands of volumes

Some records of the War Department as seen prior to their transfer to the National Archives.

of papers . . . stored in places so damp that the water, oozing from walls and ceilings . . . [had] so covered them with mold that the titles could not be read." Stamp collectors and autograph dealers stole many valuable documents, and some villain removed with a razor the signatures of such giants of American history as John C. Calhoun, Henry Clay, and John Quincy Adams from a volume of original letters. One government official is known to have sold 400 tons of records as scrap paper to make room for his office staff!

Worst of all have been the losses to fire, the principal curse of archives. The new capital city possessed not one fireproof building and procedures for fighting fires were hopelessly inadequate until the mid-nineteenth century. Even President Jefferson was seen lugging water buckets during a fire in the Treasury in 1801.

The government had scarcely settled into Washington when a fire in the War Department building consumed all its records except one ledger listing land sales. The 1801 fire at the Treasury damaged the records of the auditor's office. In 1833, fire destroyed the Treasury building as well as the Secretary's correspondence. Some years later, most of the Navy Department's records were lost to fire. The Post Office and Patent Office (which shared quarters) had their turn in 1836, when all the patent drawings and models were consumed. Again, in 1877, fire destroyed 60,000 patent models. The District of Columbia fire marshal counted 250 fires in government buildings between 1873 and 1915.

As early as 1810, prodded by Representative Josiah Quincy of Massachusetts, the House appointed a committee to investigate the condition of public records. The committee found "all the public records and papers . . . in a state of great disorder and exposure; and in a situation neither safe nor convenient nor honorable to the nation." Quincy noted the inadequate storage of patent drawings and models in the Post Office building. "Gentlemen might laugh at it and call it a gimcrack affair," he declared, "but it is the depository of the genius of the country."

His concern was echoed by President Jackson, who told Congress that

Above, left: Records of the General Accounting Office following a fire.

Above, right: Records of the Bureau of Indian Affairs in the basement of a government building. The water on the floor caused the containers to disintegrate.

Left: Fire is always a threat to archival treasures. The show-cause order served on James Madison, a key document in the celebrated case of *Marbury v. Madison*, bears the scars of the Capitol fire of 1898.

John Franklin Jameson, the eminent historian, editor, and educator, who spent more than twenty-five years as leader of the campaign for the National Archives.

Above, right: The National Archives Building by architect John Russell Pope, who designed it in the classical style "to harmonize with the Capitol, the White House, the Treasury Building, and the Lincoln Memorial." The exterior's dominant feature is the colonnade, fifty-two feet high, on each of the four facades.

"the expediency of a fireproof building for the important books and papers of the Post Office is worthy of consideration." Three years later the Secretaries of War and Navy advocated fireproof buildings for the safety of public records. "The most valuable documents," they asserted, "are now deposited in several private buildings, which have repeatedly been on fire; and which, notwithstanding every precaution for safety, cannot but be considered as liable to the most serious accidents."

But repeated warnings were ignored. When the Post Office was rebuilt after the fire of 1877, the Secretary of the Interior admitted that the new facility was better than the old one in design, but that it offered no security from fire. The wooden roof, he warned, was already charring where it touched "the defective flues it covers."

In 1878 still another proposal was made for a separate fireproof building to store government records. Montgomery C. Meigs, Quartermaster General of the Army, with the approval of the Secretary of War, recommended the construction of a "cheap building, perfectly fireproof, as a hall of records." He suggested a one-story structure with an open courtyard, in its center a tall water tower, ready to fight a fire if necessary. One part of his plan anticipated developments at the National Archives Building many years later: Meigs proposed that the open courtyard could be roofed over if the space in the original building should prove inadequate. President Hayes liked the idea and twice recommended it to Congress in his annual message. "Every paper worthy at any time to be recorded and placed in the public files," he pointed out, "may be of value at some future time, either in a historical, biographical, or pecuniary way, to the citizens of the nation."

Despite presidential interest, no hall of records came into being. After a War Department fire in 1881, the Senate finally passed an archives bill, but the expiration of the Forty-sixth Congress prevented its consideration by the House. Undaunted, the proponents pressed their efforts, introducing forty-two archives bills in the House or Senate between 1881 and 1912. All failed to pass. In retrospect, perhaps this discouraging course of events was for the best. The archival advocates had in mind only a warehouse for

When it learned that this century-old landmark—Center Market (here in 1914)—had to make way for the National Archives Building, the *Washington Post* on December 22, 1933, commented that "dignity is coming to Seventh Street, to the very spot where Bermuda onions once flourished and they grated horse radish while you waited."

safe storage. None showed awareness of the other equally important purpose of an archives: the administration of its holdings to serve the government, scholars, and the public. Ironically, the "Rebel Archives," records of the Confederacy that the federal government reconstructed and used in post-Civil War litigation, was the only example of the modern concept of archives administration in nineteenth-century America.

Near the close of the century, however, the baton of concern for archives was again picked up, this time by a small group of capable and dedicated scholars. Its two leaders were John Franklin Jameson, editor of the *American Historical Review*, and Waldo G. Leland, his student and colleague. Jameson, a nationally recognized scholar and chairman of the Historical Manuscripts Committee of the American Historical Association, realized that a place to safeguard government records was necessary before researchers could use them efficiently. Thus, the founding of a national archives became his passion. He persuaded the American Historical Association in 1899 to create a commission to report on archival problems. Later, as director of the Carnegie Institute, he authorized Leland and an associate to compile the monumental *Guide to the Archives of the Government of the United States*, published in 1904. This work presented the sordid conditions of the federal records to public scrutiny.

In 1908 the Executive Council of the American Historical Association complained that the lack of public provisions for the "orderly keeping of . . . public documents" made them "unavailable for historical work." It appointed a committee of distinguished historians to remind the president and the Congress of the importance of an archival establishment, "for researches into American history." Its members were John B. McMaster, Alfred T. Mahan, and Jameson, the committee's *force majeure* for twenty years.

Jameson knew the ways of Washington. He was willing to call the building an archives, a hall of records, or anything else Congress would agree to build. He was confident that in time the professionals who would preside over the result would create a true archives. Therefore, he concentrated his

No. 95   Taken Nov-2-193
The Archives Building
Washington, D. C.
John Russell Pope, Architect
George A. Fuller Co., Builders

efforts on pressing Congress to construct an archives building. His efforts, supported by a variety of historical and patriotic societies, were almost successful. In the final days of the Taft administration, Congress passed the Public Building Act of 1913, authorizing the Secretary of the Treasury to have plans and specifications prepared for a fireproof National Archives building to cost not more than $1,500,000. These plans, however, were not to be developed before the designers had studied the arrangement and construction of the best modern archives building in Europe.

Unfortunately, Woodrow Wilson, who succeeded Taft, was not the patron of archives that one might expect a scholar to be. Jameson feared the worst. "We shall have to see whether an Executive Order 'Let there be an Archives, W. Wilson' will be potent with the [next] Congress," he wrote Leland. "I am afraid when it should get through [the Congress] it would emerge in the shape 'Let them Archives be.'"

Wilson was not put to the test, because World War I intervened. America's entrance into the War in 1917 stopped official consideration of the project for almost a decade.

For once, however, circumstances helped the archives advocates. Because of the war, the volume of government records increased at an incredible rate, driving officials almost mad in their efforts to find space for both their staffs and their files. They stored documents in attics, basements, closets, and even abandoned doorways. Then, on January 11, 1921, a Commerce Department fire burned census records dating back to 1790 and virtually wiped out the entire 1890 census. Housed in a basement on wooden shelves, the census records were, according to a newspaper account, kept

A view of the Great Hall during construction.

Opposite: Architect John Russell Pope designed the Great Hall, like the exterior, "in monumental proportions" to give the public "a proper realization of the significance and importance of the building itself as a complete record of the history of the National Government."

Two of the medallions, each eight feet in diameter, that adorn the upper facades of the National Archives Building. These two, designed by sculptor Robert Ingersoll Aitken, symbolize (*above, left*) the Department of Justice, represented by a figure holding statute books and the "reins of guidance," and (*above, right*) the Department of Agriculture, represented by a young man clutching a sheaf of wheat and a sickle.

"in ideal conditions for total destruction." What did not burn was damaged by the water that flooded the basement. The loss was tragic, but it brought Jameson's campaign influential new support from the American Legion and the Hearst newspapers.

This revival of interest coincided with a need for the construction of federal buildings to house the expanding government. The Public Building Act of 1926 (which brought to reality the dreams of L'Enfant, George Washington, and other Founding Fathers for the capital city) included among the projected structures a National Archives building.

Two sites were lost to other development before the final decision to tear down Center Market for the archives was made. A city landmark for more than a century, the market was also called the Marsh Market because Tiber Creek, tamed into a canal in 1869, sometimes flooded the area. (The Tiber still flows under the National Archives; in fact, in the early years, its waters were used for an innovative cooling and heating system for the building.)

Bordered by Seventh and Ninth Streets, Pennsylvania and Constitution Avenues, halfway between Capitol Hill and the White House, the site was ideal. At the laying of the cornerstone on February 20, 1933, President Hoover waxed eloquent. "This temple of our history," he boasted, "will appropriately be one of the most beautiful buildings in America, an expression of the American soul. It will be one of the most durable, an expression of the American character."

John Russell Pope, the architect, took literally his commission to create a building in harmony with its federal neighbors and yet appropriate for its intended function. He chose the popular neo-classic style. For economy's sake, a limestone façade replaced the more costly granite originally planned. The change did no esthetic damage. Strong lines and simplicity serve as

a background for telling detail. Seventy-two Corinthian columns ring the solid rectangular building. At the main entrance are massive bronze doors, each weighing six and one-half tons and measuring nearly thirty-nine feet high, ten feet wide, and a foot thick. Impressive bas-relief sculptures overlook Constitution and Pennsylvania Avenues. Their symbolism was dictated by Pope, who insisted that the work be allegorical rather than realistic, "in view of the classic spirit in which the design of the building was conceived."

The central figure in James Earle Fraser's pediment facing Constitution Avenue is the "Recorder of the Archives" seated on a throne. Surrounding him are rams, representing parchment, and papyrus plants, representing paper. Beside him is Pegasus, the winged horse, a symbol of aspiration. Two groups present documents to the Recorder: one, documents of literary and historical value; the other, records of lesser significance. The dogs at each end symbolize guardianship.

Adolph Alexander Weinman's pediment faces Pennsylvania Avenue. "Destiny" is the dominant figure, his throne supported by two eagles, one representing the national emblem and the other courage. Two genii bearing the "Fire of Patriotism" rise behind him. On the left of "Destiny" is a group symbolizing the "Art of Peace." On his right is another symbolizing the "Art of War."

Thirteen large medallions decorate the upper portion of the building symbolizing the Senate, the House of Representatives, the ten major departments of government, and the Great Seal of the nation. The last mentioned was originally designed with some artistic license, but one member of the Commission of Fine Arts objected. Egerton Swartout thought the medallion should be accurate. "These suggestions may be mere quibbles,

and the answer might be that the medallion is up so high that no one could make it out very well with a spy glass," he admitted. "Still, the thing is eight feet in diameter and in Washington they have spy glasses as well as dusters."

Even more useful than "spy glasses" would be a classical education and a good imagination, because interpreting the elaborate sculptured allegories of the façade is essentially left to the observer 150 feet below. For the four statues at street level, however, chiseled inscriptions help explain the symbolism. Facing Constitution Avenue is Fraser's "Heritage," a woman holding a child and a sheaf of wheat. The pedestal bears the inscription, "The heritage of the past is the seed that brings forth the harvest to the future." Opposite her is "Guardianship," a male figure whose inscription warns, "Eternal vigilance is the price of liberty." Beside the Pennsylvania Avenue entrance are two figures by sculptor Robert Atkin. One, symbolizing the Past, is a man whose pedestal admonishes, "Study the Past." Opposite him, a woman representing the Future proclaims, "What is Past is Prologue."

Few quotations are better known in Washington than "What is Past is Prologue," words from Shakespeare's *The Tempest*. The National Archives named its scholarly journal *Prologue*. President Eisenhower, accepting the Republican nomination in 1956, told the story of a newly arrived government worker who noticed the inscription when passing the Archives in a taxi. Knowing Washington cab drivers can answer common questions about the city, he asked what it meant. "Oh, that!" the driver replied. "That's just bureaucrat talk. What it really means is—You ain't seen nothing yet."

Pope designed the interior of the building to match the monumental exterior. From the Constitution Avenue portico, the great bronze gates open into the semi-circular Exhibit Hall with its seventy-five-foot half-domed ceiling. Pope intended this chamber for the display of documents having "particular" public interest. He expected these to include the Great Charters of American freedom: the Declaration of Independence, the Constitution, and the Bill of Rights, then in the custody of the Library of Congress. On

Above, left: Construction of the National Archives Building began in 1931. Although the contract specified completion within two years at a cost of no more than five million dollars, the building required six years and twelve million dollars to complete. Part of the problem, as this photograph shows, was the swampy condition of the site.

Above, right: Construction of the building had scarcely begun when it became obvious that Pope's inner court space, intended for future expansion, would be needed immediately. Work on the interior decking, begun in December 1935, was completed within two years.

Opposite: Ringing the Archives Building are seventy-two Corinthian columns, each fifty-two feet high, which, like the sculptural decorations, were carved on the site.

the walls are murals by the painter Barry Faulkner. One, entitled "Declaration of Independence," portrays Thomas Jefferson submitting that Great Charter to John Hancock; the other, James Madison submitting the Constitution to George Washington. The lighting in the Exhibit Hall, necessarily dim to prevent the deterioration of the documents, produces a cathedral-like ambiance. Many visitors, in fact, refer to the Hall as "the Shrine," which it is—a shrine devoted to American freedom.

Pope knew that his building had to be more than a showcase. It had also to protect, preserve, and provide access to the permanent records of the federal government, protecting them while making them accessible. His original plan had several functional components: the Exhibit Hall, an administrative unit consisting of stacks and offices, and an inner court that could eventually be enclosed as the space was needed for the storage of records.

The administrative unit required rooms for receiving, cleaning, repairing, and accessioning records as well as offices, research facilities, a library, and an auditorium. Stack areas had to be self-contained for fire protection. To protect the papers, proper temperature and humidity levels had to be maintained; a building-wide air-conditioning system was needed. In the early 1930s, this technology was so novel that the Surgeon General issued a statement guaranteeing the safety of those working in "reconditioned" air.

In 1932 the George A. Fuller Company was awarded the construction contract, which specified completion within two years at a cost of five million dollars. The final tally was six years and twelve million dollars. Because of the Tiber marsh, the building required deep pilings—8,575 of them, each 27 feet deep. Another problem was the enormous weight of the structure, which Pope resolved by designing a bowl-shaped foundation, a technique not used since the days of the Romans. The economic depression added to the difficulties. Sub-contractors needed prompt payment to

Here we see pages of the Constitution and the Bill of Rights and, in the vertical case above, the Declaration of Independence.

Opposite: Often referred to as "The Shrine," the Exhibit Hall of the National Archives has on permanent display the Declaration of Independence, the Bill of Rights, and the Constitution.

Truck convoy bringing War Department records to the National Archives in 1934.

survive financially; wildcat strikes added delays. Someone, meanwhile, calculated the space needed for already existing federal records, and concluded that the Archives could not afford the luxury of an empty inner court. Construction of stacks in that space began in December 1935 and was finished a year and a half later. With all the obstacles eventually overcome, the nation finally had a unique strongbox in which to store its archival treasures.

Not until the National Archives Act of 1934 was John Franklin Jameson's dream fulfilled. In a case of the cart before the horse, or the architect before the archivist, Congress had authorized the steel and stone "National Archives" before the National Archives as a federal agency was formed or staffed or its mission defined. The organic act of 1934 established the Office of Archivist of the United States at an annual salary of $10,000 (a princely sum in that Depression era); it also gave the National Archives the status of an independent agency with a two-fold mandate: to preserve the permanently valuable records of the federal government and to administer them in a manner useful to both the government and the public.

R.D.W. Connor, the first Archivist, was the right man for the job. A former Kenan Professor of History at the University of North Carolina, Connor was the consummate Southern gentleman. He had charm, patience, and courtesy, as well as a smooth golf stroke. He was a skilled raconteur who understood the cocktail circuit and a deck of cards. These abilities, in addition to his dedication to the archival profession, helped him to advance the interests of the National Archives with the White House, Capitol Hill, agency heads, and, above all, his staff. During his tenure, voluminous and diverse records of the federal government were surveyed and the most important brought to the National Archives Building from hundreds of locations across the country. Officials reluctant to surrender their treasures succumbed to Connor's charm. By the time he returned to his beloved Chapel Hill in 1942, Connor had the satisfaction of knowing that the National Archives was safely and securely established.

Since Connor's tour of duty, the Archives has been blessed with a succession of talented Archivists: Solon J. Buck, Wayne C. Grover, Robert Bahmer, James B. Rhoads, and now Robert M. Warner, each a leader of his profession and a dedicated public servant. A distinguished scholar once questioned the wisdom of entrusting the nation's archives to appointed officials who might be "political in character, unversed in scholarship, unappreciative of the historical value of archives, uncertain and brief in their tenure of office, and comparatively inexperienced in the art of making and preserving records." So far his fears have not been realized. Politics have not yet touched the process by which the Archivist is selected and appointed, even though there was some concern on this point when the National Archives was made part of the newly established General Services Administration in 1949. From Connor to Warner, each one has embodied the ideals of the archival profession and has transmuted them into the effective administration of the National Archives. Each has thereby honored the trust begun by Charles Thomson and so carefully fostered by Waldo G. Leland and John Franklin Jameson.

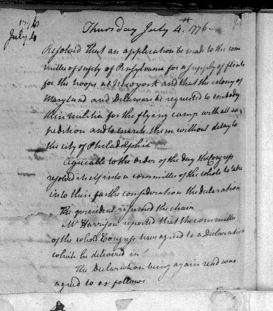

CHARTERS OF FREEDOM

ach year, hundreds of thousands of visitors come to the National Archives to see the Declaration of Independence, the Constitution, and the Bill of Rights. These Great Charters of our freedom are the most precious documents in our history. Americans from all corners of the country, like pilgrims to Mecca, bring their children to see for themselves these documents that have shaped the nation's history and life. Most of the awestruck visitors, however, know little of the difficulties that beset these documents before they could take their rightful place in the National Archives. We hope this is their last stop in an odyssey that began more than two centuries ago.

What started primarily as a protest against certain political and economic restrictions exploded into a revolution that relatively few colonists either wanted or expected. The force of events, however, made inevitable that moment on June 7, 1776, when Richard Henry Lee of Virginia introduced in the Continental Congress the resolution that changed forever this country's destiny: "That these United Colonies are, and of right ought to be, free and independent States, that they are absolved from all allegiance to the British Crown, and that all political connection between them and the State of Great Britain is, and ought to be, totally dissolved."

After endorsing Lee's resolution, the Congress appointed a committee, consisting of Thomas Jefferson, John Adams, Benjamin Franklin, Robert E. Livingston, and Roger Sherman, to draft a statement of America's case for independence. Jefferson was the primary architect of the declaration that the committee introduced in the Congress on July 2. Here it was discussed, debated, and revised. Late on the afternoon of July 4, 1776, it was formally adopted and the text turned over to John Dunlap, the official printer. The following morning, Dunlap had printed copies available for the members of the Congress to dispatch to their various assemblies, conventions, and committees of safety. We do not know how many copies Dunlap printed. Twenty-two are known to exist today, including one that was inserted in the Journal of the Continental Congress for July Fourth.

On July 19, the Congress ordered that the Declaration be "fairly en-

Opposite: After John Dunlap finished the first printing of the Declaration of Independence, a copy was attached with wax wafers to the journal of the proceedings of the Continental Congress for July 4, 1776.

grossed on parchment, with the title and style of 'The Unanimous Declaration of the Thirteen United States of America,' and the same, when engrossed, be signed by every member of Congress." (Engrossing is the process of copying an official document in a large, clear hand. The term derives from the Latin *ingrossus*, made up of the words *in* and *grossus*, meaning thick.) Timothy Matlack, a Pennsylvanian who had assisted the Congress for more than a year and who had written out George Washington's commission as commanding general of the Continental Army, probably engrossed the Declaration of Independence, using a fine sheet of parchment measuring 29¼ by 29¾ inches.

Two weeks passed before the Declaration was presented to the Congress for signing on August 2. Eventually fifty-six delegates signed it, although not all who did so were present that day. The first to sign was John Hancock, President of the Congress, who centered his signature below the text. Contrary to legend, Hancock did not sign his name extra large so that King George III could see it without his spectacles. This was Hancock's normal signature, as numerous examples in the National Archives can attest. The others, in accordance with prevailing custom, began signing on the right below the text, arranging their signatures according to the geographical location of the colonies they represented. New Hampshire, as northernmost, headed the list, which ended with southernmost Georgia. Among the late signers was Matthew Thornton, who had no room to sign with his New Hampshire colleagues. Several delegates never did sign. Among these were John Dickinson, who feared the effect of revolutionary change without an established policy for a new government, and Robert Livingston, one of the draftsmen of the Declaration, who considered its publication premature.

None of the signers could have fully anticipated the profound impact their action was to have on the course of American history. Perhaps few believed thirteen weak and separate colonies—in some cases having little in common besides their relationship to Great Britain—could secure international recognition and assistance, fight the most powerful nation on

IN CONGRESS, JULY 4, 1776.

The unanimous Declaration of the thirteen united States of America,

When in the Course of human events, it becomes necessary for one people to dissolve the political bands which have connected them with another, and to assume among the powers of the earth, the separate and equal station to which the Laws of Nature and of Nature's God entitle them, a decent respect to the opinions of mankind requires that they should declare the causes which impel them to the separation. —— We hold these truths to be self-evident, that all men are created equal, that they are endowed by their Creator with certain unalienable Rights, that among these are Life, Liberty and the pursuit of Happiness. —— That to secure these rights, Governments are instituted among Men, deriving their just powers from the consent of the governed, —— That whenever any Form of Government becomes destructive of these ends, it is the Right of the People to alter or to abolish it, and to institute new Government, laying its foundation on such principles and organizing its powers in such form, as to them shall seem most likely to effect their Safety and Happiness. Prudence, indeed, will dictate that Governments long established should not be changed for light and transient causes; and accordingly all experience hath shewn, that mankind are more disposed to suffer, while evils are sufferable, than to right themselves by abolishing the forms to which they are accustomed. But when a long train of abuses and usurpations, pursuing invariably the same Object evinces a design to reduce them under absolute Despotism, it is their right, it is their duty, to throw off such Government, and to provide new Guards for their future security. —— Such has been the patient sufferance of these Colonies; and such is now the necessity which constrains them to alter their former Systems of Government. The history of the present King of Great Britain is a history of repeated injuries and usurpations, all having in direct object the establishment of an absolute Tyranny over these States. To prove this, let Facts be submitted to a candid world.

He has refused his Assent to Laws, the most wholesome and necessary for the public good.
He has forbidden his Governors to pass Laws of immediate and pressing importance, unless suspended in their operation till his Assent should be obtained; and when so suspended, he has utterly neglected to attend to them.
He has refused to pass other Laws for the accommodation of large districts of people, unless those people would relinquish the right of Representation in the Legislature, a right inestimable to them and formidable to tyrants only.
He has called together legislative bodies at places unusual, uncomfortable, and distant from the depository of their public Records, for the sole purpose of fatiguing them into compliance with his measures.
He has dissolved Representative Houses repeatedly, for opposing with manly firmness his invasions on the rights of the people.
He has refused for a long time, after such dissolutions, to cause others to be elected; whereby the Legislative powers, incapable of Annihilation, have returned to the People at large for their exercise; the State remaining in the mean time exposed to all the dangers of invasion from without, and convulsions within.
He has endeavoured to prevent the population of these States; for that purpose obstructing the Laws for Naturalization of Foreigners; refusing to pass others to encourage their migrations hither, and raising the conditions of new Appropriations of Lands.
He has obstructed the Administration of Justice, by refusing his Assent to Laws for establishing Judiciary powers.
He has made Judges dependent on his Will alone, for the tenure of their offices, and the amount and payment of their salaries.
He has erected a multitude of New Offices, and sent hither swarms of Officers to harrass our people, and eat out their substance.
He has kept among us, in times of peace, Standing Armies without the Consent of our legislatures.
He has affected to render the Military independent of and superior to the Civil power.
He has combined with others to subject us to a jurisdiction foreign to our constitution, and unacknowledged by our laws; giving his Assent to their Acts of pretended Legislation:
For Quartering large bodies of armed troops among us:
For protecting them, by a mock Trial, from punishment for any Murders which they should commit on the Inhabitants of these States:
For cutting off our Trade with all parts of the world:
For imposing Taxes on us without our Consent:
For depriving us in many cases, of the benefits of Trial by Jury:
For transporting us beyond Seas to be tried for pretended offences
For abolishing the free System of English Laws in a neighbouring Province, establishing therein an Arbitrary government, and enlarging its Boundaries so as to render it at once an example and fit instrument for introducing the same absolute rule into these Colonies:
For taking away our Charters, abolishing our most valuable Laws, and altering fundamentally the Forms of our Governments:
For suspending our own Legislatures, and declaring themselves invested with power to legislate for us in all cases whatsoever.
He has abdicated Government here, by declaring us out of his Protection and waging War against us.
He has plundered our seas, ravaged our Coasts, burnt our towns, and destroyed the lives of our people.
He is at this time transporting large Armies of foreign Mercenaries to compleat the works of death, desolation and tyranny, already begun with circumstances of Cruelty & perfidy scarcely paralleled in the most barbarous ages, and totally unworthy the Head of a civilized nation.
He has constrained our fellow Citizens taken Captive on the high Seas to bear Arms against their Country, to become the executioners of their friends and Brethren, or to fall themselves by their Hands.
He has excited domestic insurrections amongst us, and has endeavoured to bring on the inhabitants of our frontiers, the merciless Indian Savages, whose known rule of warfare, is an undistinguished destruction of all ages, sexes and conditions. In every stage of these Oppressions We have Petitioned for Redress in the most humble terms: Our repeated Petitions have been answered only by repeated injury. A Prince, whose character is thus marked by every act which may define a Tyrant, is unfit to be the ruler of a free people. Nor have We been wanting in attentions to our British brethren. We have warned them from time to time of attempts by their legislature to extend an unwarrantable jurisdiction over us. We have reminded them of the circumstances of our emigration and settlement here. We have appealed to their native justice and magnanimity, and we have conjured them by the ties of our common kindred to disavow these usurpations, which, would inevitably interrupt our connections and correspondence. They too have been deaf to the voice of justice and of consanguinity. We must, therefore, acquiesce in the necessity, which denounces our Separation, and hold them, as we hold the rest of mankind, Enemies in War, in Peace Friends.

We, therefore, the Representatives of the united States of America, in General Congress, Assembled, appealing to the Supreme Judge of the world for the rectitude of our intentions, do, in the Name, and by Authority of the good People of these Colonies, solemnly publish and declare, That these United Colonies are, and of Right ought to be Free and Independent States; that they are Absolved from all Allegiance to the British Crown, and that all political connection between them and the State of Great Britain, is and ought to be totally dissolved; and that as Free and Independent States, they have full Power to levy War, conclude Peace, contract Alliances, establish Commerce, and to do all other Acts and Things which Independent States may of right do. —— And for the support of this Declaration, with a firm reliance on the protection of divine Providence, we mutually pledge to each other our Lives, our Fortunes and our sacred Honor.

John Hancock

Button Gwinnett
Lyman Hall
Geo Walton.

Wm Hooper
Joseph Hewes
John Penn

Edward Rutledge.

Thos Heyward Junr.
Thomas Lynch Junr.
Arthur Middleton

Samuel Chase
Wm Paca
Thos Stone
Charles Carroll of Carrollton

George Wythe
Richard Henry Lee
Th Jefferson
Benja Harrison
Ths Nelson jr.
Francis Lightfoot Lee
Carter Braxton

Robt Morris
Benjamin Rush
Benja Franklin
John Morton
Geo Clymer
Jas Smith.
Geo Taylor
James Wilson
Geo. Ross
Caesar Rodney
Geo Read
Thos M:Kean

Wm Floyd
Phil. Livingston
Frans Lewis
Lewis Morris

Richd Stockton
Jno Witherspoon
Fras Hopkinson
John Hart
Abra Clark

Josiah Bartlett
Wm Whipple
Saml Adams
John Adams
Robt Treat Paine
Elbridge Gerry
Step Hopkins
William Ellery
Roger Sherman
Samel Huntington
Wm Williams
Oliver Wolcott
Matthew Thornton

earth to a standstill, and then negotiate a favorable treaty of peace. That, of course, is just what they did. Once there was no longer a common enemy to hold the new states together, however, their loose confederation began to unravel. Each state acted like an independent country, issuing currency, taxing imports from other states, and ignoring debts incurred during the Revolution. Daniel Shays' rebellion against the Massachusetts Government in 1786, threatening widespread anarchy, was an additional factor prompting George Washington and other leaders to call for a new national government that would be strong enough to earn obedience at home and respect abroad. The result was a constitutional convention that met in Philadelphia during the following summer. Here, in a peaceful revolution, the new states changed their loose political alliance to a federal union under the first written constitution anywhere. Later, specific guarantees of individual freedom were added in a Bill of Rights.

The Constitution was not easily worked out, however. Getting delegates to attend the convention proved difficult. Of seventy-four delegates appointed, only fifty-five came. Patrick Henry, for one, refused to serve claiming he "smelt a rat." By May 14, the date set for convening, only delegates from Pennsylvania and Virginia had arrived. Ten days passed before a quorum of seven states was represented. New Hampshire had no money for sending delegates; eventually two of her four arrived, more than three months late, their expenses financed privately. Rhode Island sent no delegates at all, fearing a conspiracy to overthrow the established government.

Who were these men who decided the future of the United States? They were merchants, planters, lawyers, educators, judges, veterans of the Continental Congresses, as well as emerging politicians. Eight had signed the Declaration of Independence. The eldest, at eighty-three, was the venerable Benjamin Franklin, suffering so badly from gout that he had to be carried in a sedan chair. The youngest was Jonathan Dayton, aged twenty-seven. Jefferson, writing to Adams from Paris, called the delegates "demi-gods." Others described them in less exalted terms. One contempo-

We the People

of the Un...

insure domestic Tranquility, provide for the common defence, prom...
and our Posterity, do ordain and establish this Constitution for the...

Article. I.

Section. 1. All legislative Powers herein granted shall be vested...
of Representatives.

Section. 2. The House of Representatives shall be composed of Me...
in each State shall have the Qualifications requisite for Electors of the most nume...

No Person shall be a Representative who shall not have attained...
and who shall not, when elected, be an Inhabitant of that State in which he...

Representatives and direct Taxes shall be apportioned among the sev...
Numbers, which shall be determined by adding to the whole Number of free...
not taxed, three fifths of all other Persons. The actual Enumeration sha...
and within every subsequent Term of ten Years, in such Manner as they...
thirty thousand, but each State shall have at Least one Representative;...
entitled to chuse three, Massachusetts eight, Rhode-Island and Providen...
eight, Delaware one, Maryland six, Virginia ten, North Carolina five, S...

When vacancies happen in the Representation from any State...

the House of Representatives shall chuse their Speaker and othe...

Section. 3. The Senate of the United States shall be composed of two S...
Senator shall have one Vote.

Immediately after they shall be assembled in Consequence of the...
of the Senators of the first Class shall be vacated at the Expiration of the se...
Class at the Expiration of the sixth Year, so that one third may be chosen eve...
Recess of the Legislature of any State, the Executive thereof may make tempora...
such Vacancies.

No Person shall be a Senator who shall not have attained to the...
not, when elected, be an Inhabitant of that State for which he shall be cho...

The Vice President of the United States shall be President of the Sena...

The Senate shall chuse their other Officers, and also a President pro...
President of the United States.

...shall have the sole Power to try all Impeachment...

States, in Order to form a more perfect Union, establish Justice,
be general Welfare, and secure the Blessings of Liberty to ourselves
States of America.

Congress of the United States, which shall consist of a Senate and House

chosen every second Year by the People of the several States, and the Electors
Branch of the State Legislature.
Age of twenty five Years, and been seven Years a Citizen of the United States
be chosen.
States which may be included within this Union, according to their respective
, including those bound to Service for a Term of Years, and excluding Indians
made within three Years after the first Meeting of the Congress of the United States
Law direct. The Number of Representatives shall not exceed one for every
til such enumeration shall be made, the State of New Hampshire shall be
antations one, Connecticut five, New York six, New Jersey four, Pennsylvan
Carolina five, and Georgia three.
utive Authority thereof shall issue Writs of Election to fill such Vacancies.
; and shall have the sole Power of Impeachment.
from each State, chosen by the Legislature thereof, for six Years, and each

lection, they shall be divided as equally as may be into three Classes. The Se
ear, of the second Class at the Expiration of the fourth Year, and of the third
nd Year; and if Vacancies happen by Resignation, or otherwise, during the
pointments until the next Meeting of the Legislature, which shall then fill
irty Years, and been nine Years a Citizen of the United States, and who shall
shall have no Vote, unless they be equally divided.
, in the Absence of the Vice President, or when he shall exercise the Office of
ling for that Purpose, they shall be on Oath or Affirmation. When the Pres

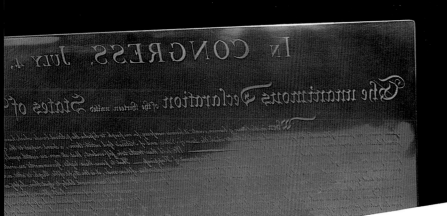

rary claimed, somewhat cynically, that "twenty assemblies of equal number might be collected, equally respectable both in point of ability, integrity and patriotism." He thought the body was tarnished by "public defaulters" among it as well as others who were "guilty of notorious peculation and fraud, with regard to public property in the hour of our distress." The truth lies somewhere between these extremes of judgment. Max Farrand, editor of the records of the Federal Convention, believes it was a representative body for the time. "Great men there were," but, he admits, there were others "utterly unfit."

No matter. These men produced a document that worked. The Constitution that was written in Philadelphia in 1787 has met challenges in good times and bad, in peace time and war time. It has enabled the original homogenous Anglo-Saxon population to absorb wave after wave of immigrants of different cultures and colors. The United States of 1787 and the United States of today might be on different planets, so great are their differences, yet the Constitution has successfully served them both.

The men who framed the Constitution were less than enthusiastic about the fruit of their labors. On September 17, when they met to sign the document, Franklin made a special appeal for unanimous approval. Too weak to read his own speech, which a colleague delivered for him, the old patriot urged the assembly to put aside personal disagreements for the public good. Despite misgivings, he was prepared to sign, because "I expect no better and because I am not sure that it is not the best." Therefore, he pleaded, could not each member who still had objections "put his name on this instrument" and "with me . . . make manifest our unanimity?" Franklin's eloquence notwithstanding, three delegates— Edmund Randolph, Elbridge Gerry and George Mason—refused to sign.

For a time events bore out the fears of the convention delegates. By January 9, 1788, only five states had given their approval—Delaware, Pennsylvania, New Jersey, Georgia, and Connecticut. The outcome appeared doubtful in such key states as Massachusetts, New York, and Virginia. In fact, not until Federalists at the Massachusetts State Conven-

An archivist examining one of the state ratifications of the Constitution. These large parchment sheets are bound into a special volume that contains the Ratifications of the Constitution and the Bill of Rights.

Opposite: The engraved copper printing plate of the Declaration of Independence executed by William J. Stone in 1823, with an impression made from it during the Bicentennial.

tion agreed to recommend a list of amendments amounting to a bill of rights did that commonwealth consent. Following her example, six of the remaining states attached similar conditions when they ratified. Ironically, ratification was attained despite the fact that the majority of citizens probably opposed the Constitution as it stood. Only the promise of amendments ensured its approval.

Clearly popular sentiment required a statement of the rights of citizens. Thomas Jefferson, generally in favor of the new government, admitted privately to James Madison that a guarantee of rights was what "people are entitled to against every government on earth." Madison, "Father of the Constitution," needed little convincing. As a representative from Virginia to the first Federal Congress, he worked zealously to persuade the House to enact amendments. It was largely through his efforts, in fact, that the House approved seventeen amendments, a list that the Senate later trimmed to twelve. President Washington, as required under the Constitution, sent these to the states for ratification in October 1789. Over the next two years, the states ratified ten of the twelve, thereby providing Americans with their now cherished Bill of Rights. (Of the two amendments not ratified, one limited the size of the House of Representatives; the other forbade members of the House and Senate to raise their own compensation.)

Anyone looking at these Great Charters of freedom today can see that they have been treated differently by the hand of time. The Constitution, even after two hundred years, is virtually pristine in condition, whereas the Declaration is barely legible. This shocks and dismays viewers, who want to know why. The reason lies in the care the documents received before they reached the National Archives. The care accorded the Declaration, unfortunately, has left much to be desired.

Once signed, the Declaration of Independence became the property of the Continental Congress and was filed in the office of Charles Thomson, Secretary of the Congress. Like other parchment documents, it was probably stored rolled from the top down. This meant that the signatures were on the outer layer of the roll, where they suffered the perils of

Congress of the United States

begun and held at the City of New York, on

Wednesday the fourth of March, one thousand seven hundred and eighty nine.

THE Conventions of a number of the States, having at the time of their adopting the Constitution, expressed a desire, in order to prevent misconstruction or abuse of its powers, that further declaratory and restrictive clauses should be added: And as extending the ground of public confidence in the Government, will best ensure the beneficent ends of its institution.

RESOLVED by the Senate and House of Representatives of the United States of America, in Congress assembled, two thirds of both Houses concurring, that the following Articles be proposed to the Legislatures of the several States, as amendments to the Constitution of the United States, all, or any of which Articles, when ratified by three fourths of the said Legislatures, to be valid to all intents and purposes, as part of the said Constitution, viz.

ARTICLES in addition to, and Amendment of the Constitution of the United States of America, proposed by Congress, and ratified by the Legislatures of the several States, pursuant to the fifth Article of the original Constitution.

Article the first..... After the first enumeration required by the first Article of the Constitution, there shall be one Representative for every thirty thousand, until the number shall amount to one hundred, after which the proportion shall be so regulated by Congress, that there shall be not less than one hundred Representatives, nor less than one Representative for every forty thousand persons, until the number of Representatives shall amount to two hundred, after which the proportion shall be so regulated by Congress, that there shall not be less than two hundred Representatives, nor more than one Representative for every fifty thousand persons.

Article the second.... No law, varying the compensation for the services of the Senators and Representatives, shall take effect, until an election of Representatives shall have intervened.

Article the third..... Congress shall make no law respecting an establishment of religion, or prohibiting the free exercise thereof; or abridging the freedom of speech, or of the press; or the right of the people peaceably to assemble, and to petition the Government for a redress of grievances.

Article the fourth... A well regulated militia, being necessary to the security of a free State, the right of the people to keep and bear arms, shall not be infringed.

Article the fifth..... No Soldier shall, in time of peace be quartered in any house, without the consent of the owner, nor in time of war, but in a manner to be prescribed by law.

Article the sixth.... The right of the people to be secure in their persons, houses, papers, and effects, against unreasonable searches and seizures, shall not be violated, and no Warrants shall issue, but upon probable cause, supported by oath or affirmation, and particularly describing the place to be searched, and the persons or things to be seized.

Article the seventh.. No person shall be held to answer for a capital, or otherwise infamous crime, unless on a presentment or indictment of a Grand jury, except in cases arising in the land or naval forces, or in the militia, when in actual service in time of War or public danger; nor shall any person be subject for the same offence to be twice put in jeopardy of life or limb; nor shall be compelled in any criminal case to be a witness against himself, nor be deprived of life, liberty, or property, without due process of law; nor shall private property be taken for public use, without just compensation.

Article the eighth.. In all criminal prosecutions, the accused shall enjoy the right to a speedy and public trial, by an impartial jury of the State and district wherein the crime shall have been committed, which district shall have been previously ascertained by law, and to be informed of the nature and cause of the accusation; to be confronted with the witnesses against him; to have compulsory process for obtaining witnesses in his favor, and to have the assistance of counsel for his defence.

Article the ninth... In suits at common law, where the value in controversy shall exceed twenty dollars, the right of trial by jury shall be preserved, and no fact tried by a jury, shall be otherwise re-examined in any Court of the United States, than according to the rules of the common law.

Article the tenth... Excessive bail shall not be required, nor excessive fines imposed, nor cruel and unusual punishments inflicted.

Article the eleventh. The enumeration in the Constitution, of certain rights, shall not be construed to deny or disparage others retained by the people.

Article the twelfth.. The powers not delegated to the United States by the Constitution, nor prohibited by it to the States, are reserved to the States respectively, or to the people.

ATTEST,

Frederick Augustus Muhlenberg, Speaker of the House of Representatives.

John Adams, Vice President of the United States, and President of the Senate.

John Beckley, Clerk of the House of Representatives.

Sam. A. Otis Secretary of the Senate.

exposure and abrasion. Since ink does not penetrate parchment but dries on the surface, it has a tendency to flake off, making the signatures vulnerable to wear. A further cause of deterioration was the excessive handling the document endured, particularly during the course of the Revolution when the Congress, and the Declaration, moved frequently.

In July 1789, the new government created the Department of Foreign Affairs and after an act of September 1789, which changed its name to Department of State, gave it custody "of all records, books, and papers," including the Declaration. The Department's first Secretary was Thomas Jefferson. Having drafted the Declaration, he now had the responsibility for its physical care. Jefferson, however, took no special pains to ensure its preservation nor did any of his successors before the War of 1812. Then the document was whisked from Washington just before the attack by British forces. According to Stephen Pleasonton, a clerk in the State Department, he and the "gentlemen" in the office packed several coarse linen bags with records, including the Declaration. These they took by cart across Chain Bridge to an unused gristmill about two miles up stream from Georgetown, where they remained overnight. On August 24, 1814, the day the British burned the government buildings, the Declaration was thirty-five miles away in Leesburg, Virginia. Not until the British fleet left Chesapeake Bay several weeks later was it returned to Washington.

From September 1814 to May 1876, the Declaration was housed in several different buildings about the city, at least one of which "offered no security against fire." At the Patent Office Building, now the National Portrait Gallery at Seventh and F Streets, the Declaration and Washington's Commission as Commander-in-Chief were exhibited together for thirty-five years exposed to sunlight in a white-painted hall opposite a window.

Appalling as this negligence was, the decisions to make copies of the Declaration may have caused additional damage to the document. Owen Tyler in 1818 and John Binns the following year published decorative copies made by expert calligraphers. The Tyler copy was especially fine, according to Acting Secretary of State Richard Rush, who collated it with the original. He considered it a "curiously exact" imitation, particularly the signatures. "It would be difficult, if not impossible," he claimed, "for the closest scrutiny to distinguish them, were it not for the hand of time, from the originals."

Perhaps more detrimental was the copy made in 1823 by William J. Stone. This was commissioned by Secretary of State John Quincy Adams, who wanted an exact copy of the entire Declaration including the signatures. Stone used a method of copperplate engraving that required a "wet sheet transfer" from the original. Surface ink of the Declaration itself was probably detached and imposed as a mirror-image on a copper plate. This reverse image was then engraved into the plate's surface and copies run off on a press.

Stone doubtless hastened the Declaration's deterioration, but his copies are today valued collectors' items. The two hundred copies of the official pressrun carry this identification at the top in small print: "Engraved by W.J. Stone for the Dept. of State, by order of J.Q. Adams, Sec. of State July 4th 1823." Stone later struck a number of unofficial copies that bear the simple identification: "W.J. Stone SC. Washn."

By the time of the Centennial Celebration in 1876, when it was exhibited in Philadelphia, the Declaration had become a faded relic, and many of its signatures were barely discernible. Despite widespread concern, little was done to save the document from further deterioration. In fact, shortly after its return from Philadelphia, it was taken from the Patent Office Building for display in the State Department library, a room heated by a fireplace where smoking was permitted. Here it remained for the next seventeen years. Fate nevertheless may have smiled on the Declaration for once, in spite of its smoky surroundings, because fire gutted the Patent Office Building soon after the transfer.

Not until 1894 did State Department officials decide to take steps to save the Declaration of Independence from further deterioration. For the next quarter of a century, it was locked in a steel safe between two sheets of glass. During this period, however, it was brought out for occasional public

Overleaf: The Papers of the Continental Congress, literally the first Archives of the United States, are boxed in special acid-free containers and stored in an ideal temperature- and humidity-controlled environment. Shown here is a shelf of the Papers and a selection of broadsides to be found in them.

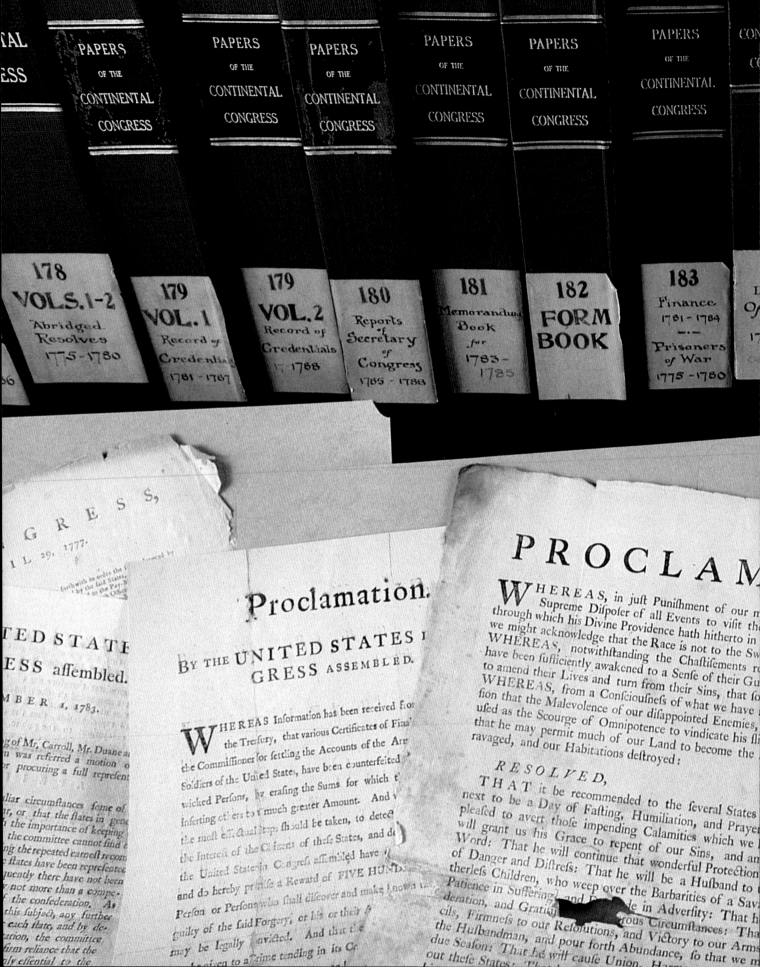

appearances, as in 1898 when it was photographed for the *Ladies Home Journal*.

The Constitution, meanwhile, had enjoyed a much less disturbed existence. Although it had suffered the same tribulations in the period between 1790 and 1814, it remained out of sight in the State Department after the War of 1812. Consisting of five pages instead of one, it was not as suitable to exhibit as the Declaration of Independence and as a result had considerably less handling.

The Declaration and the Constitution remained in storage, hidden but not forgotten, until 1920. In that year, the Secretary of State appointed a committee to study the appropriate steps for the permanent protection "of those documents of supreme value" in his custody. He was especially anxious to determine the propriety of displaying some of those documents "for the benefit of the patriotic public."

The committee's report was unsettling. Storage conditions in the State Department were poor, offering protection neither from fire nor "evil disposed persons." The committee could see no harm in displaying the Declaration of Independence because the fading was already so bad that it could not get worse. The most important recommendation, however, was for the State Department to turn over all these historical documents to the Library of Congress, which could care for them properly.

A year later, acting upon the recommendation of the Secretary of State, President Warren G. Harding issued an executive order transferring the Great Charters to the Library of Congress. There, after receiving the attention of a conservator, they were placed on display in a special case. This was their home for the next thirty years, except during World War II when they were taken to Fort Knox for safe keeping.

While the Charters were at the Library, the National Archives Building was built. Most of the people involved expected this to be the permanent home of these national treasures. The architect, in fact, had designed the exhibition hall with the Declaration of Independence and the Constitution in mind. Nevertheless, getting them to the new National Archives after

1934 was no simple matter. Although the State Department had already transferred to the National Archives the Bill of Rights together with the Amendments to the Constitution, officials at the Library of Congress felt that losing the Great Charters would diminish the status and prestige of their institution; officials of the National Archives felt just as strongly that the failure to obtain the Charters would diminish the stature of theirs.

Despite a great deal of talk, nothing was done. In 1951 the Library of Congress gave the Declaration and the Constitution permanent protection by placing them in sealed, helium-filled cases. To celebrate this event, the Library held a ceremony attended by President Truman and other dignitaries.

According to Milton O. Gustafson, a National Archives authority on the history of these documents, Archivist Wayne C. Grover decided to confront the issue. "He felt it was impossible to go on indefinitely with ceremonies that gave the impression that the documents would remain everlastingly in the Library of Congress."

Immediately after the ceremony, Grover began a dialogue with Luther Evans, Librarian of Congress, that culminated in the transfer not only of the Declaration of Independence and the Constitution, but also of the Papers of the Continental Congress and other official records of the Revolutionary War period. Grover accomplished this feat by stressing the need for safety in case of atomic war. No one could dispute the fact that the National Archives Building was one of the sturdiest in the Washington area. Furthermore, Grover knew that the law was on the side of the National Archives in its effort to gain custody of these documents. The Federal Records Act of 1950 required the transfer to the National Archives of all government records more than thirty years old, unless needed in the course of daily business. Although sorry to lose the principal documents of American history, officials at the Library of Congress agreed that logic and the law made the move inevitable. Evans made the necessary arrangements, and the transfer took place on December 13, 1952.

Considering the rude treatment these documents had suffered over the years, the pomp and ceremony for this move was spectacular. A cordon of

Overleaf: Each night the Great Charters are lowered twenty feet below the exhibit hall into a specially designed vault of steel and reinforced concrete that is sealed by massive interlocking leaves of the same material. Shown here is a technician cleaning the glass over the documents before they are raised into their display cases.

The Declaration of Independence and the Constitution arriving at the National Archives, December 11, 1952.

eighty-eight service women lined the steps of the Library of Congress as twelve members of the Armed Forces Special Police carried the six leaves (one, the Declaration of Independence; five, the Constitution), each in its helium-filled glass case enclosed in a wooden crate, and laid them on mattresses in an armored Marine Corps personnel carrier. The escort for the parade to the National Archives Building consisted of motorcycle police, a color guard, ceremonial troops, the Army Band, two tanks, and a cadre of servicemen carrying submachine guns. Additional military personnel lined the parade route along Constitution and Pennsylvania Avenues.

The formal ceremony installing the documents in the National Archives Building two days later was equally impressive. More than one hundred dignitaries crowded into the Exhibit Hall to hear patriotic speeches, solemn benedictions, and the *Star Spangled Banner* played by the U.S. Marine Band. One stirring episode was the roll call of states by the Governor of Delaware, the first state to ratify the Constitution. As he called the roll in the order in which each state either ratified the Constitution or was admitted to the Union, a service woman carrying the state flag entered the hall and stood at attention. President Truman, the chief speaker, saluted the "honorable effort" being made, "based upon reverence for the great past," to ensure that these documents would be preserved "for the ages." He particularly praised the shrine that houses the Great Charters, noting that it is "as safe from destruction as anything that the wit of modern man can devise."

The security surrounding the Declaration of Independence and the Constitution is tight. Their specially designed glass cases provide the finest physical protection possible. They are lowered each night (and in time of danger) into a vault of steel and reinforced concrete that is covered by a massive lid of interlocking steel and concrete leaves. Should the electricity fail, the guards can operate the apparatus with batteries.

The happy conclusion of this story was made possible only because great men were in charge of the Library of Congress and the National Archives in 1952. Luther Evans and Wayne Grover combined high standards of professionalism with common sense and ready wit. The latter is illustrated in the humorous exchange that followed the decision to transfer the documents. Evans chided Grover with the following limerick:

> There once was an agency rich
> Whose head had a terrible itch
> To take all records over.
> His name it was Grover,
> A two-fisted son-of-a-bitch.

To which Grover responded:

> I have read your effusions;
> I bleed with remorse.
> No further contusions
> Will come from this source.
> But to label us ''rich''
> Is outright deception.
> Better limit the Pitch
> To unimmaculate conception.

With his limerick, Evans also included a personal note. "I don't know what history will say about our friendly collusion," he told Grover, "but I can tell you that I feel darned broadminded and just a wee bit righteous, something like a fellow who gave up his gal to an ugly clumsy younger brother who wasn't very good at finding gals of his own." Grover took the kidding with good grace and offered Evans the credit for working out the transfer. "Jefferson wanted on his tombstone that he wrote the Declaration," Grover wrote. "I want on mine that I saw it safely enshrined in the Archives of the United States. If you'll be satisfied with a footnote on a tombstone, I will certainly see to it that the source is properly cited."

of the United States of America

Proclamation.

on the twenty-second day of
the year of our Lord one thousand
d and sixty two, a proclamation
by the President of the United States,
ning other things, the following,

at on the first day of January, in the
r Lord one thousand eight hundred
y-three, all persons held as slaves within
te or designated part of a State, the people
shall then be in rebellion against the
States, shall be then, thenceforward, and
free; and the Executive Government of the
ed States, including the military and naval
hority thereof will recognize and maintain
freedom of such persons, and will do no act
acts to repress such persons, or any of them,
n any efforts they may make for their actual
freedom. a That the Executive will, on the first day

one thousand eig
and sixty three, a
Independence of the
States of America, the
seventh.

the President.

Abraham Lin

William Seward
Secretary of State.

THE PRESIDENCY

The president of the United States is the public official most represented in the National Archives, whether as Chief of State, as Chief Executive of the Federal Government, or as Commander-in-Chief of the armed forces. Every public law, executive order, and proclamation of a treaty, Indian or international, bears a presidential signature, as do thousands of less formal documents. One of the delights of working in federal records is the possibility of finding a presidential letter, note, or signature that may have gone hitherto unrecognized.

From these papers, one can learn much about the character of each president and his administration. Recorded are moments of decision and indecision, of compassion and anger, even of humor and pique. The dour John Adams, in a letter to Secretary of State Timothy Pickering, refused a passport to Dupont de Nemours, complaining: "We have had too many French philosophers already, and I really begin to think or rather to suspect, that learned academicians not under the immediate inspection and control of government have disorganized the world and are incompatible with social order."

The records document many instances of presidential compassion in the use of the pardon. To grant an unpopular pardon requires strength of character, as was the case in President Ford's controversial pardon of former President Nixon. George Washington showed that mercy was not weakness when he pardoned the leaders of the "Whiskey Rebellion," to the dismay of Alexander Hamilton and other prominent Federalists.

Other presidential qualities, especially decisiveness, are revealed in Archives records. Being the nation's chief decision-maker is a major part of the job. A plaque on Truman's desk proclaimed: "The Buck Stops Here." A simple sheet of doodles by President John F. Kennedy provides unusual insight into the pressures on a president. During discussions in April 1961 about preparations for the Bay of Pigs invasion of Cuba, the President fingered a pen on a scratchpad. He wrote (and misspelled) the word "decisions" seventeen times.

President Thomas Jefferson acquired the vast Louisiana Territory from

Opposite: President Abraham Lincoln's Emancipation Proclamation, dated January 1, 1863, freeing slaves in areas "still in rebellion," thus shifting the emphasis of the Civil War from a struggle to preserve the Union to a crusade for human liberty.

Above: A listing of personal property belonging to Dupont de Nemours when he immigrated to America in January 1800, as recorded by the Collector of Customs at Newport, Rhode Island.

Right: President Kennedy was a great "doodler" and many have been preserved, including this revealing one made in April 1961 during discussions of the Bay of Pigs invasion.

35

France even though he could find nothing in the Constitution giving him the authority to make such a purchase. His bold decision doubled the size of the United States, advancing its boundary westward from the Mississippi River to the Rocky Mountains. Even Jefferson's enemies recognized the wisdom of his action. Ironically, Andrew Johnson's decision to purchase Alaska in 1867 was considered a colossal blunder by many people. Today, it is considered his greatest presidential achievement.

In some cases, papers in the Archives reveal instances of apparent presidential decisiveness, perhaps wrongly attributed. We take for granted President James Monroe's authorship of the Doctrine which bears his name, as stated in his annual message to Congress in 1823. But his warning to European powers not to intervene in the Americas was conceived, if not actually penned, by John Quincy Adams, then Secretary of State.

The use of the veto is one measure of presidential resolve. President Grover Cleveland, a Democrat, acted decisively and courageously when he vetoed the Dependent Pension Bill as well as many private bills sponsored by Congressmen on behalf of constituents who had served in the Civil War. His action earned him the undying hatred of the Grand Army of the Republic, dubbed by wits "the Grand Army of the Republican Party." Andrew Jackson, noted for his strength of will, used the veto twelve times. Although this is more than twice the combined total of vetoes by his predecessors in office, it is negligible compared to those of his successors. Eisenhower, for example, used the veto 181 times; Franklin D. Roosevelt, 631 times.

Decision-making and the presidency are inseparable. Not all decisions are as difficult and profound as those leading to Truman's use of the atomic bomb or to Wilson's entry into World War I. Many are routine, even though they may stir popular interest, as did Theodore Roosevelt's decision to change the name of the presidential residence from the Executive Mansion to the White House in 1901.

Even minor presidential decisions at times have had great impact on the course of American history. President John Adams appointed a number of

Andrew Jackson, seventh president of the United States, from an original daguerreotype made at the Hermitage just a few weeks before Old Hickory's death on June 8, 1845. Although part of the Brady Collection, Brady probably did not take the picture but had someone do it for him. Brady, in fact, later claimed that he "had Andrew Jackson taken barely in time to save his sacred lineaments to posterity."

Opposite: The Volstead Act, better known as the Prohibition Act, passed in 1919, provided for the enforcement of the Eighteenth Amendment, which forbade the sale, manufacture, and transportation of "intoxicating beverages" in the United States. One little-known fact about this legislation is that President Woodrow Wilson vetoed it. The pro-temperance forces were so great, however, that Congress had little trouble in mustering the necessary votes to override his veto.

judges in the last days of his administration. Among these were John Marshall as Chief Justice of the Supreme Court and William Marbury as Justice of the Peace. Marshall's long and effective service clearly established the Court as the strong third branch of government the Founding Fathers had envisioned. One of his first actions, however, nullified Adams's appointment of Marbury, whose commission as Justice of the Peace was rejected by Jefferson's Secretary of State. Marbury's suit to retain his commission ended in the famous decision in the Supreme Court of *Marbury v. Madison*, in which Marshall declared that a law passed by Congress and signed by a president (the Judiciary Act of 1789) could be unconstitutional, thereby invoking the now well-known principle of judicial review.

Times of crisis, as when a president dies in office, are also reflected in the Archives. So far, eight have done so. And two vice presidents thus thrust into the presidency believed it necessary to sign oaths of office —John Tyler and Andrew Johnson. Tyler took the oath, and wrote it, at Jesse Brown's Indian Queen Hotel, using a piece of hotel stationery. The Circuit Court Judge who certified the document stated that Tyler deemed himself "qualified to perform the duties and exercise the powers and offices of President, on the death of William Henry Harrison. . . . without any other oath than that which he has taken as Vice President; yet, as doubts may arise, and for greater caution, took and subscribed the foregoing oath, before W. Cranch, April 6, 1841." (Many years later, Attorney General Robert F. Kennedy ruled that a vice president, on the strength of his oath for that office, automatically inherits the powers of the highest office upon the death of the president.)

Andrew Johnson, Lincoln's successor, received a letter from the Cabinet, except for Secretary of State William H. Seward, who was injured in the same assassination plot, urging him to assume the duties of president. "The emergency of the government demands that you should immediately qualify according to the requirements of the Constitution, and enter upon the duties of President of the United States," declared the Cabinet members. The stress of the hour is evident in the hastily written letter, which has

H. R. 6810.

66

Sixty-sixth Congress of the United States of America;

At the First Session,

Begun and held at the City of Washington on Monday, the nineteenth day of May,
one thousand nine hundred and nineteen.

AN ACT

To prohibit intoxicating beverages, and to regulate the manufacture,
production, use, and sale of high-proof spirits for other than beverage
purposes, and to insure an ample supply of alcohol and promote its use
in scientific research and in the development of fuel, dye, and other lawful
industries.

*Be it enacted by the Senate and House of Representatives of the United
States of America in Congress assembled*, That the short title of this Act shall
be the "National Prohibition Act."

TITLE I.

TO PROVIDE FOR THE ENFORCEMENT OF WAR PROHIBITION.

The term "War Prohibition Act" used in this Act shall mean the
provisions of any Act or Acts prohibiting the sale and manufacture of intoxicating
liquors until the conclusion of the present war and thereafter until the
termination of demobilization, the date of which shall be determined and
proclaimed by the President of the United States. The words "beer, wine,
or other intoxicating malt or vinous liquors" in the War Prohibition Act shall
be hereafter construed to mean any such beverages which contain one-half
of 1 per centum or more of alcohol by volume: *Provided*, That the foregoing
definition shall not extend to dealcoholized wine nor to any beverage or liquid
produced by the process by which beer, ale, porter or wine is produced, if it
contains less than one-half of 1 per centum of alcohol by volume, and is made
as prescribed in section 37 of Title II of this Act, and is otherwise denominated
than as beer, ale, or porter, and is contained and sold in, or from, such sealed
and labeled bottles, casks, or containers as the commissioner may by regulation prescribe.

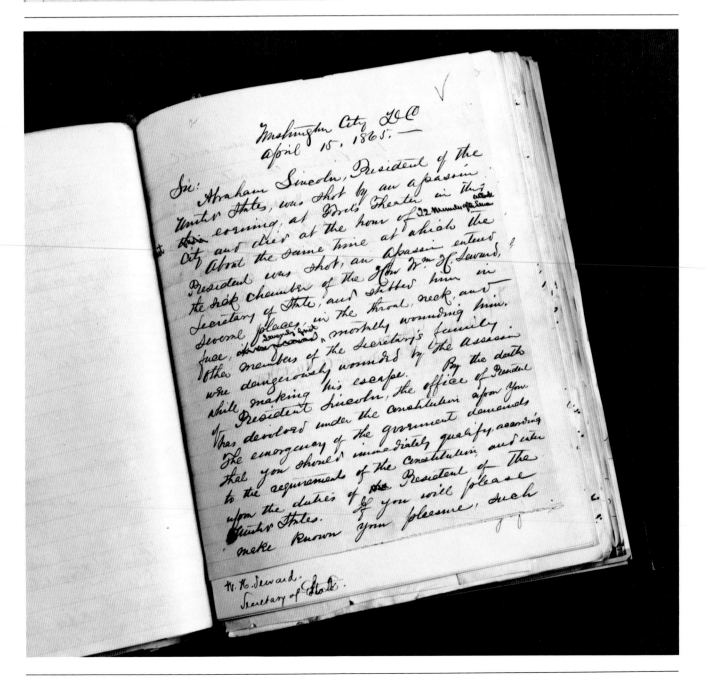

The letter Vice President Andrew Johnson received from fellow cabinet members informing him of Lincoln's assassination and asking him to assume the responsibilities of President. Note that Secretary of the Treasury Hugh McCulloch signed it twice.

numerous emendations, blotches, and strike-outs. Secretary of the Treasury Hugh McCulloch signed the letter twice, although his second signature is crossed out.

As noted at the outset of this chapter, each president is required to perform a variety of duties, whether he is suited to them all or not. He is at once Commander-in-Chief of our Armed Forces, Chief Administrative Officer of the Federal Government, and Chief of State. Only a few have been able to master the whole job.

George Washington was probably our most successful president. Having served as Commander-in-Chief throughout the Revolutionary War and as President of the Constitutional Convention, he was chosen unanimously for the presidency, the only person ever to be so honored. Widespread confidence that he would not subvert America's hard-won liberties, that he would not replace one king with another, enabled the new government to succeed. Fully aware of the importance of his role as the nation's first president, he brought substance to the office that the Constitution had only outlined; he gave the country a strong executive who worked amicably and effectively with other branches of government.

Washington, the hero of Valley Forge, Princeton, and Yorktown, was the epitome of the citizen-soldier. His success on the battlefield, followed by his success as president, may explain in part Americans' inclination to put generals in the White House. But even he had problems when it came to picking military subordinates. Two of them were defeated fighting Indians, who enjoyed their greatest victory over an American army during his administration, the so-called St. Clair Massacre. Washington finally avoided a major humiliation for the United States by sending General "Mad Anthony" Wayne into the fray. Wayne's victory over Little Turtle and his Miami warriors at the Battle of Fallen Timbers dampened their enthusiasm for war and opened the Old Northwest to white settlement.

Abraham Lincoln and Harry S Truman also had problems with generals. Lincoln replaced one after another until he found Ulysses S. Grant could deliver the victories he desperately needed to hold the Union together.

Abraham Lincoln in one view from a multiple-image glass-plate negative made by Mathew Brady on January 8, 1864.

New York, 6th April, 1789.

Sir,

I have the honor to transmit to your Excellency the information of your unanimous election to the office of President of the United States of America. Suffer me, Sir, to indulge the hope, that so auspicious a mark of public confidence will meet your approbation, and be considered as a sure pledge of the affection and support you are to expect from a free and an enlightened People.—

I am, Sir, with sentiments of respect,

y^r m^t hb. serv^t,

J L

His Excellency
George Washington, Esqr

Truman's "general" troubles were of another sort. Whereas Lincoln needed a crushing victory, Truman wished to avoid the one that Douglas MacArthur wanted to give him in Korea. The war in Korea had limited objectives, but MacArthur insisted upon total victory. He argued so stubbornly that Truman finally sent the order relieving him of his command. Truman was not the first president to dismiss a popular general, but he did it in a manner that raised a storm of protest and made MacArthur a folk hero. Critics sneered that a "two-bit President had fired a five-star General." Nevertheless, scholars now credit Truman with confirming the republican principle of civilian supremacy over the military.

Being a good president does not necessarily mean being a good administrator, although Washington was an excellent executive, thanks to his experience in managing his large plantation as well as the Continental Army. The government of his day was tiny compared to today's bureaucracy, of course. Each of his successors has had to deal with an increasingly complex administrative situation. The last president to supervise personally the entire government may have been Polk, who literally worked himself to death. He attended to all administrative details, ran executive departments when their supervisors were away, and kept a detailed diary as well. He seldom left Washington for vacations and was usually at his desk until past midnight. As a result, Polk was so exhausted that he died only 103 days after leaving office.

A problem common to all presidents has been the difficulty in finding competent executive assistants. Cleveland once grumbled that if the president ever had great policy in mind, "he had no one to help him work it out." This complaint had previously been voiced by President-elect Garfield: "I am more at a loss to find just the right man for Private Secretary than for any place I have to fill," he claimed. "The man who holds that place can do very much to make or mar the success of an administration. The position ought to be held in higher estimation than Secretary of State."

The president is also our nation's chief diplomat. He formulates and executes foreign policy. He appoints and supervises the diplomatic corps,

President Lincoln inspecting the headquarters of the Army of the Potomac on October 1, 1863. The man facing Lincoln is General George B. McClellan, who was removed from command a month after Alexander Gardner took this photograph.

Opposite: The letter notifying George Washington of his unanimous election as President of the United States, April 6, 1789. The initials are those of John Langdon, president of the Senate.

Overleaf: This picture of Indian delegations—Pawnee, Ponca, Pottawatomi, Sac, and Fox—visiting the president of the United States may well be the earliest photograph of the White House. Taken by an unknown photographer in front of the South Portico on December 31, 1857, it was probably commissioned by Charles Mackay, who featured the Indians in a story for the *Illustrated London News.* The photograph is now in the Brady Collection of the Archives.

President Franklin D. Roosevelt and
General Dwight D. Eisenhower tour-
ing an American base in Sicily, December 8, 1943. At left is General Patton.

negotiates treaties with other nations, administers foreign aid, and nowa-
days serves as a good-will ambassador, visiting foreign countries and receiving world rulers and dignitaries on their visits here.

Washington was superb in this role, but his successors were not all so
gifted. Polk, for example, thought receiving announcements of royal births
was ridiculous. Once, when the Russian ambassador announced the birth
of an imperial grandchild, Polk apologized for not being able to reciprocate.
He was especially irked that he had to acknowledge each announcement
in writing. "Had I not found such to be the settled practice," he confided
to his diary, "I never would have signed or sent such answers." President
Theodore Roosevelt also had little patience for some of the courtesies of
state. He resented the flowery language used in diplomatic correspondence.
"Politeness is necessary," he remarked, "but gushing and obviously insin-
cere and untruthful compliments merely make both sides ridiculous; and
are underbred in addition."

One diplomatic requirement for all presidents until late in the nineteenth century was the entertainment of Indian leaders who came to the
capital to solidify relations between their tribes and the United States. To
the American Indians the president personified the majesty and strength
of the nation, and they called him the Great Father (never the Great White
Father) in the hope that he would be generous to his impoverished children.
Meetings between the Great Father and these delegations varied little from
administration to administration as ceremonial occasions. Serious business
was seldom transacted, for this was left to officials who administered Indian affairs at the cabinet level.

Only recently have presidents served as their own ambassadors of
international good will. Until 1906, when Theodore Roosevelt visited
the Panama Canal, no American president had left the United States
while in office. Since then, of course, foreign travel has become almost
routine. Richard Nixon, for example, promoted globe-trotting into notable
achievement in foreign affairs. His visit to the People's Republic of
China in February 1972 was the first high-level contact between the

President Truman awarding the Distinguished Service Medal to General Douglas MacArthur during the Wake Island Conference, October 1950.

Below: President Truman's proposed order to General MacArthur removing him from command during the Korean War.

PROPOSED ORDER TO GENERAL MacARTHUR TO BE SIGNED BY THE PRESIDENT

I deeply regret that it becomes my duty as President and Commander in Chief of the United States military forces to replace you as Supreme Commander, Allied Powers; Commander in Chief, United Nations Command; Commander in Chief, Far East; and Commanding General, U. S. Army, Far East.

You will turn over your commands, effective at once, to Lt. Gen. Matthew B. Ridgway. You are authorized to have issued such orders as are necessary to complete desired travel to such place as you select.

My reasons for your replacement, ~~which~~ will be made public concurrently with the delivery to you of the foregoing order, will be communicated to you by Secretary Pace. *and are contained in the next following message.*

/s/ Harry S Truman

United States and the added responsibility which has been
entrusted to me by the United Nations, I have decided that
I must make a change of command in the Far East. I have,

Opposite: Page one of the draft, with his handwritten changes, of the message President Franklin D. Roosevelt delivered to Congress the day after the Japanese attack on Pearl Harbor.

two nations in decades. As he stated before his historic visit, he hoped it would "become a Journey for Peace, peace not just for our generation but for future generations on this earth we share together." Although some benefits of his visit may remain in question, he established an atmosphere of rapport between China and the United States, which is considered a major success in an otherwise troubled presidency.

Many documents in the Archives reflect the activities of presidents-to-be as well as of presidents-that-were. All of our chief executives except Cleveland and Wilson served the U.S. government before their election to the highest office. Thirteen were vice presidents; nine were cabinet members; eighteen were members of the House of Representatives; sixteen were senators; and twenty-five served in the armed forces. Their early public service was not always at a lofty level. Safe in the Archives is Abraham Lincoln's appointment as postmaster of New Salem, Illinois, in 1833. Here also is documentation of Lyndon Johnson's service as Texas State Director of the National Youth Administration between 1935 and 1937. The work of Captain Ronald Reagan in producing training films during World War II is noted in Department of the Army records.

Some presidents have returned to public office after the end of their administrations. President Adams appointed George Washington Lieutenant-General in 1798 and placed him in command of all armies of the United States. John Quincy Adams ran for Congress, serving seventeen years in the House of Representatives before he collapsed on the floor of the House. William Howard Taft turned to a professorship at the Yale Law School after his defeat by Woodrow Wilson. But in 1921 President Harding named him Chief Justice of the Supreme Court, a post which he filled until 1930. Herbert Hoover retired from public life until President Truman summoned him to coordinate World War II relief planning. Deeply touched, Hoover sent Truman his thanks: "When you came to the White House, within a month you opened the door to me to the only profession I knew, public service, and you undid some disgraceful actions that had been taken in the prior years. For all of this and your friendship, I am deeply grateful." Hoo-

DRAFT No. 1 December 7, 1941.

PROPOSED MESSAGE TO THE CONGRESS

Yesterday, December 7, 1941, a date which will live in ~~world history~~ *infamy*

the United States of America was ~~simultaneously~~ *suddenly* and deliberately attacked

by naval and air forces of the Empire of Japan.

The United States was at the moment at peace with that nation and was *still in*

~~continuing the~~ conversation with its Government and its Emperor looking

toward the maintenance of peace in the Pacific. Indeed, one hour after

Japanese air squadrons had commenced bombing in *Oahu* ~~the Philippines~~

the Japanese Ambassador to the United States and his colleague delivered

to the Secretary of State a formal reply to a *recent American* ~~former~~ message. ~~from the~~

~~Secretary.~~ *While* This reply ~~contained a statement~~ *stated* that diplomatic negotiations *it seemed useless*

~~must be considered at an end,~~ *it* contained no threat ~~and no~~ hint of *war or*

armed attack.

It will be recorded that the distance ~~of Hawaii, and especially~~ of

Hawaii from Japan makes it obvious that the attack ~~was~~ *was* deliberately

planned many days *or even weeks* ago. During the intervening time the Japanese Govern-

ment has deliberately sought to deceive the United States by false

statements and expressions of hope for continued peace.

Herbert Hoover served as chairman for the Commission for Relief in Belgium, which aided that country throughout World War I. Following the shipment of 697,116,000 pounds of flour to Belgium, the emptied flour sacks were embroidered or painted by artists, or decorated in convents or girls' schools. They were then returned to Mr. Hoover and the American people as an expression of gratitude.

Opposite: During each administration the president of the United States gives and receive gifts. The photograph shows only a small portion of the approximately 951 Head of State gifts and their storage crates received by President Richard M. Nixon. Among these are a jar from Masada, Israel, 73 A.D, a statue of the goddess, Isis, from Egypt, sixth century B.C., silver and ebony bookends from Mexico, a tea service from the Soviet Union and a Louis XVI clock from France. One Domestic gift included in this photograph is the hand-sewn American flag on a handkerchief made by Col. John Dramesi while he was a prisoner of war in North Vietnam. He was able to smuggle this flag out when he was released.

ver went on to serve as Chairman of the Commission of Organization of the Executive Branch of Government under both Presidents Truman and Eisenhower.

For the first century and a half of our history, the personal and state papers generated during a president's term of office were considered his private property. All of the chief executives from Washington through Hoover took their papers with them when they left office, but Franklin D. Roosevelt changed this practice by donating his presidential papers, along with a building to house them, to the United States government. Roosevelt did this because he had a unique sense of history, and he was a collector. He collected anything and everything—stamps, historical manuscripts, naval prints, ship models, Dutch tiles, paintings, books, and even bird calls. "If he had done nothing else," claims historian Samuel Eliot Morison, "he would have gone down in history as a great collector."

He was furthermore a preserver, a habit inherited from his mother and cultivated by his informal tutor, William Chase. "Never destroy anything!" Chase admonished the future president. Roosevelt realized early that his collections had outgrown the capacity of an ordinary residence. In 1934 he confided to a friend his hope that someday Hyde Park would have a fireproof building where "historical documents" could be safely kept. By the summer of 1938 he knew what he wanted. On the Fourth of July, he brought together the two prime movers of what was to become the Franklin D. Roosevelt Library: Archivist of the United States R.D.W. Connor and Frank C. Walker, a Pennsylvania lawyer who later became Postmaster General. Roosevelt proposed to establish a depository, financed by private money and presented as a gift to the federal government, to be administered by

the National Archives. Two considerations kept him from giving his papers outright to the Archives: (1) his fear that the building might be damaged in time of war and (2) his knowledge that much of his material was not directly related to the federal government. Like any true collector, he did not wish to see his treasures dispersed. Within three years, Franklin D. Roosevelt had his library, just as he designed it—a one-story Dutch colonial structure of local fieldstone, built in the Hudson Valley on land the Roosevelt family had owned for four generations.

The most famous of Franklin D. Roosevelt's hobbies was stamp collecting. This saw him through the terrible days of recuperation from polio, the disease that left him crippled. As president, he could indulge this hobby to a degree undreamt of in the history of philately. No stamp went to press without his personal approval; during his administration the Post Office published 134 commemoratives and forty-nine regular issues. What he liked got printed; what he disliked was discarded. He even suggested ideas for stamps, like the one he proposed to celebrate the impending Polar voyage of his friend, Richard E. Byrd. Roosevelt drew a rough sketch of what became the "Byrd Antarctic Expedition II" stamp—a global map with dotted lines indicating the routes of Byrd's previous flights. Upon examining the die proof, the President turned to the artist, pointed to the route of Byrd's 1927 transatlantic flight, and said: "He landed further up than that." The artist checked, found him to be correct, and made the alteration.

The housing of his collections helped Roosevelt solve a problem that had troubled his predecessors in office: what to do with the gifts they receive but cannot keep. The men who drafted the Constitution thought they had taken care of the matter in Article I, Section 9, which provides that "no Person holding any Office of Profit or Trust . . . shall, without the consent of Congress, accept of any present, Emolument, Office, or Title, of any kind whatever, from any King, Prince, or foreign State." Such a rule was needed, explained Alexander Hamilton, because the president might be "tempted to betray the interests of the State for the acquisition of wealth."

Realizing that a refusal to accept gifts from foreign governments could

Above, left: Having heard from Ambassador to England Joseph P. Kennedy that his son Robert was an avid stamp collector, President Roosevelt sent the nine-year-old a packet of stamps from his own collection, prompting this reply.

Above: President Franklin D. Roosevelt with his stamp collection.

Opposite, top left: President Wilson's Inaugural Parade, March 4, 1917.

Opposite, top right: Herbert Hoover and President Calvin Coolidge leaving the White House for the Capitol on Inauguration Day, March 4, 1929.

Opposite: Ulysses S. Grant's inauguration, March 4, 1869, in a magnificent photograph by Mathew Brady. The cracks in the picture are on the original negative, a typical condition for many of the glass plates received by the National Archives.

Overleaf: Gifts and letters from the King of Siam to the President of the United States, February 14, 1861. The king was Somdetch Phra Paramendr Maha Mongkut, better known as the enlightened monarch in Margaret D. Landon's book *Anna and the King of Siam* and later in the musical *The King and I.*

be viewed as an expression of ill will, the first two presidents adopted a relaxed attitude about this restriction. Jefferson, however, refused anything but pamphlets, books, or similar items of so little value as to be "below suspicion." He did not permit his daughter to keep a cashmere shawl given to her by the Tunisian ambassador; the shawl was sold at auction and the proceeds placed in the Treasury.

Abiding by Article I, Section 9, has produced several comic incidents. In 1839, the U.S. Consul at Tangiers was confronted with a pair of lions from the Emperor of Morocco intended for President Martin Van Buren. Since refusal to accept the gift could have meant the messenger's beheading, the consul lodged the lions in one of the rooms at the consulate, pending instructions from the Department of State. (The lions were eventually sold at auction in Philadelphia for $375.) During Lincoln's term, the King of Siam capped a commercial treaty with the United States by giving the president a handsome sword, a pair of elephant tusks, and a daguerreotype of himself and one of his children. He offered also several pairs of elephants for breeding, since the United States had none of these wonderful beasts of burden. By explaining that steam engines were a more efficient form of transportation in the United States, Lincoln managed to avoid accepting the elephants. The other gifts he accepted as "tokens" of good will for the American people, promising to place them in "the archives of the government, where they will remain perpetually as tokens of mutual esteem." The sword, daguerreotype and one tusk are in the vault of the National Archives today.

Although few gifts are as exotic as lions and elephants, each president receives his share of ancient pottery, jeweled daggers, cigarette holders, canes, and assorted oddities. Now, thanks to the Presidential Libraries, the nation has appropriate places in which to display them.

One library, of course, does not make a system. Roosevelt created the basic concept, but Truman and Eisenhower gave it impetus by following his example. In 1955, Congress passed the bipartisan Presidential Libraries Act, which provides the system's charter. Under its terms, the authority to

accept land, buildings, papers, and "other historical materials" belonging to each president was conferred upon the Administrator of General Services, who, in turn, delegated the authority to the Archivist of the United States. Because of this legislation, a network of unique cultural institutions spans the country. It includes the Harry S Truman Library in Independence, Missouri; the Dwight D. Eisenhower Library in Abilene, Kansas; the Herbert Hoover Library in West Branch, Iowa; the Lyndon B. Johnson Library in Austin, Texas; the John F. Kennedy Library in Boston, Massachusetts; the Gerald R. Ford Library in Ann Arbor and Museum in Grand Rapids, Michigan; the Richard M. Nixon Library, planned for San Clemente, California; and the Jimmy Carter Library, to be located in Atlanta, Georgia; as well as the Franklin D. Roosevelt Library in Hyde Park, New York. These Libraries are administered as an integral part of the National Archives under the aegis of the General Services Administration.

The idea of Presidential Libraries did not originate in the twentieth century. George Washington considered establishing a kind of records repository on his estate at Mount Vernon. The Adams family, in fact, did build a library, which went to the Massachusetts Historical Society. But the leap from inspiration to execution proved formidable, with the result that much presidential material was lost. The wastage of Washington's papers began immediately upon his death. Martha destroyed almost all the correspondence between herself and her husband. Bushrod Washington, the President's nephew, shipped most of the papers to Richmond for John Marshall to use in writing a biography. By the time Marshall returned them twenty-five years later, they had been damaged by rats, dampness, and neglect. Meanwhile, Bushrod had made gifts of Washington's memorabilia to friends and relations, a letter here, an autograph there. Some letters were cut into pieces to spread them further.

At great cost and trouble over the last century, most of Washington's known papers have been retrieved and are now in the Library of Congress, as are some of the personal papers of twenty-two other presidents. Still, there are enormous lacunae in the documentation of the presidency, be-

The John F. Kennedy Presidential Library.

An exhibit case at the Gerald R. Ford Presidential Library, which contains Bicentennial presents President Ford received from citizens across the country.

Below: Campaign buttons from the collections of the Presidential Libraries.

cause papers were deliberately destroyed, lost in fires, or dispersed. Many of John Tyler's papers were lost when Richmond burned in 1865. Warren G. Harding's wife took it upon herself to destroy most of his papers after his death. Other collections have been as good as lost because of the incredibly long periods during which families have withheld them from the public. Lincoln's papers, for instance, were not opened to research until 1947, eighty-two years after his death; the papers of John Quincy Adams remained closed for 128 years after he left the presidency.

Presidential Libraries have helped to change this. By 1950, only five years after the Roosevelt Library had opened, the bulk of Franklin D. Roosevelt's papers, both personal and public, had been opened for research. The same speed of access has been true at the other Libraries. Even more important, of course, is the certainty that the papers will not be dispersed or lost. The Libraries have finally tamed what one historian has called "the winds of housecleaning and neglect."

Critics call the Libraries monuments, and they are a particularly suitable kind of monument. Because the twentieth century has witnessed enormous growth in both the power and the scope of the presidency, one can no longer understand the office through papers alone. As James O'Neill, director of the Presidential Library System, points out: "The impact of the presidency is to be found in the whole range of objects from handwritten note to video tape, from presentation dagger to political cartoon—even in those idiosyncratic collections of Ming vases, gavels, Bibles, guns, and ship models that capture the museum visitor's eye." Although the presidency is an institution, presidents are individuals, and each gives the office a distinct style of leadership. This, O'Neill believes, is what makes the combination of papers and "other historical materials" in a Presidential Library unique and valuable. "The library reflects the man, and, like the presidency itself, it exists not for the few but for the many, not for scholars alone but for the nation as a whole."

YOU HAVE STRUCK
A NOBLE BARGAIN

he greatest trove of treasures in the National Archives is the records of the Department of State, largely because the State Department kept important documents for the entire federal government before there was a National Archives. Thus, the Declaration of Independence, the Northwest Ordinance, and the Emancipation Proclamation are examples of State Department records. So are the passenger list for the *Lusitania*'s final voyage, the announcement of Queen Victoria's marriage to Prince Albert, and a "wanted" poster for Butch Cassidy and the Sundance Kid. In these files are passports, treaties (including those with Indian tribes), presidential proclamations, executive orders, and similar documents of state. Among the most fascinating are the diplomatic and consular files, thousands of bound volumes that contain despatches accumulated since 1786 from every U.S. post abroad, reflecting our country's rise to world power.

America was born into a strife-torn world. Its survival depended largely on the quality of its diplomats. One of the best was Benjamin Franklin, who engineered treaties of friendship and alliance with France in 1778. These treaties, our nation's first, were central to American victory in the Revolution. Franklin viewed the British surrender at Saratoga, in October 1777, as a diplomatic as well as military windfall. He played so well on French fears that England after this defeat might make concessions to the colonies in return for peace, thereby restoring the British Empire, that France promptly signed two treaties with the United States. One gave American shippers special privileges, the other gave the new republic a powerful ally.

Franklin was the first American Minister (the title Ambassador was not used until late in the nineteenth century) to be received by a foreign government. His home in Passy, in fact, was the center of American diplomatic activity in Europe during the Revolution. He also had the honor of being one of the Plenipotentiary Commissioners who negotiated the peace treaty with Great Britain ending the war. Thomas Jefferson, who followed him as Minister to France, when asked by a French official if he was Franklin's replacement, replied: "No one can replace him, Sir; I am only

Opposite: Napoleon Bonaparte, then First Consul of the French Republic, and Talleyrand, his Foreign Minister, signed the Louisiana Purchase Treaty on April 30, 1803. Like many treaties of this period, it includes an ornate skippet, here a gold-washed silver box containing a wax impression of the French seal.

Dodge City "Peace Commissioners"
about 1890. Left to right: Charles
Bassett, W. H. Harris, Wyatt Earp,
Luke Short, L. McLean, Bat Master-
son, and Neal Brown.

Below: When Butch Cassidy and the
Sundance Kid were suspected of having left the country, the Pinkerton
Detective Agency sent copies of their
"wanted" poster to various American installations abroad; hence their
presence among the records of the
State Department.

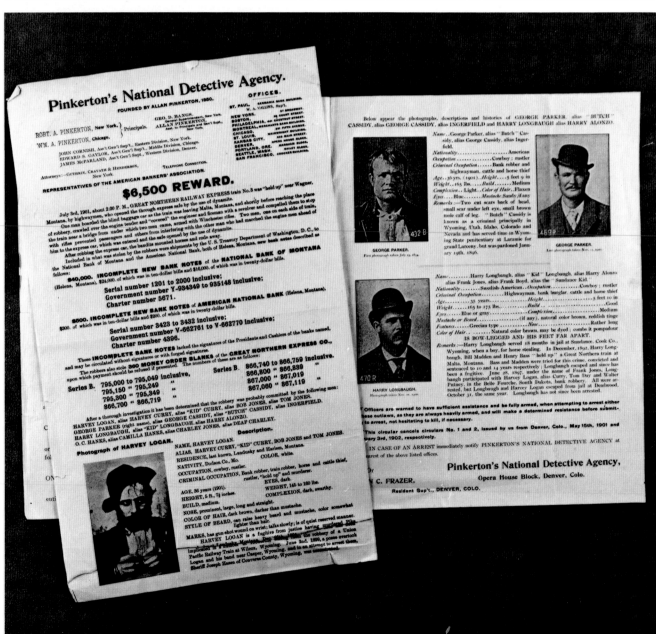

his successor."

Had it not been for the rivalry between England, France, and Spain, the course of American history might well have been entirely different. Each of these powerful nations had interests in North America, but each was more concerned with undermining the other than in taking risks for North American territory. Franklin and the other Founding Fathers realized this and, once they had won the Revolution, avoided further alliance. Non-alignment became the watchword of the young republic, which viewed the Atlantic Ocean as a huge moat. As a result, America for more than a century managed to steer clear of major foreign controversy, while using the European political situation, through shrewd negotiations, to achieve a series of stunning territorial acquisitions.

During a century of relative isolation, the United States enjoyed explosive geographical growth, the result of a series of international treaties that enabled the nation to increase from thirteen to fifty states. (Some Americans called it Manifest Destiny; the Indians probably would have called it Manifest Greed.) Among these treaties, now carefully preserved in their original and often colorful form in the National Archives, are : the Treaty of Paris, 1783; the Louisiana Purchase, 1803; the Adams-Onis Treaty with Spain, 1819; the Oregon Treaty with Great Britain, 1846; the Treaty of Guadalupe-Hidalgo with Mexico, 1848; and the Alaska Purchase with Russia, 1867. The records show that these treaties often resulted from the sort of diplomatic skill that Franklin displayed in 1778. Just as often they reveal blind luck and international stupidity. Two, in fact, the Louisiana Purchase and Guadalupe-Hidalgo, came about because the U.S. negotiators disobeyed their instructions.

The United States obtained Louisiana because President Jefferson wanted to acquire New Orleans from France. Since this seaport was vital for the livelihood of Americans living along the Mississippi River and its tributaries, Jefferson authorized U.S. Minister to France Robert Livingston and Special Envoy James Monroe to pay up to ten million dollars for the City of New Orleans and limited additional territory. Livingston and Monroe haggled

The legend with this photo reads: "Judge Roy Bean, the 'Law West of the Pecos', holding court at thé old town of Langtry, Texas in 1900, trying a horse thief. This building was court- house and saloon. No other peace officers in the locality at that time."

Overleaf: Three treaties that have played major roles in the history of the United States. Left: Treaty of Alliance with France, the first nation to acknowledge our nation's inde- pendence, signed in 1778. Under its terms, France provided military assis- tance that may have been decisive in the American victory. Right: Alaska Purchase Treaty, signed in 1867, which gave the United States its first noncontiguous territory. Foreground: Treaty of Guadalupe Hidalgo. Signed with Mexico on February 2, 1848, it added nearly two million square miles to the United States, including pres- ent-day California, Arizona, Nevada, Utah, New Mexico, and parts of Colo- rado and Wyoming.

Napoleon Bonaparte's signature on the Louisiana Purchase Treaty, April 30, 1803.

Opposite, top: A detail of one of the earliest cipher messages of U.S. diplomacy. In the years after the American Revolution, American sailing ships were often in peril on the high seas. In 1795, France, for example, ordered the capture of any vessels, American or otherwise, suspected of carrying merchandise of Great Britain, with whom she was at war. In an attempt to negotiate an end to the seizure of ships, the United States government in 1796 dispatched John Marshall, Elbridge Gerry, and C.C. Pinckney to France to request a treaty of commerce and friendship. Although the French Foreign Minister refused to see them, they were approached by three French intermediaries—designated X, Y, and Z—who demanded a bribe of $240,000 as the price for negotiations. This demand, detailed in the coded despatch sent back to Washington, prompted the legendary response from Congress: "Millions for defense, Sir, but not one cent for tribute!"

for an emotion-filled week with French Foreign Minister Talleyrand, then agreed to pay fifteen million dollars for the entire tract of land claimed by France. The American envoys had little knowledge of what they had purchased. Talleyrand claimed ignorance as well. He insisted that the United States take Louisiana as the French had received it from Spain a few years earlier. "I asked him how Spain meant to give them possession," Livingston later reported.

"I do not know," Talleyrand shrugged.

"Then you mean that we shall construe it our own way?" Livingston asked.

"I can give you no direction," Talleyrand responded. "You have made a noble bargain for yourselves and I suppose you will make the most of it."

Noble bargain indeed! Louisiana turned out to be a vast empire, bigger than France itself. The unexpected opportunity came because Napoleon, beset with troubles at home and concerned that Spain would expand her influence in North America, had suddenly directed Talleyrand to cede the entire tract.

Another case involving a U.S. negotiator who violated his instructions resulted in the Treaty of Guadalupe-Hidalgo, signed February 2, 1848. While General Winfield Scott pursued Santa Ana around northern Mexico, President Polk sent Nicholas Trist, Chief Clerk of the State Department, to that country to negotiate a peace. No sooner had Trist arrived in Mexico City, however, than he fired off despatches critical of Scott and behaved in a generally inappropriate manner. Polk ordered his recall, but the envoy refused to leave. In cheerful disregard of his instructions, he concluded a treaty with Mexico. Trist, as it turned out, may have been wiser than his Washington superiors, for he opened negotiations with the Mexican moderates who had come to power. Among other provisions, the treaty ceded a vast region—half of Mexico—to the United States for fifteen million dollars. Polk may have been unhappy with his emissary, but he approved the treaty nonetheless.

The Alaska Purchase also caused difficulty for its chief proponent,

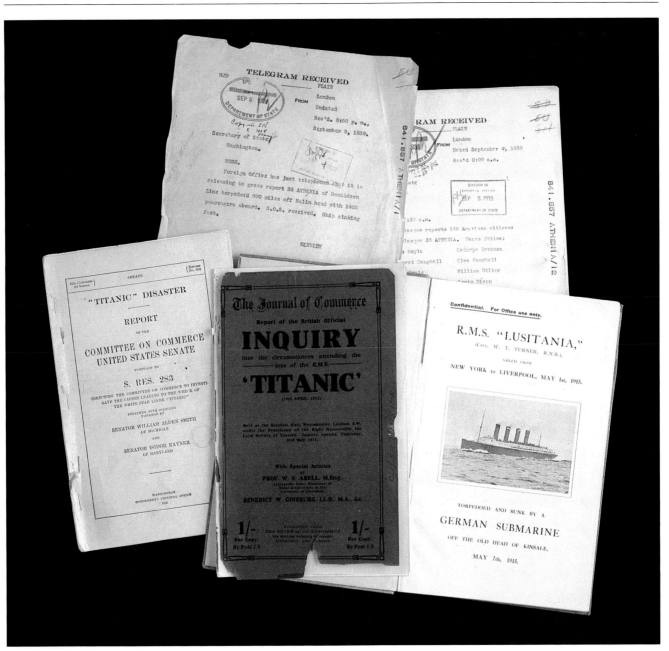

Below: Information on virtually any topic in American history can be found in the National Archives. Here is a sampling of documents and publications relating to maritime history—in this case, ship disasters—to be found among records of the Department of State.

Bret Harte.

Opposite: The Treaty of Commerce and Navigation between the United States and the Kingdom of Belgium, signed at Brussels on November 10, 1845.

Secretary of State William H. Seward. After the Civil War, there was little interest in territorial expansion. Seward, however, took advantage of an opportunity to acquire a chunk of real estate that its financially troubled owner viewed as a frozen asset. When he offered the Russians $7.2 million for Alaska, they eagerly accepted the money, signing the treaty in the State Department at four o'clock on the morning of March 30, 1867. When the news became public, the press ridiculed the purchase, dubbing it "Seward's Folly," the "Polar Bear Garden," and "Seward's Ice Box." Some Congressmen threatened to disavow the treaty, but it was eventually approved, and many people even then realized that Seward may have struck his own "noble bargain" for the United States. Among them was the author Bret Harte, who expressed his opinion with this prescient poem:

> T'aint so very mean a trade,
> When the land is all surveyed.
> There's a right smart chance for fur-chase
> All along this recent purchase.
> And, unless the stories fail,
> Every fish from Cod to Whale;
> Rocks too; mebbe quartz, let's see.
> T'would be strange if there should be,
> Seems I've heard such stories told,
> Eh, why, bless us, yes its gold!

Until recently, treaties involved two forms of diplomatic "art." One, of course, was the skill demonstrated in the negotiations; the other was the craftsmanship reflected in the preparation of the documents themselves. Until about 1920 the "exchange copy" of a treaty was often handsomely bound in fine leather embossed with a coat of arms or other elaborate ornamentation. Sometimes a wax impression of the state seal was contained in a silver or gold box called a "skippet" and attached to the treaty with silk or metallic cords.

In the "art" of diplomacy the United States differed little from its national counterparts. Although the new republic attempted to practice an

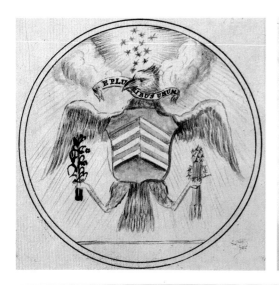
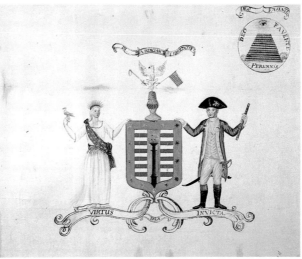

austerity compatible with its Puritan idealism, Americans abroad soon found diplomatic elegance to be a necessity. As John Adams reluctantly observed: "We must submit to what we cannot alter."

Accordingly, the Continental Congress, in 1782, designed a Great Seal for the United States. In effect a national coat of arms, the seal has a simple design that has remained essentially unchanged ever since. It consists of a displayed eagle, a constellation of thirteen stars, an olive branch, arrows, and a shield.

Until 1824, the United States used the original die for the Great Seal for the pendant seals on treaties, but its small size—only 2¼ inches in diameter —compared so unfavorably with European pendant seals that the State Department decided to order a more imposing one. Seraphim Masi, a Washington jeweler, produced a die nearly five inches in diameter. Known as the Old Treaty Seal of the United States, this was used on all American treaties for the next half century, making them as ostentatious as those received from the European nations. Although the ornate "exchange copies" are normally to be found in foreign archives, several remain in the National Archives because, for one reason or another, they were never delivered.

The United States used pendant seals until Secretary of State Hamilton Fish decided to end this colorful—and expensive—practice in the early 1870s. The last American treaty to bear one was probably the Treaty of Washington, signed in 1871 with Great Britain. It was also about this time that the Masi die disappeared, not to surface again until 1947 when two State Department employees found it while clearing trash from a storehouse. Now it has a permanent home in the National Archives, where it recalls the romantic age of international diplomacy.

Other examples of diplomatic art are letters of credence, especially those from the nineteenth century. Usually called credentials, these are formal documents that heads of state furnish to their chief diplomats for presentation to the heads of the governments to which they are assigned. One of the finest examples in the National Archives of a letter of credence as a work of art was presented by Chang Yen Hoon, Chinese Minister to the

Above, left: Charles Thomson's design for the obverse of the Great Seal of the United States, adopted June 20, 1782.

Above: William Barton's design for the Great Seal of the United States was rejected except for the small drawing in the upper right corner, which was adopted for the reverse of the seal. This same design also appears on the back of the dollar bill.

Opposite: The first die for the Great Seal of the United States and the much larger die of the Old Treaty Seal made by Seraphim Masi, which the United States began using in 1825 in order to make the pendant seals for American treaties as impressive as those received from European nations.

Overleaf: In the nineteenth century, Letters of Credence were the credentials diplomats presented to the countries to which they were sent. This one was given by Chang Yen Hoon, Chinese Minister to the United States, to President Grover Cleveland on April 29, 1886.

大清國

大皇帝問

大美國

大伯理璽天德好

貴國與中國換約以來睦誼攸關夙敦和好

茲特派二品頂戴三品卿銜候補四品京

堂張蔭桓為駐紮

貴國都城欽差大臣並令親賫

國書以表真心和好之據朕稔諗該大臣明練

有為忠誠素著辦理交涉事件必能悉臻

妥協朕恭膺

United States, to President Grover Cleveland on April 29, 1886. Inscribed in Chinese characters surrounded by a gold dragon border, the scroll is wrapped in an ornate yellow silk case embroidered in a multicolored flower and dragon design; even the ties securing the case are embroidered. Essentially, the letter informed Cleveland that Chang Yen Hoon was "upright and experienced in public affairs" and would give "mutual satisfaction in the discharge of his diplomatic duties."

Chang Yen Hoon proved to be an excellent diplomat, highly regarded in Washington. Upon his return to China, he served as an advisor to the Emperor Kwang Shu during his reform movement; but when the Empress Dowager gained control of the government, she ordered him beheaded. Thanks to the intervention of the American and British Ministers to China, his life was spared temporarily. He was banished to hard labor in Mongolia. Unfortunately, the Empress Dowager had her original order carried out when the foreign legations were besieged during the Boxer Rebellion.

For the United States, the ultimate in diplomatic art accompanied Commodore Perry's mission to Japan in 1854, which successfully opened the island empire to Western trade. The gifts Perry carried with him were both

Nathaniel Hawthorne.

Below: A sampling of diplomatic despatches, now bound into volumes, from Nathaniel Hawthorne, Washington Irving, George Bancroft, Lew Wallace, and James Russell Lowell—eminent literary figures who served in the State Department.

Opposite: A silk scroll with a water-color painting by an eyewitness to the Battle of Yalu, a major naval engagement in the Sino-Japanese War of 1894–95. It was given to Sheridan Read, U.S. Consul in Tientsin, China, who sent it to the State Department in September 1895 with the note: "As it is of considerable historic interest as well as a curio, and a specimen of Japanese art, I venture . . . it may be found worthy of a frame and a place in the Department's offices."

ber of government positions until after the election of 1876. Because his support of local Republicans and the national administration in that election rankled his clients and neighbors in Fauquier County, Virginia, he readily accepted the post at Hong Kong when President Hayes offered it to him. By that time, Mosby's wife had died and his six children were living with relatives.

Mosby proved to be as adept a consular officer as he had been a Confederate ranger. By the time he finished his tour of duty, he had earned the respect of most of the ship captains calling at Hong Kong, who repeatedly sought his help in righting wrongs inflicted at other ports; he had won the thanks of the Chinese government for disrupting the traffic in Chinese women for "immoral purposes"; he had gained the admiration of local journalists for his efforts on behalf of social justice; and, when he left Hong Kong, local merchants gave him an ivory-headed cane as a token of their respect. The one thing he did not come away with was increased personal wealth, as had his predecessors, who had managed to acquire tidy sums from the various "unofficial" duties they had collected while in Hong Kong.

By coincidence, two Civil War generals—James Longstreet (C.S.A.) and Lew Wallace (U.S.A.)—served as Ministers to Turkey. This was only one of several parallels in their careers. Both men suffered humiliation as a result of their Civil War service: Longstreet was harshly criticized for ordering Pickett's charge at Gettysburg; Wallace was relieved of command because of the high number of casualties the Union Army suffered at Shiloh. Both were authors: Longstreet wrote his memoirs, *From Manassas to Appomattox*; Wallace, his epic novel, *Ben Hur*. When Longstreet left Turkey in 1881, he was succeeded by Wallace, who received the appointment to Constantinople because President Garfield had been fascinated by *Ben Hur*. "I expect another book out of you," noted Garfield in his letter of appointment. "Your official duties will not be too onerous to prevent writing it."

Wallace, like most other nineteenth-century authors who joined the foreign service, was more concerned with fiscal security than with literary

明治廿七有八乙未春稍月清國
於天津寫之
内田雲庸匣

Two of the literary figures who once worked for the Department of State: James Russell Lowell (at left) and Washington Irving.

creativity. We, of course, are the ultimate beneficiaries. The National Archives today has shelf upon shelf of despatches penned by those gifted writers, some of the most articulate messages ever drafted by government employees.

How did these men of letters get their diplomatic posts? By political influence, naturally. Nathaniel Hawthorne wrote a campaign biography for Franklin Pierce, his college classmate, and was rewarded with a consulate in Liverpool. Washington Irving, another literary giant, was named by his friend Martin Van Buren Secretary of the U.S. Legation in London and then Minister to Spain. William Dean Howells' campaign biography of Lincoln eventually earned him the consul's post in Venice. James Russell Lowell, a member of the electoral college from Massachusetts, swung his vote to Hayes, whose tight presidential battle with Tilden remains controversial to this day. Hayes received the presidency; Lowell's prize was three years as Minister to Spain followed by five more as Minister to London.

Not all these men were suited to their diplomatic duties. The introverted Hawthorne found meeting the public very uncomfortable, and he detested office routine. When he ended his foreign service career after four unhappy years, he declared: "I have received and been civil to at least ten thousand visitors since I came to England, and I never wish to be civil to anybody again." Bret Harte proved to be as much a misfit as Hawthorne. He lasted two years as consul in Krefeld, Germany, where he turned over most of his duties to his clerk. When a transfer to Glasgow did not change his attitude, he was asked to resign.

James Russell Lowell, on the other hand, relished his role as diplomat. He was established as one of America's major authors when he accepted the post of Minister to Spain in 1877. He enjoyed being the lion of society. Nevertheless, despite a heavy schedule of meetings and lectures, he maintained a steady flow of despatches to the State Department. Many of them are delightful to read; Lowell seldom missed the chance to inject humor. One despatch concerns an opportunistic Frenchman named Fourcarde, who smuggled oil into Madrid in the artificially enlarged bosoms of women.

As Lowell explained to his superiors, the plan was so ingenious that he could not resist recounting it:

> The Frenchman's object was to smuggle petroleum into Madrid without paying the *octroi* (tax). To this end he established his storehouse in the suburbs, and then hiring all the leanest and least mammalian women that could be found, he made good all their physical defects with tin cases filled with petroleum, thus giving them . . . the pectoral proportions of Juno. Doubtless he blasphemed the unwise parsimony of Nature in denying to women in general the multitudinous breasts displayed by certain Hindu idols. For some time these seeming milky mothers passed without question into the unsuspecting city and supplied thousands of households with that cheap enlightenment which cynics say is worse than none. Meanwhile, Mr. Fourcarde's pockets swelled in exact proportion to the quaker breastworks of the improvised wet nurses. Could he only have been moderate! Could he only have bethought him in time of the *ne quid nimis*. But one fatal day he sent in a damsel whose contours aroused in one of the guardians at the gates the same emotions as those of Maritornes in the bosom of the carrier. With the playful gallantry of a superior he tapped the object of his admiration and—it tinkled! He had "struck oil" unawares. Love shook his wings and fled; Duty entered frowning; and M. Fourcarde's perambulating wells suddenly went dry.

Some of the art of diplomacy—whether verbal or visual—is only a distant memory. The artfully composed despatches, like Lowell's description of the "quaker breastworks," have given way to cablegrams, telephone calls, and other rapid forms of communication in our fast-paced society. The colorful trappings of the diplomatic tradition disappeared even earlier, for they necessarily suffered the same fate of the imperial courts that had created and sustained them.

GREAT FALLS OF THE YELLOWSTONE

THE AMERICAN LAND

The dominant factor in shaping our country and our character has been the land, which lured millions of colonists, immigrants, and refugees to these shores. We fought and destroyed Indians for it. We waged wars over it. We rewarded our soldiers with it. We farmed it, mined it, and lumbered it; we reclaimed it, despoiled it, and, perhaps belatedly, conserved it. We have mapped it, sketched it, and photographed it. We have regulated it, sold it, and preserved it. And most of what we have done to the land is documented in the National Archives.

The story of the land is primarily that of the public domain—that vast area the United States acquired as it extended its sovereignty over more and more Western territory. The passage of the Northwest Ordinance, which established a policy for acquired territory, stands as a great American political innovation. After their experience as colonists, the representatives of the newly established United States had decided that the new republic should not build a colonial empire. On October 10, 1780, they resolved: "That the unappropriated lands that may be ceded or relinquished to the United States . . . [shall be] formed into different republican states which shall become members of the federal union and have the same rights of sovereignty, freedom, and independence as the other states." To govern the land ceded to it under the Treaty of Paris, in what was then named the Northwest Territory, the Confederation Congress in 1787 approved the Northwest Ordinance, outlining the steps by which territories could attain statehood. The procedures thus established were followed by each new state from Kentucky to Hawaii (except Texas and California, which were never territories) as it entered the Union.

The continental limits of the United States were reached rapidly because the Founding Fathers decided to expedite the transfer of the public domain from federal to private ownership. The trouble with this decision was that Indian tribes occupied most of the land earmarked for the country's future growth. Although the Northwest Ordinance also specified that "the utmost good faith shall always be observed towards the Indians" and that their "lands and property shall never be taken from them without their consent,"

Opposite: William Henry Jackson's photographs of Yellowstone made his reputation, since they were the first to be published of that fantastic region. Thanks in part to his album, *Yellowstone's Scenic Wonders,* and the drawings by his friend Thomas Moran, Yellowstone became the first national park in America in March 1872.

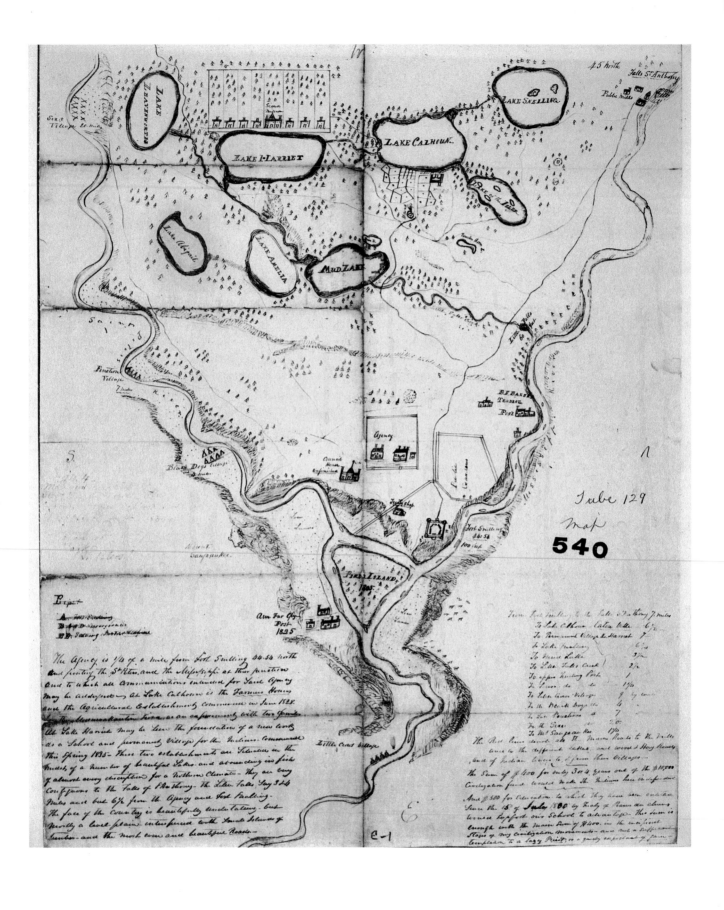

Tube 129

Map

540

C-1

 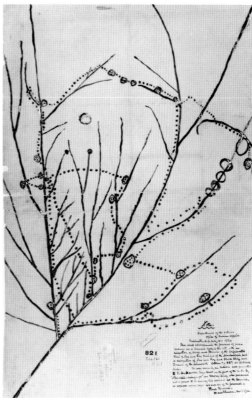

the federal government did little to hold back the White tidal wave that eventually engulfed the continent. Those tribes that resisted the Whites were crushed; those that befriended them ultimately suffered the same fate as their militant brothers but avoided the bloodshed.

The story of the red man's retreat is found in the National Archives. It is recorded in the treaties that the United States negotiated with the Indian tribes it encountered from New England to California. It is portrayed in dramatic detail in the more than seventeen thousand maps and drawings that come from the Bureau of Indian Affairs. A map of the St. Peters Indian Agency is typical of the jewels to be found among them. Drawn in 1835 by the agent, Lawrence Taliaferro, the 21 by 17 inch map is no marvel of cartography, but it does tell us much about the Ft. Snelling area, site of the future cities of St. Paul and Minneapolis, then a pioneer community at the leading edge of civilization. Taliaferro painstakingly located roads, buildings, and Indian villages, so that the Superintendent of Indian Affairs, William Clark, five hundred miles away at St. Louis, could have a clear idea of this remote but important outpost. The agent probably expected his rather awkward chart to be discarded, but Clark appreciated maps. Thus, 150 years later, it offers Americans a glimpse of a primitive area before it had completely surrendered to axe and plow.

To survey and sell the public lands required a vast bureaucracy. Although the Treasury Department at first handled the sale of public lands, it was the General Land Office, established in 1812, that transferred most of the public domain to private ownership. The basic operating unit was the District Land Office, and the first one opened in Steubenville, Ohio, on July 2,

Above, left: Man and Chief and The Chief Whom They Look Upon, Pawnee delegates to Washington photographed by Mathew Brady in January 1858. Although Indians were popular subjects in the early days of photography, it was not easy to get them to pose. Not only did they balk at the clamps necessary to keep photographic subjects from moving, but also many of them believed that a photograph captured some of their spirit.

Above, right: This map of the Mississippi River Valley was used by Chief No Heart of the Iowas during treaty negotiations in Washington in 1837 and shows Indian villages, trails, rivers and streams, and tribal boundaries.

Opposite: Lawrence Taliaferro's map of the Fort Snelling area in 1835.

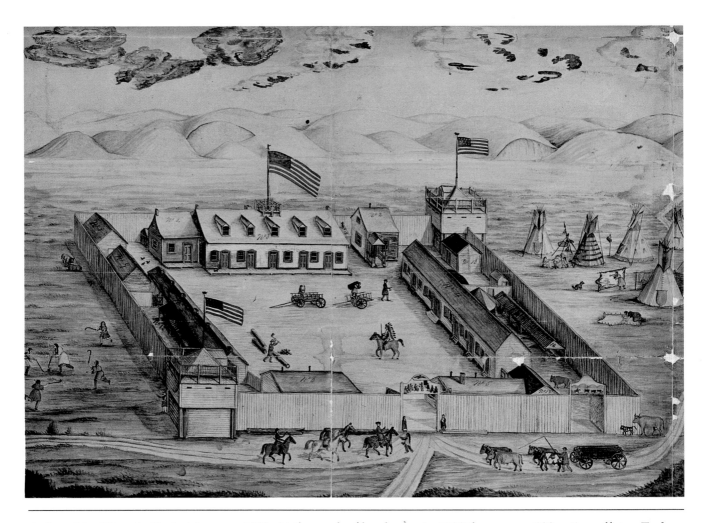

A view of Fort Pierre by Frederick Behman, an employee of the Chouteau Fur Trading Company. This watercolor, made in 1855, was sent to the War Department when the Chouteau Company negotiated the sale of the once-important trading post to the United States. Behman's rendition may not have been entirely truthful, however. On the basis of the drawing, the government paid $36,500 for the fort, but when army officers took possession they found both the stockade and the buildings in need of repair. Today the city of Pierre, South Dakota, is on the site.

Opposite: A detail showing Indian signatures on the Treaty of Greenville, negotiated by General "Mad Anthony" Wayne after the decisive Battle of Fallen Timbers, which ended Indian control over what is present-day Indiana and Ohio.

1800. At the peak of land sales in 1890 there were 123 active offices. Today the number is fewer than 25.

In the process of selling the public domain invaluable federal records were created. The surveyor's field notes, which were used to make survey plats, are the basic record by which public lands are identified, described, and measured. The tract book is a ledger maintained by a township and constitutes a geographical index to initial transactions conveying title from the U.S. government to the first patentee. Land entry papers, or case records, consist of the papers accumulated in processing each initial application to the federal government for land, and these now number in the millions. The patent, or deed, is the end product of each transaction. Through these and related records in the National Archives, it is possible to trace the advance of settlements in the United States from the "Seven Ranges"of Ohio, which were the first public domain lands surveyed, to the Pacific Ocean.

Three pieces of legislation enacted in 1862 pertain directly to the public domain. Each was a great giveaway; each did much to shape our country's future growth. To encourage construction of a transcontinental railroad, the Pacific Railroad Act promised a would-be builder one-half the land in alternating twenty-mile strips along either side of the tract. The builder could sell the land, presumably to settlers, and thus raise the money to

Chipwa's

Mee-ne-doh-gee-jogh

Pee-wan-she-me-nogh

Wey-me-gwas

Gob-mo-a-tick

Che-go-nickska
(an Ottawa from Sandusky)

Sho-pe-ne-be...

Naw-ac (for himself
and brother it-so-me-the

Nes-nan-se-ka

Kee-jass (or Sun)

Ottaway

Ka-ba-ma-saw
(for himself & brother
Chi-sau-gan

Sug-ga-nunk.

Wap-me-me
(or white pigeon)

Wa-che-ness (for himself
and brother Pendargos) Shok

Web-she-cub-naw...

La-Chasse.

Putawatamic's of the River Saint Joseph.

Putawame's

Ne-que-haugh-aw.

Shah-goo-see-kaw.
(or Captain Reed.)

Au-goosh-away.

Kee-no-sha-meek

La-Malice.

Ma-chi-we-tah

Tho-wo-na-wa.

Se-baw.

Mash-i-pe-naish-i-wish
(or bad bird)

Naw-sho-ga-she.
(in Lake Superior)

Ka-tha-wa-sung

Me-sass

Ne-me-kass
(a little Thunder)

Pe-shaw-kay.
(young ox)

Nan-guey.

Ottawa's

Chipawas

U.S. Indian Treaty Commissioners and Sioux leaders in conference at Fort Laramie in April 1868. Among the commissioners, seated third from the left is General William T. Sherman, who served as commander of the western division of the army after the Civil War.

Opposite: Daniel Freeman, for many years reputed to be the first homesteader to claim land under the Homestead Act of 1862, filed his claim on January 1, 1863, at the Brownsville, Nebraska, land office and received the first certificate issued at that office. His 160 acres were located in Cub Creek Valley about five miles west of Beatrice, Nebraska. To finalize his claim, he certified that he had built a house "part log & part frame 14 by 20 feet one story, with two doors two windows, shingle roof board floors . . . a comfortable house to live in."

finance construction. Thirty million acres were granted in the act, and Congress doubled the amount two years later.

The Morrill Act, named after its sponsor, Senator Justin Morrill of Vermont, committed the federal government to grant public lands to the states to help them establish educational institutions. Each state received 30,000 acres in the form of "land scrip" for each of its congressional districts. Although some states squandered their revenues, this endowment laid the foundation for a system of state colleges and universities, now known as land-grant colleges, that brought higher education within reach of millions of Americans.

The Homestead Act, which gave away the most land, is perhaps the best known of the three. It provided 160 acres of public land to any adult citizen who paid a small registration fee and farmed the land for five years. Ironically, the act was not the great agent of democracy popular opinion would have us believe. Comparatively few Americans could afford to travel to the western plains and then purchase the seeds, livestock, and tools necessary to establish a farm, even if the land itself was free. Most of the land given away under this program went to speculators, cattlemen, miners, and other entrepreneurs. Of some 500 million acres dispersed by the General Land Office between 1862 and 1904, only 80 million went to true homesteaders like Charles Ingalls in *Little House on the Prairie*. In fact, more small farms were established under the act in the twentieth century than in the nineteenth.

Among Americans well-served by the Homestead Act were freedmen who found haven in Kansas, a state with ample homesteading lands and a reassuring Abolitionist history. Some of the first Black immigrants came from Tennessee soon after the Civil War and settled in the southeastern corner of the state, where they established Singleton Colony. Ben Singleton —"Old Pap"—was a former fugitive slave who formed the Edgefield Real Estate and Homestead Association in 1869 to encourage freedmen to buy farms in Kansas. "Ho for Kansas," proclaimed one of his flyers, which offered "Brethren, Friends and Fellow Citizens" homes and "Transportation

Witnesses to scenes such as this must have coined the expression "doing a land-office business." The crowd is waiting for the 9 A.M. opening of the land office in Perry, Oklahoma Territory, September 29, 1893.

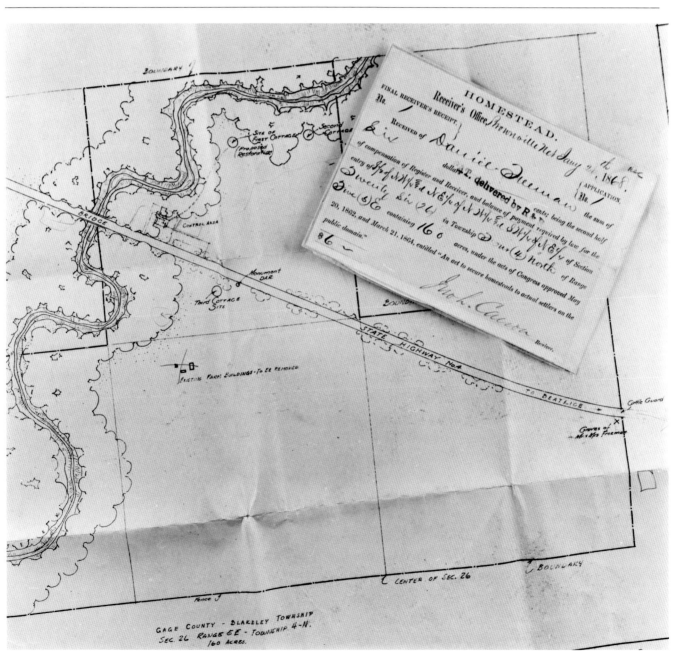

Scale of Forty Chains to an Inch.

Township N.º V. Second Range.

contains 21,139 Acres. Surveyed in 1786 by

Abralem Martin

N.º 36.	N.º 30. Date of Patent, March 10.th 1788. Hon.ble Arthur Lee. 640 A.º	N.º 24. Date of Purchase, Dec.r 1796, by Rob.t Caldwell of Ohio C.º Virginia. 640 a.º	N.º 18. Date of Patent April 27.th 1788. Robert Kirkwood. 640 a.º	N.º 12. D. of P. April 10.th 1788. Jn.º Fowlkes. 640 a.º	N.º 6.
N.º 35.	N.º 29.	N.º 23.	N.º 17. D. of P. April 27.th 1788 W.m M.c Kennan 640 a.º	N.º 11. Reserved.	N.º 5.
N.º 34.	N.º 28.	N.º 22. Date of Patent April 27.th 1788. Jn.º Lyon. 640 A.º	N.º 16. Reserved.	N.º 10. Date of P. April 27.th 1788. W.m M.c Kennan 640 a.º	N.º 4. D. of P. July 26.th 1788 Jn.º Covenhoven jr. 558¼ a.º
N.º 33.	N.º 27.	N.º 21. D. of P. April 27.th 1788 Jn.º Learmouth 640 a.º	N.º 15. D. of P. April 27.th 1788. Rob.t Kirkwood. 640 a.º	N.º 9. D. of P. April 27.th 1788. Rob.t Kirkwood. 640 a.º	N.º 3. D. of P. March 10.th 1788. Abijah Hammond. 182¼ a.º
N.º 32.	N.º 26. Reserved.	N.º 20. D. of P. April 27.th 1788. Jn.º Learmouth. 640 a.º	N.º 14. Date of P. April 10.th 1788. Benj.n Manning. 640 a.º	N.º 8. Reserved.	N.º 2. Arnold H. Dohrman 46¾ a.º
N.º 31. D. of P. April 27.th 1788. Doctor R. Johnson. 640 a.º	N.º 25.	N.º 19. Date of P. April 10.th 1788 Jacob Martin. 640 a.º	N.º 13. D. of P. April 10.th 1788. W.m Manning. 640 a.º	N.º 7. Date of Purchase, Dec.r D.º 1796, by Jn.º Carpenter of the N.W. Territory. 640 a.º	Dat. of March 10.th 1788. Abijah Hammond. 1½ a.º

OHIO RIVER

HQ.

Rates cheaper than ever known before" to Blacks willing to make the long trek to Kansas.

Other Black colonies lured settlers with their own broadsides. One boosted Hodgeman County, "the best place for climate and for soil for the smallest capital." Here, on the high, windblown plains of western Kansas was established Nicodemus, the most famous of the Black towns. Named for a legendary slave who possessed an uncanny knack for prophecy, Nicodemus was Horatio Alger country, its customs varying little from other towns in rural America. In 1887, it boasted five stores, three land companies, three livery stables, a baseball team, a literary society, several lodges, and a band. It celebrated the Fourth of July and its own Founding Day (September 1). Eventually, drought, dust storms, and economic change decimated the once flourishing community as they did hundreds of other prairie towns. Its population dwindled to almost nothing. In 1953, the post office was closed.

These Black colonies were orderly and well planned. By contrast, in the "Exodus Movement" of 1879, 4,000 panic-stricken and leaderless Blacks fled from Mississippi and Louisiana, knowing little about Kansas and even less about establishing communities. The migration of "Exodusters" had been spurred by fear of hooded nightriders and a false rumor that free transportation, land, and mules awaited them in Kansas. Eventually, the Kansas Freedmen's Relief Association, with $90,000 in money and supplies from concerned citizens across the nation, settled them on homesteads.

Cheap land attracted Americans, and so did gold. As soon as the first flash of "color" showed in the sparkling waters of California's American River in 1848, gold fever swept the country, sparking a mad rush for the earthbound riches of the West. Over the next three decades, first California, then Colorado and Nevada, and finally Montana and Idaho, experienced the

When the original landowners in areas ceded to the United States by Mexico filed land claims with the federal government, they often included highly graphic plats prepared in the manner of seventeenth-century European maps. This one of the Rancho San Miguelito was submitted to the General Land Office by José Rafael Gonzales in 1852.

Opposite: The first land surveyed under the Land Ordinance Act of 1785 is pictured in this map of Township 5, Range 2, in an area known as Ohio's "Seven Ranges." This act regulated the disposition of public land throughout the nineteenth century. It also introduced the grid system of land division—into sections, townships, and ranges—a feature of the American landscape that is readily apparent to anyone who flies across the United States.

The Loomis Hotel in Torsina, Alaska, 1903.

boom-and-bust cycle of the mining frontier. Coming as they did during the tumultuous Civil War era, the gold and silver strikes attracted sympathizers, draft dodgers, and veterans from both sides of the conflict. Southerners predominated, judging from the place names—Atlanta, Dixie, Leesburg, Secession Ridge, Secesh River—that adorn Western territorial maps.

Chinese immigrants were also attracted to the diggings, thanks to the Central Pacific Railroad Company which brought as many as twelve thousand of them to this country to construct the western end of the transcontinental railroad. Once the railroad was completed, the Chinese laborers scattered across the West seeking homes and employment. Many became miners. Of the 6,572 miners in Idaho in 1870, 3,853 were Chinese as were seven of the territory's physicians.

Unfortunately, the Chinese had to endure the hostility of their White neighbors. In Rock Springs, Wyoming, in September 1885, a mob killed several Chinese residents, burned their homes, and destroyed property worth an estimated $147,000. Although no one was punished, the federal government indemnified the survivors for losses, distributing the money through the Chinese legation. When the legation discovered that there were several repetitious claims totaling $480.75, it returned the excess money to

the Treasury to show good faith.

Home makers, town builders, and railroaders invariably followed the get-rich-quick miners, and with them came the need for government. On the mining frontier, the Northwest Ordinance, now almost a century old, served as the model even though it did not always work as smoothly as the Founding Fathers had envisioned. According to one historian, "the early years of organization in each western territory were characterized by disruptive, confused, intensely combative, and highly personal politics that can best be described by the term *chaotic factionalism*."

This was certainly Idaho's territorial experience, which one writer described as a "cruel joke." Created by President Lincoln in March 1863, the territory occupied an area larger than the present state of Texas and included Montana and much of Wyoming. Lewiston, the capital, was illegal; it was located on an Indian reservation and thus could not serve as the seat of government. Lewiston was only three hundred miles west of Virginia City (Montana) as the crow flies, but to attend the territorial legislature delegates from that community had to make a months-long, two-thousand-mile trip. They travelled by horseback south to Salt Lake City, then by stage to San Francisco, where they boarded a ship bound for Portland.

These photographs of the Anadarko townsite taken two days apart—August 6 and 8, 1901—from the same spot indicate the "boom town" phenomenon that marked the Oklahoma land rushes.

Above: Homesteaders pose beside their covered wagon in the Loup Valley of Nebraska, about 1886.

Above, right: Covered wagons were the mobile homes for thousands of pioneers. This is the interior of the wagon John Bemmerly used in 1849 for his trek from Ohio to the California gold fields.

Opposite: Drawings from the Northwest Boundary Survey of 1857–62 by James Madison Alden. Top: "Lake near summit [of] Kishenehn Pass, Rcky Mtns." Bottom: "Canon of Palouse River looking South from a point just below the falls (Great Falls)."

From there a riverboat took them up the Columbia and the Snake to Lewiston.

Between 1863 and 1890, when Idaho became a state, the territory had sixteen territorial governors, five of whom never set foot on their domain. One of the most colorful was the second, Caleb Lyon of Lyonsdale, whom President Lincoln appointed in 1864 to preside over the newly reduced territory. (In that year Montana Territory was created and the Idaho-Montana border was established along the line of the Bitterroot Mountains, thus forming the narrow panhandle of present-day Idaho.) A New Yorker, Lyon has been variously described as "pompous," a "dandy," a "poet," and an "eccentric," but one thing he was not was a pursuer of lost causes. Viewing the governmental chaos in Lewiston, he laid plans to move the capital to Boise. With the help of sympathetic legislators, he "escaped" to Walla Walla in Washington Territory and sent Territorial Secretary C. deWitt Smith into Lewiston to fetch the seal and documents, which its citizens, suspecting such an attempt, had placed under guard. Smith eventually smuggled the seal and an armload of papers out of the now defunct capital, arriving in Boise on the same day Lincoln was assassinated. Although President Johnson reappointed Lyon and Smith, they had little success in taming the rebellious territory, which seemed destined to a contentious future. Northern Idaho wanted to be part of Washington, southern Idahoans were being wooed by Nevada, while the eastern part of the territory was filling up with Mormons who thought it was part of Utah. It was the Mormons who established Franklin, the first purely agricultural community in the territory and the site of its first school.

Complementing the written records of American land development in the National Archives are remarkable visual records, many of them produced by the survey teams that fanned out across the new nation to determine its geographical configurations. Artists were as important as the cartographers and surveyors, because they often prepared panoramic sketches to document landscape features that appeared on the maps. Some of the early government artists were educated as topographic engineers,

William Henry Jackson, whose life virtually spanned the first hundred years of photography, from 1843 to 1942, is best remembered for the western views he took during his nine seasons as a member of the Hayden Survey team. More documentary than interpretive, his photographs show the land as he found it. Today these images are invaluable to scholars interested in measuring geological, ecological, and botanical changes that have occurred in the American landscape over the past century. *Above:* Fort Hall, Idaho, 1871. *Opposite:* Hanging Rock, Colorado, 1872.

usually at West Point. Those not skilled at free-hand sketching relied on the *camera lucida*, a drafting device, to obtain accurate and quick proportions, which were colored as time permitted.

Some of the most interesting art in the Archives is the product of the surveys that determined the border between the United States and Canada. The Northeast Boundary Survey of 1840–42, which set Maine's border, was directed by Columbia University Professor James Renwick. He attempted the most ambitious visual record of the American landscape to that time. Familiar with the new daguerreotype process of photography introduced in Europe just the year before, Renwick invited Edward A. Anthony, a young West Point–trained engineer, to bring his daguerreotype equipment on the survey. Renwick also hired several engineer-artists who used the *camera lucida* and Anthony's daguerreotype images as the basis for watercolor sketches. Renwick later submitted the daguerreotypes and sketches to the State Department with his final report. Only the watercolors are extant today. A treasure in themselves, they are also a tribute to the fortitude and dedication of these early government artists who, as they worked, were often besieged by flies, mosquitoes, and incessant rain.

The Northwest Boundary Survey, which established our border with Canada from the crest of the Rockies to the Pacific, also produced a set of magnificent watercolors. The artist was James Madison Alden, a U.S. naval captain and skipper of the steamer *Active*. The sixty-four drawings he prepared have a special quality of their own, thanks to his eye for light and shadow, color, and perspective.

HANGING ROCK, CLEAR CREEK CAÑON, COL.

CARBON LAKE
FROM THE EAST,
SIERRA NEVADA IN THE DISTANCE

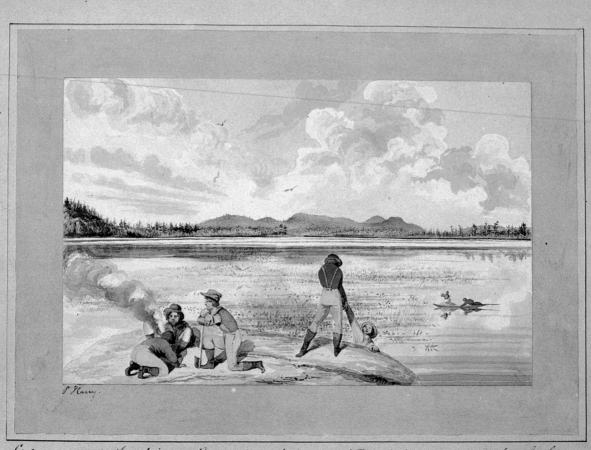

Co-cum-go-moe Mountains - Bearing from about N.10°.W. to North as seen from the Southern
End of Co-cum-go-moe-sis Lake, near its outlet into Co-cum-go-moe Lake (Penobscot Water)

In the period from 1867 and 1878, four major scientific expeditions explored and mapped large areas of the West. One of the four, which were eventually merged to form the U.S. Geological Survey, was the Geological and Geographical Survey of the Territories led by Ferdinand Vandeveer Hayden. He employed a young artist-turned-photographer named William Henry Jackson, one of the greatest of the American landscape photographers. Hayden also invited Thomas Moran, an outstanding landscape painter, to accompany his expedition. Congress later purchased Moran's paintings of Yellowstone Falls and the Grand Canyon of the Yellowstone for $10,000 each. Moran's paintings, Jackson's photographs, and Hayden's lobbying were later instrumental in getting Yellowstone established as the nation's first National Park in 1872. Besides the pictures of the spectacular scenery, Congress was persuaded by the logic that the area's volcanic activity made it valueless for mining, while the high altitude made it worthless for farming. Thus, it was perfect for public recreation.

Another agency, the Reclamation Service, compiled a remarkable pictorial record of the West. Although established in 1902, its roots go back to the great surveys, whose teams determined that sufficient water existed in the mountains to supply the needs of Western farmers if it was properly managed. Government officials were concerned that the arid character of the Western lands would lead to intense development of the few river valleys but leave virtually unoccupied the dry mesas and deserts. To stimulate development of the latter, Congress passed the Desert Lands Act in 1877 and the Carey Act in 1894. The first allowed individual families to claim 640 acres of arid lands if they would irrigate them, and the second gave vast tracts of desert lands to states that would oversee the development of irrigation projects financed through private or state monies. Neither legislation proved satisfactory: private or state funds were rarely sufficient to bring an irrigation project to completion. As a result, Congress established the Reclamation Service (later the Bureau of Reclamation), and gave it the responsibility of erecting the huge storage reservoirs and conduits —tunnels, canals, ditches—needed to transform millions of desert acres in

Opposite, top: In 1859, topographical engineer James Hervey Simpson completed one of the most useful surveys of the Utah Territory before the Civil War. Members of his party made beautiful landscape views in watercolor, like this one titled "Carson Lake from the East, Sierra Nevada in Distance," which were not published with his report but remain with his manuscript maps.

Opposite, bottom: Co-cum-go-muc-sis Lake by P. Harry, a drawing from the Northeast Boundary Survey of 1840–42. This drawing, as well as the one on pages 146–47, gives no indication of the harsh conditions under which the artists worked—surrounded by swarms of black flies and mosquitoes, or drenched with seemingly incessant rain.

Photographs by Walter J. Lubken, who documented many Reclamation Service projects for the Interior Department before World War I. *Above:* Opening day of the Gunnison Tunnel in Montrose, Colorado, then the center of a rich farming community of 4,000 people. *Opposite:* The symmetry of these timbers gives no hint of the troubles encountered in constructing the six-mile-long tunnel built to divert water from the Gunnison River to the Uncompahgre River. High levels of carbon dioxide at times drove the men from their work, while heat and humidity rotted the timbers, which had to be replaced by concrete.

seventeen Western states into green, productive farmland.

While building those dams, lakes, and parks, the Reclamation Service documented its work with more than 60,000 photographs taken by more than 150 amateur and professional cameramen—project engineers with office Brownies as well as local commercial photographers. Their instructions were two-fold: illustrate every phase of construction and highlight the pleasant life of surrounding town and country with an eye to encouraging future settlement.

Of this army of photographers, one stands out, Walter J. Lubken, a contract photographer with the Department of the Interior. He documented Reclamation Service projects from New Mexico to Washington State, twenty-six in all. The son of German immigrants, Lubken grew up in Pendleton, Oregon, on the edge of the Umatilla Reservation. His earliest photographs are of the Umatilla Indians. His services were much in demand by project engineers and government officials, who often called upon him to travel with them and record their visits to various construction sites. As a result, the National Archives has more than 5,500 examples of his work, ranging from staff pictures to sensitive, evocative views of Western life and scenery.

Among the most significant visual records of the American land are the aerial photographs. Made in the late 1930s and early 1940s for the Agricultural Stabilization and Conservation Service, these survey more than 85 percent of the contiguous United States. Their value lies in what they reveal about changes in the landscape. Environmentalists and engineers use them to measure eroding shorelines and changing riverbeds; archeologists

find them invaluable in spotting prehistoric habitation sites. Officials in New York recently used them to identify problems caused by the dumping of chemical waste in Love Canal. According to a noted geographer, the aerial photographs are "more complete, more detailed, and more reliable than all the documents in the Archives relating to the use of the American land." To visualize their potential, he declared, "one only needs to imagine what an extraordinary value would today be placed on similar air coverage of Virginia or Iowa or California could it have been taken 100 years ago."

Since so much attention in this book has been given to Washington, D.C., the first national city, it is only appropriate we give some attention to the second national city. This is Port Angeles, Washington. Its citizens claim the distinction because Abraham Lincoln established it by presidential proclamation in 1862.

Few spots in the United States can rival Port Angeles for natural beauty. Located on the Olympic Peninsula in the most northwesterly corner of the United States, the town rises from the Straits of Juan de Fuca to a steep bluff where wooded hills climb to the snow-clad Olympic Mountains. A mile-long spit of land—Ediz Hook—protects the deep harbor.

Settlement began almost immediately after the S'klallam Indians signed the Treaty of Point No Point in 1855 giving title to the land to the federal government and, according to the 1860 decennial census, the community had 33 single males, two families, and two children. The strategic location made it ideal for a lighthouse and customs house, a fact not lost on Victor Smith, a special agent for the U.S. Customs Service. Through his efforts

Overleaf: A *camera lucida* sketch from Metjarmette Mountain by J.W. Glass, Jr., done during the Northeast Boundary Survey of 1840–42.

Mount Dowd
J. 8/44

α

J W Glass f

Camera Lucida Sketch — from MchYarmette Mount

and

the ridges on right are the Highlands between Metgarmette Dept
Etchemin —

Congress passed and Lincoln signed the legislation establishing the city, reserving 4,000 acres for future use by the Army and the Navy. Within a short time, Port Angeles boasted a post office, lighthouse, customs house, weather station, and signal post. Although the customs house is gone, the city remains an American international port. Because it overlooks every vessel passing into Puget Sound, the city has been important to our nation's efforts to halt traffic in illegal aliens, liquor, and drugs. Each of these activities is documented in the National Archives.

Military records also have much to tell us about Port Angeles. Not only was it a port of call for the Great White Fleet on its epic journey early in this century, but it was also a popular haven for the naval squadrons that operated in Puget Sound each summer. The community had a special role in World War I because its timber was vital to aircraft construction. Port Angeles was also important during World War II as it was part of the Pacific Coast defense line established to prevent Japanese submarine and air attacks. The community now received a coast artillery unit and a coast guard station.

Because one half of the 65,000 square miles of the Olympic Peninsula are forested mountains, the records of the Park Service, Forest Service, and regulatory agencies are also resources for the history of the area. President Grover Cleveland created the Olympic Forest Reserve despite lack of enthusiasm from the lumber interests, and Theodore Roosevelt established Mount Olympus National Monument in the center of the National Forest, all of which information can be gleaned from records in the National Archives.

What better way to conclude this brief discussion of the American land than to recall the poem Robert Frost read at President John F. Kennedy's inauguration in 1961.

> The land was ours before we were the land's.
> She was our land more than one hundred years
> Before we were her people.

Both Frost and Kennedy are now gone, but the land remains and so do the records that document the land and her people.

Walter J. Lubken. *Opposite:* Before building Arrowrock Dam near Boise, Idaho, construction engineers used diamond drills, like the one shown here, to test the subsurface. They found granite 90 feet below the river. *Above:* Roosevelt Lake covers the Tonto Basin, once the domain of the Tonto Apaches and later the site of Roosevelt, Arizona, a town that now lies 220 feet below the surface.

GENEALOGY

enealogists have long cherished the National Archives and are its most numerous and faithful patrons. In recent years, the often complex searching to develop a family tree has evolved into writing complete family histories. Alex Haley's *Roots* had enormous influence on this trend. Because of the book and the subsequent television series, millions of Americans awakened to the excitement of writing family history instead of compiling lists of names and dates. They now want to make those ancestors come alive, to take pride in their accomplishments, to appreciate their sorrows and failures, to place their lives into the broad perspectives of the American past.

For any family historian, the National Archives holds unparalleled treasures. Few Americans have not left some trace in government records. Here are census population schedules, passenger arrival lists, military service records, pension files, homestead applications, allotment maps—the documents needed to dissolve the mists of time, to cast the light of history on that seasick girl who arrived at Ellis Island or that frightened boy who fell at Gettysburg.

The basic resource for genealogy is the federal decennial census, mandated by the Constitution and taken every ten years since 1790. Relatively little information was collected in the early censuses, however. Until 1850, for example, the names of only heads of households were recorded. Nor is it always an easy matter to find information about someone on a census schedule. After fixing the date, you must know the state, county, town, and—in the case of large cities—the ward or enumeration district in order to find that elusive ancestor. Nevertheless, patience and tenacity can be richly rewarded. The National Archives has available on microfilm the census schedules from 1790 through 1910 (except for the 1890 schedules, most of which were destroyed by fire).

Most family historians begin their quest with a handful of names, but one researcher began with fifty-seven—all from Worthington, Massachusetts, and all neatly inscribed in indelible ink on a signature quilt, a family heirloom for more than a century. Through the census schedules, she was able

Opposite: A poster published by the Bureau of Census.

Opposite: Simon Fobes was eighty-two years old when he applied for a pension under the Act of 1832. As proof of service, he submitted the original warrant promoting him to sergeant, a document the old veteran of Bunker Hill had obviously treasured throughout his long life.

to date the quilt (about 1850) and to explore the complex world of a mid-nineteenth-century community. Five of the family names appeared in the first federal census in 1790. The number increased until 1850 when all the names can be found on the Worthington census. By 1860, half of the names had disappeared from the schedules. The quilters were obviously neighbors, for their names appeared close together on the census pages. By checking federal maps, the researcher found that their homes formed an arc covering five or six miles. Most of the men of the families were farmers; a few occupied themselves in other ways—toymaker, shoemaker, mechanic. One individual listed himself as a "gentleman." The people whose names appear on the quilt were typical of the Worthington community, for they were all natives of Massachusetts, as were four-fifths of their neighbors. Worthington itself was suffering a population decline (its peak had been in 1810). As New England became industrialized, young people drifted away from the rural communities. By 1860, many of the people whose names were on the quilt had moved to Northhampton or Springfield; one couple have moved to Illinois.

Military service records and pension application files are another major source of genealogical information and the National Archives has millions of them. This is fortunate, for these are among the most interesting, especially the Revolutionary War Pension and Bounty Land Warrant Application Files. Between 1789 and 1878, Congress passed several acts to provide pensions and free land to Revolutionary War veterans, their widows, and other dependents. Because the veterans did not always save, or even receive, discharge papers and because fires destroyed many federal records, applicants generally appeared in court and described under oath the service that entitled them to benefits. They also submitted diaries, letters, and other documents—even Continental currency and draft notices—as evidence to support their claims. Relatives faced even greater challenges when trying to prove their relationship to veterans; they submitted family bibles, marriage certificates, and family registers. As a result, some remarkable treasures of family history can be found in these files.

Roger Enos, Esqr, Colonel of the first Battallion of
A New Levies from the State of Connecticut &

To Simon Fobes

Reposing Especial Trust of Confidence in Your Skill Courage of
Good Conduct I do Appoint Authourize & Constitute You the Said
Simon Fobes, A Serjeant in Said Regiment all the Duties of Which Office
You are faithfully to Discharge of You are to Obey all Your Superiour
Officers in all their Commands According to Military Discipline & all
Under You are to Obey You as their Serjeant & for Your
So doing this Shall be Your Sufficient

WARRANT

Given Under my hand this 7th day of September AD 1778

Roger Enos Col.

Warrant
September 7th 1778

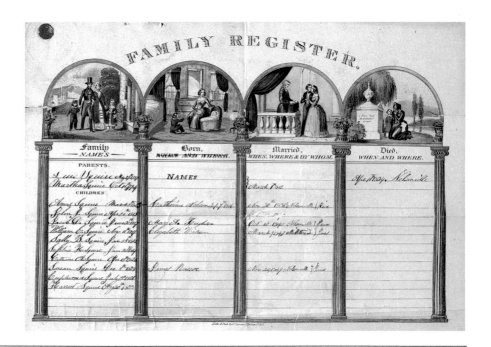

Frakturs remained popular in this country until the early nineteenth century, when the development of lithography made possible the mass printing of family register forms at relatively low cost. Among these printed registers is one published by the famous lithographer Nathaniel Currier.

The most handsome are illuminated manuscripts, usually birth, baptismal, and wedding certificates, which form a little-known but fascinating part of America's folk art heritage. Both German- and English-speaking immigrants brought to this country the tradition of decorating important family papers. Drawn by schoolmasters, clergymen, and itinerant artists, the simple certificates were frequently the principal form of artwork found in pioneer homes.

More than one hundred of these colorful examples of American folk art are held by the National Archives. The German-language certificates, called *fraktur* after the broken lines of their Gothic letters, include the works of some of the most important of the German-American folk artists. Many of these craftsmen still remain anonymous even though their work is well known to scholars and collectors. There is the "Flying Angel Artist," whose drawings of pairs of these heavenly spirits are his trademark. The "Stony Creek Artist" is known from the area of Virginia where his work is often found. The "Wetzel-Geometric Artist" was named both for the family recorded on one of his certificates and the manner in which he decorated them. The so-called "Weak Artist" was only recently identified as Conrad Trevits, thanks to clues found in the pension application that contained an example of his work. While modern viewers may consider these certificates charming and quaint, the original owners regarded them as truthful statements of faith and family. According to Monroe H. Fabian, a curator at the Smithsonian Institution and a *fraktur* authority, "they are intended to be and did become passports of social and religious affiliation. With their marginal decorations, they have also become some of the most brilliant leaves on American family trees."

Other treasures are also to be found in these files—letters, diaries, and official documents. Elish Bostwick's commission as an officer in the Continental Army is annotated with his recollections of the Revolution. They

Typical of family treasures submitted to the government by pension applicants after the Revolutionary War is this sampler.

Below: Because government records were often poorly kept or destroyed by fire, applicants for federal pensions and bounty lands sometimes had to submit family records, like these Bibles, to support their claims.

Above, opposite and following pages:
Among the most decorative documents in the National Archives are
the *frakturs,* specimens of an art form
originating in sixteenth-century Germany that takes its name from the
broken lines of its embellished script.
Revolutionary War veterans or their
survivors submitted more than one
hundred of these hand-drawn birth,
marriage, baptismal, and death certificates to the government when they
applied for pensions or other benefits.
Written in both German and English,
the *frakturs* remain a little-known but
fascinating aspect of America's artistic heritage.

include this sage advice from a battle-wise officer to his troops: "Take care
now and fire low! One man wounded in the leg is better than a dead one for
it makes two more to carry him off. So leg them, damn 'em, I say leg them!"

Bostwick's recollections also contain the only known descriptions of Nathan Hale, whose regret that he had but one life to give for his country has
stirred the imaginations of generations of American school children. Although written in 1826, fifty years after Hale's execution as a spy, Bostwick's
statement rings with authenticity:

> I will now make some observations upon the Amiable
> and unfortunate Capt. Nathan Hale whose fate is so well
> known; for I was with him in the same Regt. both at Boston
> & New York & until the day of his tragical death; & al-
> though of inferior grade in office was always in the habit of
> friendship & intimacy with him; & my remembrance of his
> person, manners & character is so perfect that I feel in-
> clined to make some remarks upon them; for I can now in
> imagination see his person & hear his voice—his person I
> should say was a little above common stature in height, his
> shoulders of a moderate breadth, his limbs strait & very
> plump; regular features—very fair skin—blue eyes—flaxen
> or very light hair which was always kept short—his eye-
> brows a shade darker than his hair & his voice rather sharp
> or piercing—his bodily agility was remarkable. I have seen
> him follow a football & kick it over the tops of the trees in
> the Bowery at New York (an exercise which he was fond of)—
> his mental powers seemed to be above the common sort—
> his mind of a sedate and sober cast, & he was undoubtedly

SPRING REMEMBER YOUR ANCESTORS SUMMER

Register

Of James & Mary Platts FAMILY
He was Born August 21 1755 & MARRIED
April 6. 1780 She was Born
Jan. 22 1755 & by him hath the following
CHILDREN.

NAMES	BORN	DIED
James Platts	Sept August 22 1755	the January 9 1835
Mary Warner	Jan 22 1755	
Mary Platts	August 22 1780	
Suky Platts	June 14 1782	the January 9 1835
Nancy Platts	March 29 1785	
Salley Platts	Sept. 10. 1787	
Mehitabel Platts	Feb. 22 1790	
Abigail Platts	Jan. 14 1892	
James Platts	May 6 1794	July 1829
Wesley Platts	July 1 1797	
Eliza Platts	May 11 1800	March 20 1832

AUTUMN WINTER

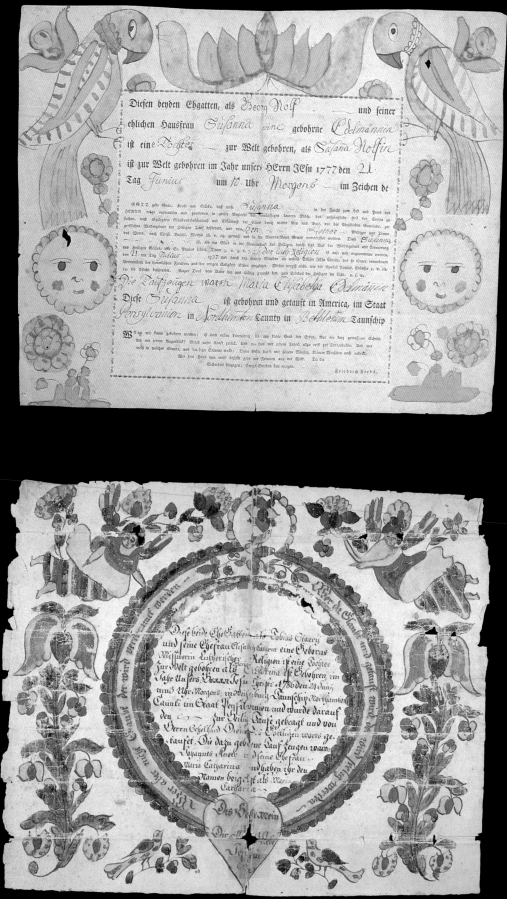

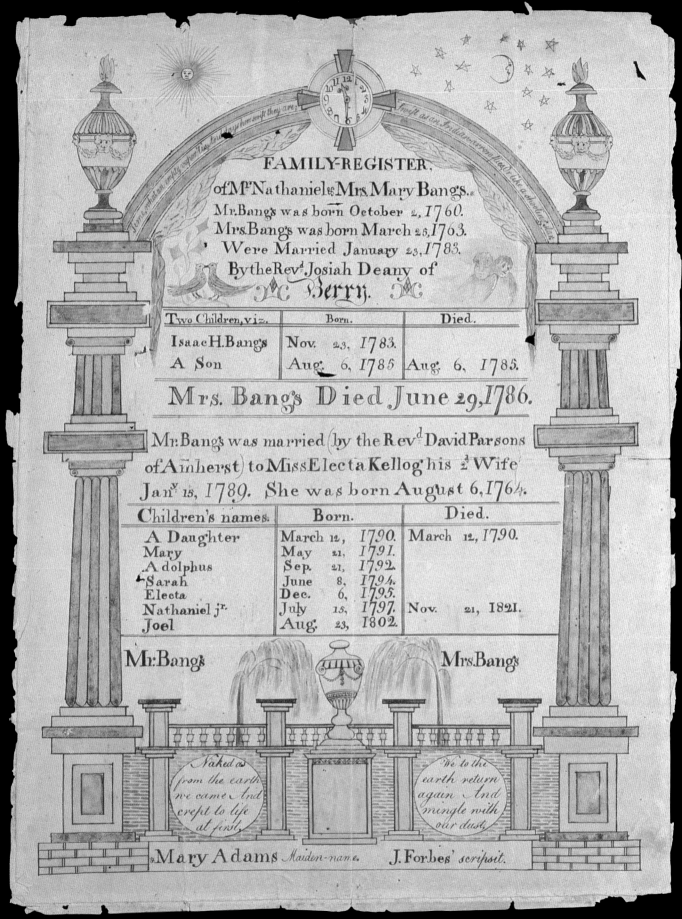

FAMILY-REGISTER,
of Mr Nathaniel & Mrs Mary Bangs.
Mr. Bangs was born October 2, 1760.
Mrs. Bangs was born March 25, 1763.
Were Married January 23, 1783.
By the Revd Josiah Deany of
Berry.

Two Children, viz.	Born.	Died.
Isaac H. Bangs	Nov. 23, 1783.	
A Son	Aug. 6, 1785	Aug. 6, 1785.

Mrs. Bangs Died June 29, 1786.

Mr. Bangs was married (by the Revd David Parsons
of Amherst) to Miss Electa Kellog his 2d Wife
Jany 15, 1789. She was born August 6, 1764.

Children's names.	Born.		Died.
A Daughter	March 12,	1790.	March 12, 1790.
Mary	May 21,	1791.	
Adolphus	Sep. 21,	1792.	
Sarah	June 8,	1794.	
Electa	Dec. 6,	1795.	
Nathaniel jr	July 15,	1797.	Nov. 21, 1821.
Joel	Aug. 23,	1802.	

Mr. Bangs   Mrs. Bangs

Naked as from the earth we came And crept to life at first.

We to the earth return again And mingle with our dust.

Mary Adams Maiden-name.   J. Forbes' scripsit.

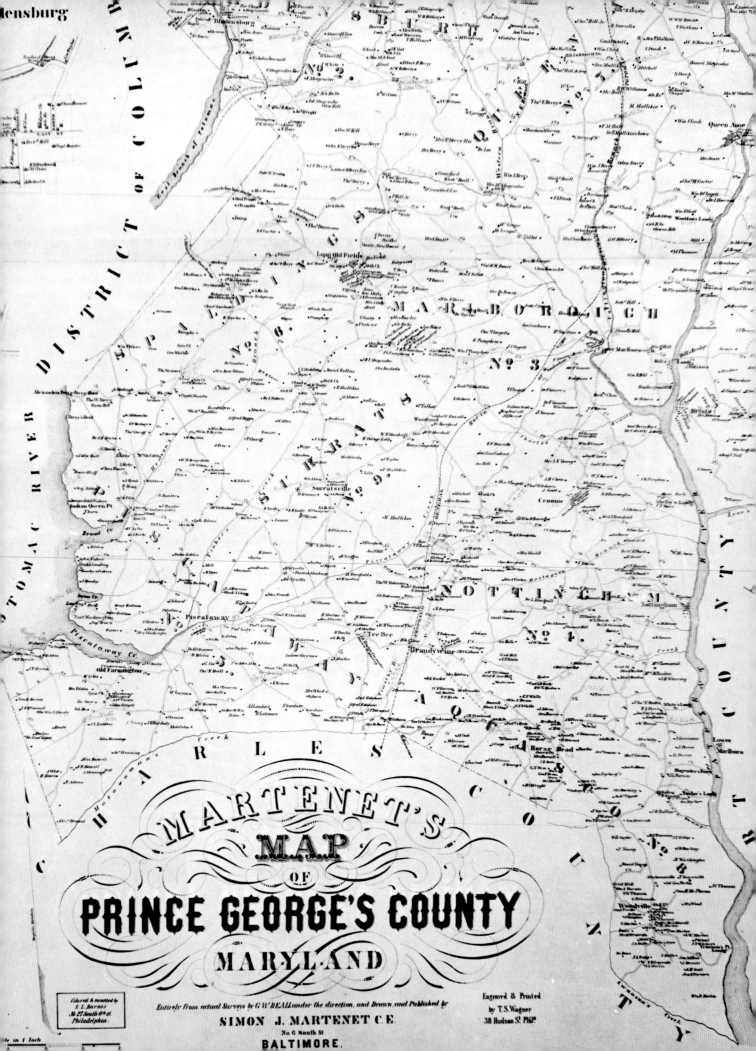

Pious; for it was remarked that when any of the soldiers of his company were sick, he always visited them & casually prayed for & with them in their sickness. a little anecdote I will relate: one day he accidentaly came across some of his men in a bye place playing cards—he spoke—what are you doing—this won't do,—give me your cards, they did so, & he chop'd them to pieces, & it was done in such a manner that the men were rather pleased than otherwise.

Civil War pension files can also reward lucky researchers, like the one who found a medal on a Virginia battlefield inscribed with the name of Benjamin F. Chase, 5th Volunteer Infantry of New Hampshire. A request to the National Archives for information produced ten original letters the soldier had written to his family. The letters graphically portray an earnest teenager from Meredith, New Hampshire, who did not enlist because of the burning issues of slavery or abolition, Union or states' rights. He wanted to travel and earn some money. What little he did earn he shared with his father, who had eleven children to support. Each letter home included money—usually five dollars, once as much as twenty-one. Although Benjamin kept a few dollars for himself, he worried that his parents believed he was squandering money. "i dont buy eny of the foolish stuff," he assured them. "You may think i do but i certain dont." But soldiers had to pay high prices even for basic commodities: cheese was forty cents a pound, butter fifty cents, tobacco sixty cents, "and every thing else is the same."

Like many recruits of 1861, Benjamin was delighted with his new experiences and confident of a short war. "What a good ride we shall have going south," he boasted in one of his first letters. Even after three months in uniform, his enthusiasm remained high. "All of the boys in our tent are

Freedmen clearing the battlefield of Cold Harbor, one of the bloodiest engagements of the Civil War. This photograph was taken in May 1865, eleven months after the battle and only a few weeks after Lee had surrendered at Appomattox Court House.

Opposite: This map of Prince George's County, Maryland, is unusual in that it shows the names of landowners. Although privately published in 1861, it was found among records of the Chief of Engineers.

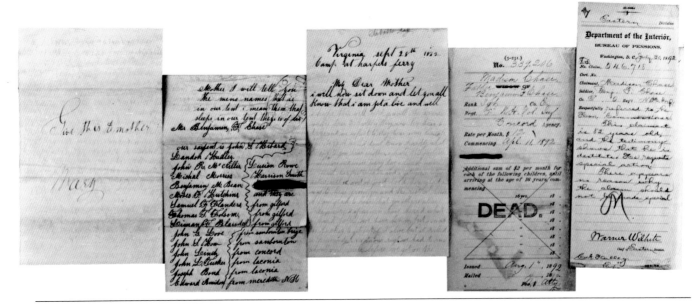

When Benjamin Chase's parents applied for a pension, they submitted nearly a dozen letters they had received from their eighteen-year-old son, who fell at Fredericksburg. These family mementos now are valued sources of first-hand information about the life of a typical Union volunteer during the Civil War.

Opposite: Land office plats are valuable to genealogists. This 1822 plat from Alabama includes the names of several allottees, although most sections are identified by file entry numbers or the letter "P" for patent number. Each township plat covered thirty-six square miles and was subdivided into sections one mile square. The income from section 16 in each township was reserved for educational purposes, as was indicated by the artist who drew a schoolhouse on this plat.

very well indeed and enjoying their health first rate," he wrote on January 8, 1862. "i hant been a mite home sick sense we ben out hear and have not ben a mite sick ether. Mother dont worrough a bout me a mite for i think we shall be home before long."

The novelty of army life quickly wore off thereafter. While encamped at Harrison's Landing, a few miles above Richmond on the James River, his company had to form every morning at 3 A.M. because the officers feared a dawn attack. Lice, "those hateful things," were constant companions. The food had long since become tiresome. How he yearned for a familiar meal of good brown bread and beans! Most of all, he wanted the war to end so he could go home, a forlorn hope that became more unlikely with each Confederate victory.

Ben's first taste of combat was at Fair Oaks on June 1, 1862. He wrote home the next day to assure everyone of his safety. His regiment lost 175 men, his company 28. "Oh it was a dreadfull battle i tell you. it was a wonder that i didnt get killed for i was right among them. all the boys [who] got killed and wounded . . . stood right beside of me. Oh how the bullets did fly."

That summer as the 5th New Hampshire fought hard engagements from the Peninsula to Antietam, Ben became less and less optimistic about surviving the war. "i was so lucky to get out of it alive," he admitted after the bloodbath at Antietam. "i thought to myself if thear mothers could only see . . . [their dead sons] they would be crasy." As for himself, he prayed constantly for that "happy day" when he could speak to his own mother again. "When will that day come? i cant tell that, perhaps it will soon, and perhaps never."

The Chase family was never reunited. Two months later eighteen-year-old Benjamin fell at Fredericksburg during a federal assault best described by a Northern war correspondent: "It can hardly be in human nature for men to show more valor, or generals to manifest less judgment."

Twenty years later Ben's mother applied for a government pension. She included the letters to prove how much the boy's financial support had

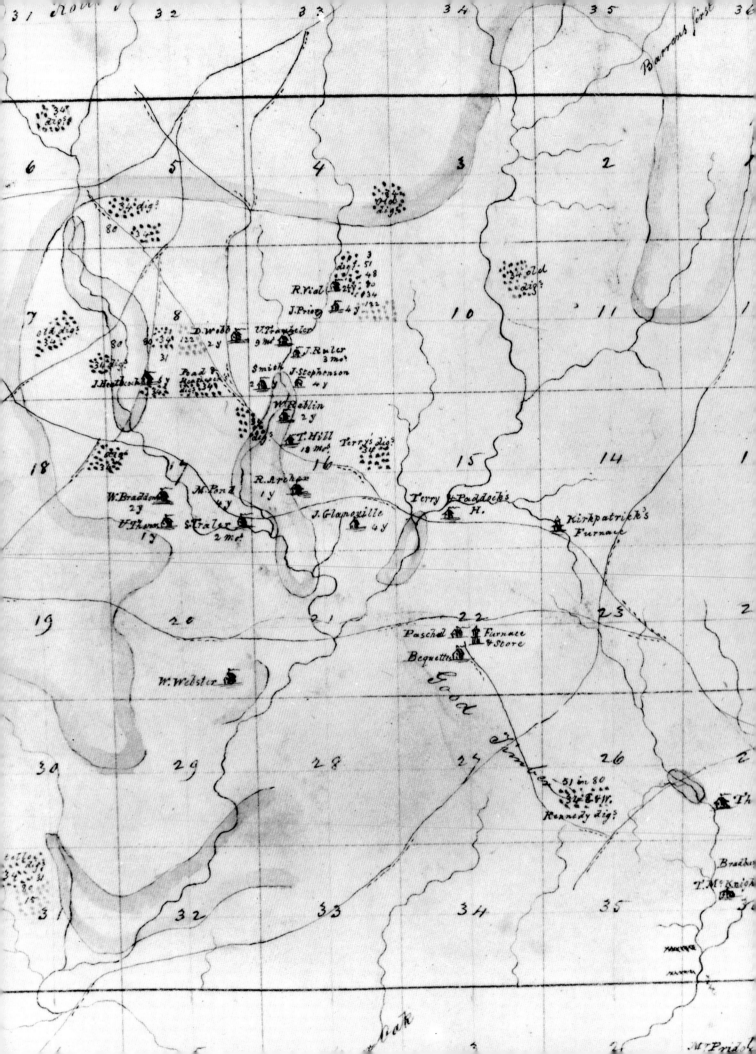

meant to the family. Additional testimony came from a sister, who described the emotional impact of his death on their mother. "Before the war she was chearful and singing about the house, but afterwards was sad and dejected and has never been heard to sing a word since."

There was grief in Confederate homes as well. (Confederate service records, but not pension applications, are also in the National Archives.) The Hite family of Luray, Virginia, certainly paid a fearful price for its Southern loyalties. Daniel and Rebecca Hite saw five of their six sons go off to war. Two joined the Luray Home Guards and surrendered with Lee at Appomattox. Three joined the 33rd Virginia Infantry, part of Stonewall Jackson's famed foot cavalry, and died: John at First Manassas, William at Gettysburg, David at the Wilderness.

Genealogical information is also to be found in land ownership and allotment maps. Large in scale, each map generally covers only a small local area of the United States and gives either a land entry number or the patentee's name. To use these maps effectively, however, the researcher must understand the township, range, and section system of coordinates developed by the General Land Office, which had responsibility for surveying and mapping the public domain in the states north of the Ohio River and west of the Mississippi, except Texas and Hawaii. The only states in the South to which the system applies are Alabama, Florida, Louisiana, and Mississippi.

In addition to the local land office plats, the National Archives has maps drawn for special surveys of the public domain; these often show the names of the original owners. The first public land survey in the United States was made only one year after Thomas Jefferson proposed it in May 1784. One of these plats from eastern Ohio shows a portion of land surveyed in 1786 by Absalom Martin of New Jersey and reveals that he then purchased some of the most desirable tracts along the Ohio River. Today, Martins Ferry is located on one of these tracts.

Perhaps the most unusual of the special survey maps is one of southwestern Wisconsin, which was prepared under the direction of David Dale

Opposite: The invaluable genealogical information to be found on the David Dale Owen map of southwestern Wisconsin is evident from this detail showing Linden Township. Pascal Bequette owned property in section 22.

The censuses of 1850 and 1860 included separate schedules for the slave population of the United States. Shown here is a page from the 1850 slave schedule for the District of Columbia along with photographs that show freedmen working as laborers in Alexandria and the slave pen of Price, Birch & Company, also of Alexandria.

Opposite: The Bureau of Refugees, Freedmen and Abandoned Lands, more commonly known as the Freedmen's Bureau, was established at the close of the Civil War to assist the former slaves, most of whom were homeless and destitute. It issued rations, clothing, and medicines and cooperated with benevolent societies in establishing schools and conducting marriage services for the freedmen. The drawing of a freedmen's school embellishes a letter written to the bureau by the teacher; the photograph is of an Episcopal church in Beaufort, South Carolina, that served for a time as a store for freedmen.

Owen in 1839. Measuring 68 by 94 inches on a scale of one inch to one mile, it is the product of one of the most ambitious geographical-geological reconnaissances in our nation's history. Pressured by speculators and miners who wished to occupy this mineral-rich region, the General Land Office authorized Owen, son of the founder of the Utopian community at New Harmony, Indiana, to conduct a special survey. Owen and about 150 surveyors and geologists tramped over four thousand square miles of woodland and prairie, carefully delineating geographical and cultural features —residences, mills, furnaces, smelters, and even a shot tower. The names of the owners or occupants of these structures, more than five hundred, also appear on the map.

Using the names found in one township in the area of Owen's survey, archivist Jane F. Smith demonstrated the depth of documentation federal records can bring to the writing of local and family history. She relied primarily on census schedules, military service and pension application files, and General Land Office records to prepare a fairly complete profile of Linden Township, which consisted of twenty-seven families. Not only did she confirm Owen's findings, but she also provided more precise identifications for most of the individuals he had listed. In fact, only two of the twenty-seven names did not appear in the records she checked. Tracing the names through the 1840, 1850, 1860, and 1870 censuses, she found that nine of the pioneers were still living in Linden Township thirty years later.

It was possible to write a rather complete biography of one of the pioneers,

165-C-393
Whittier School, Bainbridge, Ga, 1869.
Bainbridge, Ga.
Apr. 8, 1869
AND SHALL CLEAVE TO HIS WIFE: AND THEY TWAIN SHALL BE ONE FLESH.
Certificate of Marriage.
This Certifies, That
have this day been joined in
With Freedom, Fidelity and Purity.
By authority vested in me by the Assistant Commissioner of the Bureau of Refugees, Freedmen and Abandoned Lands, acting in pursuance of the law of Congress Act, March 3rd, 1866,
I HAVE UNITED IN MATRIMONY
Mr
Miss
Done at
Parish of
State of La.
this
day of
186
The State of Alabama, County.
TO ANY ORDAINED OR LICENSED MINISTER OF THE GOSPEL, JUDGE OF THE CIRCUIT OR PROBATE COURTS, OR JUSTICE OF THE PEACE FOR SAID COUNTY—Greeting:
THE RITES OF MATRIMONY
BETWEEN
AND
Given under my hand and Seal this
day of
American Independence the
year.
A. D. 18
(L. S.)

UNITED STATES OF AMERICA.

State of Maryland,   } ss:
City of Baltimore,

I, _Miss C. Moon_, do swear that I was born in the _State of Virginia_, on or about the _12th_ day of _Decr. 1840_, that I am a NATIVE AND LOYAL CITIZEN OF THE UNITED STATES, and about to travel abroad

Sworn to before me, this _18_ day   _C. Moon._
of _August_, 1873

S.E. Sangston
                     Notary Public.

I, _H. A. Tipper_, do swear that I am acquainted with the above-named _Miss C. Moon_, and with the facts stated by _her_, and that the same are true to the best of my knowledge and belief.

Sworn to before me this _18_ day   _H. A. Tipper_
of _August_, 1873

S.E. Sangston
                     Notary Public.

Description of _Miss Charlotte Moon_

Age: _33_ years.	Mouth: _full_
Stature: _5_ feet, _7_ inches, Eng.	Chin: _round_
Forehead: _mileo_	Hair: _Dk Brown_
Eyes: _Brown_	Complexion _rather fair_
Nose: _regular_	Face: _full_

I, _Charlotte Moon_, do solemnly swear that I will support, protect, and defend the Constitution and Government of the United States against all enemies whether domestic or foreign and that I will bear true faith, allegiance, and loyalty to the same, any ordinance, resolution, or law of any State, Convention, or Legislature to the contrary notwithstanding: and further, that I do this with a full determination, pledge, and purpose, without any mental reservation or evasion whatsoever; and further, that I will well and faithfully perform all the duties which may be required of me by law. So help me God.

Sworn to before me, this _18_ day   _C. Moon._
of _August_, 1873.

S.E. Sangston
       Notary Public

a man named Pascal Bequette, because he had held many positions that were reflected in federal records during his long and active life. He operated a smelter and store, helped incorporate a railroad, and fought in the Black Hawk War. He also served as a postmaster, school inspector, grand juror for the U.S. District Court, and receiver of public monies, a post he held in both Wisconsin and California, to which he emigrated during the Gold Rush.

For the most complete story, federal records should be used to complement local records and published works. Nevertheless, as many historians have discovered, federal records often provide the only available documentation, especially in pioneer communities before local governments were able to make and preserve adequate records of their own.

Invaluable material is tucked away in seemingly unlikely places in the National Archives. Consider the records of the State Department. Not everyone will enjoy the good fortune of the genealogist seeking information about an ancestor who had, according to family legend, served as a United States Consul in France. The researcher knew no further details than his ancestor's name. By examining appointment cards, which are arranged alphabetically, and by checking lists of consular offices by post, he determined that the person in question had been appointed consul at Nantes on July 4, 1884. The official correspondence and application and recommendation files (seventy-one letters of support were found for this one person) yielded a great deal of additional information. The man had died at his post in 1889; his wife died four years later. Her identification included her maiden name. Since the State Department had to ship their bodies home, the records showed the name of the ship, the port from which it sailed and its destination, and the names of a son and daughter listed as next of kin. The most exciting find was a letter the applicant had written when seeking the consular post. He had enclosed his photograph to prove his physical fitness despite his advanced age. He was sixty-nine at the time.

In another example, State Department records document the life and death of Charlotte (Lottie) Moon, who spent some forty years as a Baptist

Opposite: A passport issued to Charlotte "Lottie" Moon, a Baptist missionary who spent some forty years working in China.

Opposite: Government officials in 1882 gave Indians on the San Carlos Reservation in Arizona brass tags, like those shown here, to identify them and to prevent "hostile" or non-reservation Indians from receiving rations on issue day. More reliable as a head count was the annual enumeration, standard practice on most reservations by the end of the nineteenth century.

missionary in China. According to a newspaper clipping found in her State Department file, the seventy-one-year-old missionary was returning to America when she died aboard ship on December 24, 1912. Her passport application, dated August 18, 1873, includes her physical description, date of birth, and signature. Her name also appears in U.S. consulate post records in a register of citizens residing at Tengchow, Shantung Province. Because she died at sea, the U.S. Consular Court for the District of Cheefoo, China, probated her will, and a copy is in the records.

However, before one becomes excited about doing research in State Department records (or any other body of records in the National Archives, for that matter), it is important to remember that the search can be time-consuming and fruitless.

For family historians looking for information about their Black or Indian ancestors the research will undoubtedly be more difficult. Black genealogists will be especially frustrated because the standard resources—census schedules, passenger arrival lists, pension application files—are virtually useless for ancestors who were slaves. Regarded as property, their names seldom appear in official records.

Nonetheless, the situation is not entirely bleak. Freedmen do appear in the records. One such is Edward Ambush, a resident of Washington, D.C. According to the emancipation and manumission records in the District Court of the United States, he purchased his freedom for $150 on June 19, 1841. From that day on, he built a personal history that can be traced in the National Archives. Tax records document the purchase of a house worth $250. Living in that house, according to the 1850 census, were five people: Edward, Elizabeth (probably his wife), one-year-old Joseph (probably his son), a free Black woman named Letty Thomas, and five-year-old Charles (probably her son). "Realizing the uncertainties of life," Ambush had prepared a will, which was probated upon his death in 1865. Elizabeth received the "homestead" and Joseph received an adjoining lot. Ambush's personal possessions were valued at $67.10. The most expensive item was a family bible worth $25, which indicates where he had placed his priori-

6 Jane Smith | Jane Smith | Daug

Husband 40
Wife 40
1 Ood.il.con
2 Lah.con.con
Son 7

1 Meel.thewa
2 Gualha see ava
3 Skay.vetay
4 Tell.hoo

1 El.quatha
2 Subqaba
3 Mr.eka

S. C. Apache

Number	Indian Name	English Name	Relation
1	Tea.vu		Husban

White Mountain Apache

1888
Census of Indians
on the
San Carlos Reservation
Arizona Territory
Tonto Apache

Coyotero Apache

Number	Indian Name	English Name	Relation

Relation
Widow
Son
Son
Son

2221 — DEPT ARIZONA — OFFICE OF INDIAN AFFAIRS — REC'D AUG 30 — 1888
21825
San Carlos Indian Agency, A.T.
August 2nd, 1888.
Acting Indian Agent.
5179 — DEPARTMENT INTERIOR INDIAN DIV. — RECEIVED OCT 24 1888

Requests to be furnished with a number of tags to re-tag the Indians on the San Carlos Reservation—present supply being nearly exhausted. Encloses five brass tags as samples; also requests that dies be furnished him for stamping tags and describes kind required; also requests five of the old form descriptive books for keeping the record.

5179 — DEPARTMENT INTERIOR INDIAN DIV. — RECEIVED OCT 24 1888
Com. Indian Affairs.
October 23, 1888.
Returns certain papers rel. to providing Indians with tags on the San Carlos Res. with disapproval of same.

Indian Name	English Name	Relation	
1 Skel.pah		Husban	
2 Nahl.le.gah		Wife	
Ye.cay		Daug	
Oog.gun.na.kay.			
On.aos.		Son	
Ake.ash.			

1 Len.nay		
2 Wid.ady		Sister
3 Neth.te.jule	Son	8
1 girl under six years		

1 Mark.koo.hay	Uncle	31
2 Dah.le.bas.ky	Mother	45
3 Nah.cay.ulta	Aunt	40
4 Das.te.hay	Brother	13
5 Chock.oo.Tah.la	Nephew	10
1 girl under six years		
1 Na.tar.lah	Brother	48

Daughter
Husband
Wife
Sister
Sister
Husband
Wife
Wife
Son

Yuma

	English name	Relation
	Mr. Seiler	husband
		wife
		son
		son
		daughter
	Kitty	widow
		son
	Capt. Snooks	husband
		wife
		daughter
		father
		son

As part of the government's continual but often fruitless efforts to make Native Americans adopt White ways, President Cleveland in 1893 appointed the Commission to the Five Civilized Tribes—the Cherokees, Creeks, Choctaws, Chickasaws, and Seminoles—to persuade them to accept individual allotments of land, give up their tribal governments, and come under federal and state laws. Reformers believed that Indians who owned their own tracts of land would be more inclined to become farmers and thereby become self-sufficient. With the allotment, each Indian was also to receive full U.S. citizenship. John Parchmeal, an Oklahoma Cherokee, was one of many Indians who did not want to participate in the program. The note on his allotment certificate, written in the Cherokee syllabary, reads: "I don't want this paper or the land. I return the paper and don't want anymore."

Opposite: Under the terms of a treaty of July 8, 1817, the United States granted land reserves of 640 acres to each of those Cherokee Indians who wished to become citizens and remain east of the Mississippi River. Thomas and Jesse Raper (Rapier), White men married to Cherokee women, submitted these documents to the First Board of Cherokee Commissioners to support their claims to the reserves when the Cherokees were moved west during the 1830s. The Rapers remained in North Carolina.

ties. Although much of this information can be found only for Washington, D.C., residents, it is a fine example of how one can trace a seemingly obscure individual through Archives records.

Much more information can be found in other federal records for Alexander T. Augusta, the first Black man to hold a medical commission in the United States Army. Although born in Norfolk, Virginia, he managed to emigrate to Canada, where he graduated from medical school in 1856. Augusta probably would have remained in Canada had it not been for the Civil War. Upon learning that the United States planned to employ Negro troops, he appealed to President Lincoln for an appointment as a surgeon to one of their regiments. "I was compelled to leave my native country . . . on account of prejudice against colour," he explained, but if he had the opportunity "to be in a position where I can be of use to my race," he wanted to return. Augusta was appointed Regimental Surgeon of Colored Volunteers in April 1863. He reached the rank of lieutenant colonel before resigning his commission in 1867 to accept an appointment to the Howard University Medical School, thereby becoming the first Black to serve on the faculty of any medical school in the United States.

For the family historian, Dr. Augusta's federal career makes fascinating reading. In the National Archives are his letter to Lincoln, numerous documents regarding his appointment as a medical officer, as well as his commission and oath of office. Other documents are also there, documents that reveal the burden carried by someone crossing the color barrier: a petition from fellow officers protesting his appointment, a request for pay commensurate with his rank, a letter to a court martial board that described an unpleasant episode that resulted from his attempt to ride a streetcar (which led the Senate to rule that public transportation in the District of Columbia must be open to people of all colors). Following his death in 1890, Augusta's widow applied for a pension based on his war service. In her pension file is a record of their marriage, at St. Mary's Catholic Church in Baltimore on January 12, 1847, and a copy of Augusta's death certificate.

Indian genealogy offers it own challenges. First of all, few documents in

the National Archives dated prior to the mid-nineteenth century are useful for Indian genealogy. Not until the tribes were placed on reservations could accurate records be kept on individual Indians. Names do appear from time to time on documents such as treaties, but seldom can an Indian line be traced for more than a generation or two from such sources. Even when Indian names were recorded, they were written as the scribe heard them. The difficulty in pronunciation, in fact, encouraged school teachers and clergymen to rename their students after prominent White leaders like John C. Calhoun, Thomas Jefferson, and George Washington. A further complication is the fact that most Indians did not use surnames. Thus, their names seldom had any similarity to the names of other family members.

Information available for Indians living since the 1880s is very extensive, however. For most federally recognized tribes, the National Archives has land allotment records, census schedules, and annuity payment rolls (records of monies Indians received for lands they sold to the government or for other stipulated reasons in treaties). Many Indians also worked for the government, especially as army scouts. For them the National Archives has military service records and, usually, pension application files.

Fascinating material can be found in Indian school records. Because most were under federal jurisdiction, their records are in federal custody. Perhaps the best known of these institutions is the Carlisle Indian Industrial School in Pennsylvania which opened in 1879 and enrolled almost five thousand students. The first government-operated non-reservation boarding school, it received a great deal of publicity because its athletic teams competed successfully with the colleges of the time. Academically, however, it offered little more than a grade school education and fell into disfavor because so few graduates ventured into White society. Its most famous student was Jim Thorpe, a member of the Sac and Fox Tribes, and one of our nation's most gifted athletes. His school file is a biographer's delight, filled with newspaper clippings, photographs, and other memorabilia.

Another prominent American whose Indian ancestry is documented by records in the National Archives is Will Rogers, the cowboy humorist. Proud

Opposite: Genealogical treasures are sometimes found in federal records. This family tree and marriage license were submitted to the Bureau of Indian Affairs in 1907 by members of the Brown family as proof of their Choctaw ancestry.

of his Indian heritage, he once boasted: "My ancestors didn't come on the Mayflower, but they met the boat." Rogers got the laugh and the Archives has the proof of his Cherokee ancestry. His family is identified on the Guion Miller Roll, prepared in 1906 to identify Cherokees eligible to receive an award from the Court of Claims. Rogers could trace his ancestry back to 1817, when his great-great-grandfather, Thomas Cordery, registered "in right of his wife," so that his family could accept a 640-acre allotment. In so doing the family avoided the turmoil of the government's Indian removal program which subsequently forced most of the Cherokees to emigrate to Indian Territory.

As you can see from these vignettes, excitement can result from doing family history. Not every family boasts an Alexander Augusta, a Benjamin Chase, a Lottie Moon, or a Jim Thorpe, but every one has heroes and heroines of its own, people who worked and played, who enjoyed success and endured failure while working at the business of everyday life. Their stories also deserve to be told, and a wonderful place to search is the National Archives.

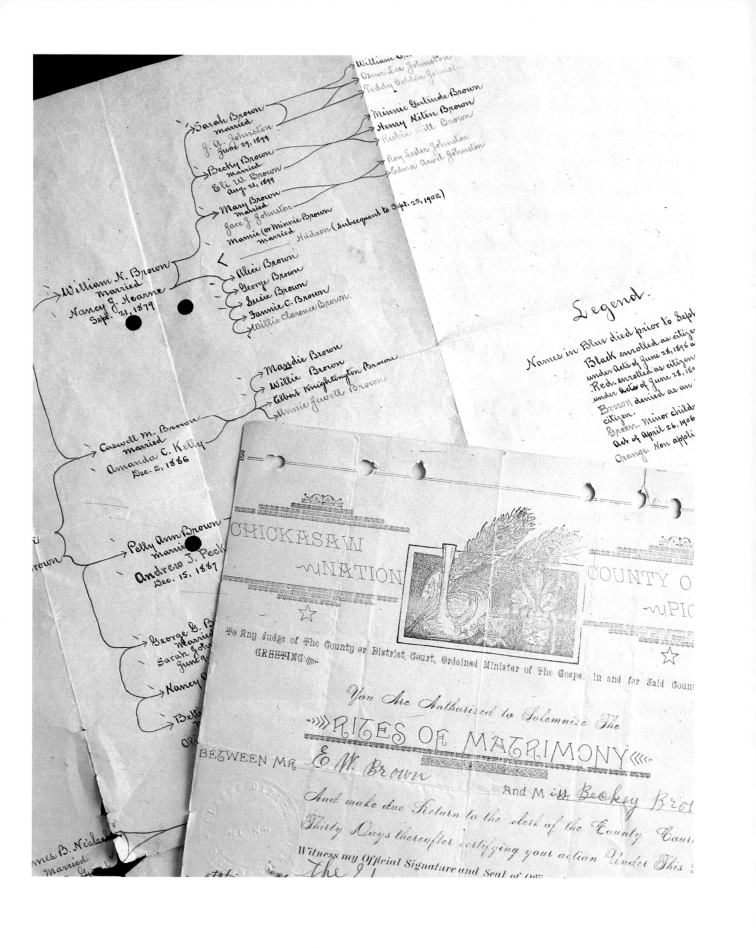

Sarah Brown
married
J. A. Johnston
June 29, 1899

Becky Brown
married
Eli W. Brown
Aug. 21, 1899

Mary Brown
married
Jace J. Johnston

Mamie (or Minnie Brown
married
Hudson (subsequent to Sept. 25, 1902)

Alice Brown
George Brown
Susie Brown
Fannie C. Brown
Willie Clarence Brown

William R. Brown
married
Nancy J. Hearne
Sept. 21, 1879

William C. Johnston
Oscar Lee Johnston
Teddy Golden Johnst.

Minnie Gertrude Brown
Henry Niten Brown
Rubie Bill Brown
Roy Lester Johnston
Edna Arvel Johnston

Maudie Brown
Willie Brown
Elbert Knightington Brown
Annie Jewell Brown

Caswell M. Brown
married
Amanda C. Kelly
Dec. 2, 1886

Polly Ann Brown
married
Andrew J. Peck
Dec. 15, 1887

George G. B.
married
Sarah Joh.
June

Nancy

Bettie
Oli

James B. Nichol
Married

Legend.

Names in Blue died prior to Sept.

Black enrolled as citizen
under Acts of June 28, 1896 a

Red. enrolled as citizen
under Acts of June 28, 189
citizen.

Brown. denied as a
citizen.

Green. Minor child
Act of April 26, 1906

Orange. Non appli

CHICKASAW
NATION

COUNTY O
PIC

To Any Judge of The County or District Court, Ordained Minister of The Gospel in and for Said Coun
GREETING:

You Are Authorized to Solemnize The

RITES OF MATRIMONY

BETWEEN Mr E. W. Brown

And Miss Becky Brow

And make due Return to the clerk of the County Cour

Thirty Days thereafter certifying your action Under This

Witness my Official Signature and Seal of Of

the 2 l

Special Archives

ot all the treasures in the National Archives are documents in the traditional sense. Photographs, maps, drawings, magnetic tapes, and motion pictures are federal records as much as census returns, military pension files, and bounty land warrants; they merely have a different format. These nontextual records present special storage and handling problems. As a result, each type—magnetic tape, motion picture film, photography, cartography—is administered separately from the textual records.

Information in machine-readable form is the fastest growing and least understood area of records preservation and use. "Machine-readable" means that a mechanical aid is required to read the information. Although the term includes punch cards, disks, and the like, most government-produced machine-readable information is preserved on magnetic tape.

Contrary to popular belief, these records are not a recent development. The electro-mechanical processing of information began a century ago when Herman Hollerith, a former employee of the Bureau of the Census, devised a system to process cards in which holes had been punched to represent census data. Hollerith noted that it took until 1887 to tabulate the 1880 census and he anticipated total frustration with the next one. Thanks to his system, however, the 1890 census was tabulated in less than three years. Thereafter, the use of punched cards by federal agencies grew steadily, and the government became the major user after the Social Security Act was passed in 1935. Now the government had to maintain employment records for thirty million people, a feat that meant punching, sorting, and checking as many as 500,000 cards a day. World War II imposed even greater strains on government record keepers. As a result they enthusiastically embraced electronic computers, when these became available after the war. Univac installed the first one in the Bureau of the Census for the 1950 census; today, more than 24,000 are used in the federal government.

The government's use of computer tape has grown with corresponding rapidity. In 1970 the Civil Service Commission had 6,800 reels of tape; by 1975 the total was 23,429 reels—a 300 percent increase in five years. Archi-

Opposite: The Assembly Line by Jolan Gross Bettelheim, 1943. This lithograph on the theme of mass production was part of an Office of War Information series compiled in 1944.

Opposite, top: Henry Peabody (1856-1951), as William Henry Jackson, zealously photographed landscapes, historic sites, and geological formations. His pictorial legacy, received by the National Archives after his death, includes turn-of-the-century photographs of California attractions. Here we see Cliff House, San Francisco.

Opposite, bottom: Hand-painted glass slides, selected from more than seven hundred, used at St. Elizabeth's Hospital from 1872 to 1910 in the treatment of mental patients from the army, navy, and the District of Columbia.

Following pages: In 1941 the Interior Department commissioned Ansel Adams to create a photo mural for its Washington office depicting the majesty of nature as preserved in the National Parks. Before World War II halted the project, Adams took more than two hundred views of the West, now kept in the National Archives. Shown here are the geyser "Old Faithful" erupting at dusk and the church at Taos Pueblo in New Mexico.

vists believe this growth has been the general trend in most federal agencies.

Counting reels is not the most reliable method for estimating the information being processed by computers because the technology changes so quickly. In the early 1960s a 2,400-foot reel could store the information equivalent to about fifteen 500-page books. Today, the same size reel can accommodate 120 books. It is estimated that 85 percent of the statistical information now processed by federal agencies is computer-based. Within another decade virtually all of it will be.

Whatever one may think of tape, and many still curse it, no one can deny it is a space saver. This alone makes it attractive to budget-conscious managers. Poverty studies by the Office of Economic Opportunity of data from the 1960 and 1970 censuses are good examples. To print the 1970 study alone, containing summary statistics for every county in the United States, would require millions of sheets of paper. This same information is carried on forty-one reels of tape.

Archivists were slow to accept the new technology. They generally regarded machine-readable information as nonrecord, a view illustrated by the decision in July 1936 to destroy eight million punch cards carrying information from the 1930 census because tabulations had been printed.

The task facing the National Archives relating to this new form of records is awesome, to put it mildly. The federal government now has about twelve million reels of magnetic tape in use or storage. The numbers are not so much the problem, however, as the differences in preserving tape and paper. Paper is used only once for storage of information; magnetic tape, on the other hand, can be used repeatedly without affecting its condition. Some federal agencies have erased valuable information to supply tapes for other projects. Magnetic tape is also very fragile. Fingerprints, dust, moisture, heat—all can cause permanent damage. Furthermore, tapes need to be rewound and cleaned regularly to prevent erosion of information.

Obsolescence is another problem. Rapid advances in computer technology can render tapes unusable in as little as fifteen years. The Census Bureau in 1975 realized with dismay that 6,500 reels of tape from the 1960

53900 THE CLIFF HOUSE, SAN FRANCISCO.

Henry Peabody photograph of the
Sutro Baths, San Francisco.

census could be processed only by equipment that was no longer manufac-
tured and could no longer be repaired. Because of this problem, the National Archives may one day convert information now on tape to a different
storage medium. Several systems using laser beam technology to record
and compress data on a photo-sensitive stock are now on the market and
archivists are watching their development.

One last disadvantage is that a computer is needed to read the information recorded on tape and a researcher may not be able to interpret a print-
out. A code book is usually necessary to decipher symbols representing
such qualities as race, sex, and marital status. Little wonder, then, that
many researchers hesitate to use computer tape. Nevertheless, those who
make the effort are rewarded with a wealth of information that would have
been impossible to assemble a generation ago. (Text storage systems which
present a line or page of text on the screen do not require code books and
user resistance is being rapidly overcome.) Imagine having at one's finger-
tips information from newspapers back to 1819 about political violence in
the United States! That study is available, as are a computerized history of
the American herbicide-spraying program in Vietnam, an income tax pro-

file compiled from thousands of individual returns each year since 1966, and dozens of other research opportunities of equal magnitude. Like it or not, computers are here to stay, and the implications for scholars are being confronted by the National Archives.

Archivists were also slow to decide that photographs merit preservation. The British took no official notice of them until 1946, when the Master of Rolls ruled that photographic materials "must in certain circumstances be treated as Public Records." A similar lack of appreciation for the archival value of photographs existed in this country, even though the federal government had early recognized the usefulness of the camera in its work. Less than two years after Louis Jacques Mandé Daguerre announced his invention in 1839, a daguerreotypist accompanied a party surveying the disputed Northeast boundary between Maine and Canada. Unfortunately, none of his pictures is known to be extant.

Similarly lost to posterity is the original work of Eliphalet Brown, Jr., a daguerreotypist who accompanied Commodore Matthew C. Perry on his mission to Japan in 1853. Brown's work survives only as engravings, based on his daguerreotypes, in Perry's three-volume report.

The Coal Mine Administration commissioned Russell Lee to document living conditions in mining areas. His "Saturday afternoon street scene," taken in 1946, depicts leisure-time pleasures available to miners in Welch, West Virginia.

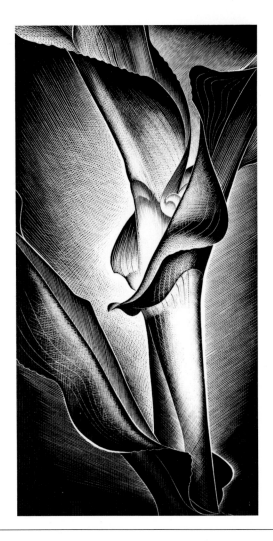

In 1944, the Office of War Information compiled original prints by sixty of the nation's finest graphic artists for use in an overseas exhibition designed to present a composite picture of America and her people "to dramatize the idiosyncracies of one nation for other nations." The following five examples (and the one on page 178), all originally in black and white, are from that group.

Above: Growing Corn by Paul Landacre, 1938. This wood engraving calls attention to the fact that corn was a botanical contribution of the New World.

Opposite: Nightmare by Rockwell Kent, 1941. The organizers of the exhibition chose this lithograph because it represented "psychological exploration" or "interior adventure."

Like all early government photographers, Brown had to supply his own equipment and supplies, a fact revealed when he appealed for additional compensation for his services. An official investigation disclosed that Perry was not authorized to employ a photographer. Nevertheless, the Congressional committee conducting the investigation recognized that Brown's service had been "very essential" to the success of the mission.

By the end of the nineteenth century, federal employees were as ready to use their cameras as their pens and typewriters in the performance of their duties. Photographs supplemented the written records of exploration, and photographers became important members of the exploration and construction parties that penetrated the West after the Civil War. The U.S. Geological Survey made brilliant use of the camera in raising public awareness of the nation's natural resources, and the National Archives now has some 1,900 original glass-plate negatives and 2,500 contemporary prints in 12 bound volumes from that office, including landscape photographs of the West that are recognized masterpieces by John K. Hillers, William Henry Jackson, and others.

Despite the wealth of government photographs, the guide to federal archives published in 1904 by Claude Halstead Van Tyne and Waldo Gifford Leland failed even to mention their existence! The second edition, pub-

lished three years later, has only two entries for photographs. One refers to the collection from the Office of the Geological Survey discussed above; the other entry, under records relating to the Civil War, describes the priceless group of 7,500 prints and 5,500 collodion glass negatives now called the Mathew Brady Collection. The guide ignored the thousands of construction photographs of government buildings found in the Office of the Supervising Architect of the Treasury. This collection, now in the National Archives, includes at least one hundred photographs of the construction of the Treasury Building Extension completed in 1867. It overlooked a file of a Lighthouse Board photographs dating from 1855 documenting the construction of lighthouses, buoys, and depots around the country. The entry for the Bureau of Fisheries omits descriptions of six hundred photographs illustrating the 1887–93 cruises of the steamer *Albatross* and an equal number of views of seal rookeries in the Bering Sea taken in the 1890s. In fact, Van Tyne and Leland could have mentioned photographs among the records of almost every government bureau. "The failure to do so," archivist Joe D. Thomas points out, "is an indication of the prevailing attitude at that time that photographs were not considered archives."

An early survey of federal agencies by the National Archives disclosed 2,346,598 still picture negatives scattered among many government depositories. The prospect of their imminent acquisition led to the formation of a special unit to manage these records. Within a year the unit had custody of 47,141 items, a number that has grown until today it has more than four million black-and-white or color photographs, posters, and artworks from 140 government agencies.

Vast as these holdings may seem, the National Archives has not been able to save more than a fraction of the American photographic legacy. The

Farewell by Raphael Soyer, 1943. A lithograph portraying people as a troop train leaves New York City.

Opposite, top: Morning Train by Thomas Hart Benton, 1943. This lithograph shows a soldier leaving for war from a rural way station in the Mississippi Valley.

Opposite, bottom: The Return from Work by Bention Spruance, 1937. One of four lithographs in the series "The People Work," this one depicts urban transportation from the pedestrian to subways and buses.

number of irreplaceable photographs lost through carelessness or thoughtlessness cannot be estimated. Even more terrible is the attrition of original negatives, because it was standard practice in the nineteenth century to discard them once prints had been made. For example, the Office of Army Engineers discarded all 80 large collodion glass negatives of Charleston, S.C., taken in 1865 by Selman Rush Seibart. Luckily, the Engineers did retain copy prints, now in the National Archives. But to the purist, original negatives and captions give prints their true value as archives.

Photographs, like other government records, are accessioned by the National Archives only after they have fulfilled their intended purposes. With a few exceptions like the Brady collection, they were part of the work of a government agency. Many of them, nevertheless, are both artistically and historically significant. The War Relocation Authority and Bureau of Agricultural Economics photographs taken by Dorothea Lange in the 1940s, the photographs of the Army Air Service in World War I and the Navy in World War II by Edward Steichen, and the photographs taken by Ansel Adams for the National Park Service are to photography what the Old Masters are to painting.

Few government photographers considered themselves artists or historians; however, their purpose was to record specific events accurately. In doing so, they compiled a pictorial history of the United States from the Civil War to the present time. Here is recorded the constantly changing face of America—her cities and her people—with vividness and immediacy.

From these photographs we can learn much about the development of the art of photography. Compare Mathew Brady's study of William Tecumseh Sherman taken immediately after the Civil War with the shot of General Dwight D. Eisenhower by an anonymous army photographer on the first day of the Normandy Invasion. The differences are remarkable. In Brady's time candid photography was unknown because an exposure required 20 seconds. A photographer could not capture a public figure without his cooperation. The candid picture of Eisenhower conveys a kind of intimacy not possible in Brady era portraits. As the photo historian Alan

General Dwight D. Eisenhower on the first day of the Normandy Invasion.

Opposite: William Tecumseh Sherman in a photograph by Mathew Brady.

Opposite: Introduced as evidence before the International Military Tribunal at Nuremberg in 1945–46, pictured here are three of seven volumes of Mauthausen concentration camp death books with vital statistics of deceased inmates including names, date and place of birth, type of prisoner and cause of death; and a cannister of Zyklon gas (introduced as evidence in 1948) similar to those used at the Auschwitz-Birkenau extermination complex in the annihilation of millions of persons.

Below: Confiscated by the U.S. Army after World War II, these albums belonged to Eva Braun, who was a professional photographer as well as Adolf Hitler's mistress. They include shots of Berchtesgaden, Hitler's triumphal entry into Paris, and Nazi officials, in addition to numerous family photographs dating back to her childhood.

As World War II threatened, home-front sacrifices included Fred's Lunch Room in the Wallabout Market area of Brooklyn, razed in early 1941 to permit expansion of the New York Navy Yard.

Trachtenberg declares, the candid picture gives the illusion of being present as emotion unfolds. "Reading photographs," Trachtenberg points out, "does not require a special skill, only a special attention and an active curiosity." Those who make the effort, he says, can participate "in the continual public process of making sense of history, of interpreting the past from the perspective of the present." For that reason, he declares, "the National Archives collection is a national public resource of immeasurable value. It provides an opportunity to realize one of the oldest ideals of democracy, of making 'every man an historian.'"

The Act of 1934 establishing the National Archives also authorized it to "accept, store, and preserve motion picture films and sound recordings pertaining to and illustrative of historical activities of the United States." As a result, the National Archives boasts one of the largest audiovisual collections of its kind. The collection includes videotapes as well as sound recordings and edited and unedited motion picture films. The material, though generally restricted to federal records and to news and public affairs programs concerning the United States government, is remarkably rich and varied.

The sound recordings alone are an amazing resource, virtually a voice library of the twentieth century! Dating from 1896, they total 115,000 phonographs, disks, magnetic tapes, wire recordings, and other formats, reflecting the development of sound technology and the government's early interest in it. To hear them all would require 30,000 hours of listening time. On them are the voices of heroes and villains—Charles Lindbergh and Winston Churchill, Adolf Hitler and Benito Mussolini—as well as of every American president since William McKinley. Here, too, can be heard

some of the most memorable moments of American broadcasting—the wreck of the dirigible *Hindenburg*, the Fireside Chats, and those stirring words that rallied our nation after the attack on Pearl Harbor: "Yesterday, December 7, 1941, [is] a date which will live in infamy!"

Even more impressive is the motion picture footage, consisting of more than 140,000 reels of film. This means 105 million running feet or 20,000 hours of viewing time. To see it all, you would have to devote about ten years, watching film eight hours a day, five days a week. The videotapes, primarily television daily news programs from the three major networks, would require 5,000 hours of viewing time.

Although the earliest film in the National Archives was made in 1894, only a handful of items pre-date World War I. One is *An American in the Making*, released by the Bureau of Mines in 1913, which depicts the assimilation of a European immigrant into a steel manufacturing community. For the most part, however, the motion picture footage is of more recent vintage and consists of non-fiction or "actuality" film such as documentaries, training films, and information films. There are also a few feature films relating to historical events. Significant collections given to the Archives include newsreels, such as the March of Time, Universal Newsreels, and Fox-Movietone News; the Ford Film Collection, donated by the Ford Motor Company; and the Harmon Foundation Collection, which contains films about minorities in the United States and about missionary work in Africa and India.

World War II is easily the subject most represented in the unit's holdings. Besides such well-known documentaries as the *Why We Fight* series, *The Negro Soldier* (1944), and *The Battle of San Pietro* (1945), there are films on the

A documentary—albeit dramatic—photograph of massive gears destined for American warships, taken in 1943 by Dimitri Kessel for the Office of War Information.

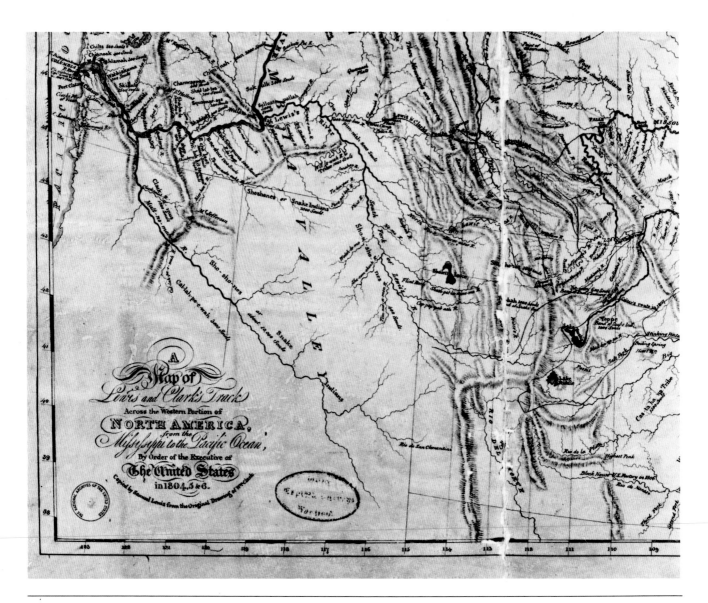

Published in 1814, this map based on observations by Lewis and Clark provided the first approximately correct positions for the Missouri and Snake Rivers. It also depicted complex mountain ranges instead of the single chain that characterized the work of earlier cartographers.

Opposite: Detail from the Second English edition of John Mitchell's 1755 map of the British Colonies in North America. The original cloth backing bears the notation "Mitchell's Map. The copy used by the framers of the Treaty of 1783." Although it served to determine the boundaries between the United States and Great Britain after the American Revolution, its relatively small scale and numerous inaccuracies eventually led to disputes between the two powers.

bombing of Japan, films on behind-the-lines activities of the Office of Strategic Services, and films produced by the war-related civilian agencies. Here, too, is the film bank where movie-makers come for their combat footage, when they need a shot of Japanese kamikaze pilots attacking an American task force or marines storming ashore at Tarawa. The World War II holdings include not only American films but also those of past allies and enemies—British, Russian, German, Italian, Japanese.

The German films are especially interesting. Perhaps the best known is *Triumph of the Will* (1935). Directed by Leni Riefenstahl for the National Socialist German Workers' Party, the film is a record of the 1934 Nuremberg Rally staged by the Nazis for propaganda purposes. *Triumph of the Will* captures some of the intangibles of Nazism: its idealism, mystique, and the personal charisma of Hitler. Interesting, too, are several hours' worth of black-and-white and color footage from the personal collection of "home-movies" of Eva Braun, Hitler's mistress. These silent films of relatives and friends contain the only known shots of Braun and Hitler together.

The documentaries, however, are the jewels of this unit. *Seeds of Destiny*

(1945), although rarely seen in theaters, has brought in more money than any other film in history, except such blockbusters as *Star Wars* and *E.T.*, in form of donations to humanitarian and anti-war causes. The film is a portrayal of the ravages of war on children. Another documentary, *The Negro Soldier*, is hailed by scholars as "a watershed in the use of film to promote racial tolerance." Originally intended as an orientation film designed to ease racial tensions in a still segregationist army during World War II, the film enjoyed widespread civilian acceptance and inspired a series of Hollywood post-war "message" films—*Intruder in the Dust* (1949), *Home of the Brave* (1949), *Storm Warning* (1950)—that promoted racial tolerance.

The film credits of the government documentaries are almost a *Who's Who* of the film and entertainment world for that period. Woody Guthrie, the well-known balladeer, composed music and lyrics for *The Columbia* (1949), a documentary depicting the construction of the Roosevelt Dam complex in the Pacific Northwest. Henry Fonda was one of the narrators for *The Battle of Midway* (1942), directed by John Ford. Joining Ford as filmmakers for the government during World War II were Frank Capra, John Huston, William Wyler, and Darryl Zanuck. Capra, the Sicilian immigrant famous for his films depicting American idealism (*Mr. Deeds Goes to Town*, 1936, and *Mr. Smith Goes to Washington*, 1939), produced the most successful documentaries of the war effort. According to film specialist William T. Murphy, Capra's seven orientation films known as the *Why We Fight* series remain "the most ambitious effort to teach modern history with motion pictures. They established the pattern for the many post-war television compilation-documentaries, although none of them ever equaled the model."

The United States government entered the modern documentary film movement in 1936 when it released *The Plow that Broke the Plains*, the first in a series known as "the films of merit." Products of the New Deal and the inspiration, largely, of one man, Pare Lorentz, a 29-year-old West Virginian, *The Plow*, *The River*, *The Land* (directed by Robert Flaherty), and others in the series were intended to clarify public perception of critical issues. No issue was more critical in the early 1930s than the plight of subsistence farmers,

men tilling marginal soil, deeply in debt, and being dislocated by the thousands because of depressed prices, drought, and dust bowls. Roosevelt set up the Resettlement Administration (later the Farm Security Administration) to assist these people. Many persons in and out of government knew that most of the farmers' ills resulted from generations of land abuse and that the only permanent cure lay in widespread conservation measures. The problem was how to convey this message to the general public.

The Resettlement Administration, therefore, included a comprehensive information staff to explain the agency's program to those who would be affected by it and to those whose taxes supported it. It used photographs, press releases, and magazine articles in addition to exhibits, radio spots, and movies. The agency assembled a crew of still photographers who attracted national recognition with their sensitive, evocative shots of dust storms, tenant farmers, and migrants. Today, the photographs of Dorothea Lange, Walker Evans, Ben Shahn and their colleagues are considered works of art as well as historical documents.

Powerful though they were, the photographs could not reveal the violence of a dust storm in action. Furthermore, many Americans considered the crisis exaggerated. But the dust bowls were real, and each year they destroyed thousands of acres of land, the result of overgrazing, overplowing, and drought. By 1934 the Dust Bowl extended from Texas to North Dakota. On one day alone that year, May 11, winds scoured away an estimated 300,000,000 tons of top soil. If the public refused to believe the photographs and news stories, the Resettlement Administration would try movies.

Lorentz, a movie critic, had never before produced, written, or worked on any part of a motion picture. What he lacked in experience, he made up for in imagination, self-confidence, and energy. He was hired in June 1935. Eleven months later *The Plow that Broke the Plains* was premiered. The film shows the three main causes of Great Plains exploitation: overgrazing by cattle, overplowing by the early settlers, and intense overcultivation during and after World War I by speculators. Lorentz offered neither solutions nor indictments. Film historian Richard Dyer MacCann points out, "the

Stills from *The Plow That Broke the Plains*, the documentary film produced by Pare Lorentz to awaken the American people to the causes behind the dust bowls of the 1930s. *Above:* A two-horse walking plow of the type used to break the virgin sod of the Great Plains lies in the yard of an abandoned farmstead, an obvious victim of the dust storms it helped create. *Above, left:* A farmer carries furniture to a truck as he prepares to abandon his farm to encroaching sand, which has formed window-level drifts.

BRICK
BUILDINGS.
50'x120'

U.S.

STONE
CHURCH

REPUBLICAN BLDG.
BRICK, IRON & STONE 70'x150'

Y.M.C.ASSN.
BRICK
(80'x150') BUILDINGS.

AVEN

picture leaves the audience with two main reactions—a sense of hopelessness at the size of the problem, and a sense of guilt which the history of the Western Plains lays upon us all." Lorentz was more modest. He had merely hoped, he said later, to tell the story of the Plains with emotional value. "Our heroine is the grass, our villain the sun and the wind, our players the actual farmers living in the Plains country."

Another dimension in the history of America's expansion and development can be viewed in the approximately two million maps and charts, two hundred thousand architectural and engineering drawings and eight million aerial photographs that also form part of the special collections of the National Archives. The collection provides a graphic record of America's expansion and development and adds a spatial dimension to many of the significant events in our country's history.

These cartographic archives are the product of thousands of individuals, and the information they contain is as diverse as the functions of the agencies that utilized them. Here is the work of celebrated nineteenth-century American explorers such as Meriwether Lewis and William Clark, Robert E. Lee, William Tecumseh Sherman, Zebulon Pike and John Charles Fremont. Some bear the signatures of presidents from James Monroe to Franklin D. Roosevelt and others are the work of distinguished cartographers, scientists, geologists and architects. Most are the work of federal employees simply performing their duties.

One of the more significant series of these records came from the Office of the Chief of Engineers. For almost a century and a half, army engineers had been responsible for most of the mapping of the United States. An especially significant series of nineteenth-century maps was prepared by the Corps of Topographical Engineers and deposited in a central file on civil works. This eventually became the greatest collection anywhere of cartographic documents relating to Western explorations, military campaigns and operations, and internal improvement projects such as canal, river, road and harbor surveys.

This series is so rich in outstanding maps that of course only a few can

Opposite: Map of a coal mine under the proposed site for the U.S. Post Office in Scranton, Pennsylvania. Only after a mining engineer certified that there would be no danger "of any fall" either to the mine or the building was the post office constructed.

be mentioned here. There is, for instance, a map completed by Nicholas King in 1806, based on sketches by William Clark drawn while the Lewis and Clark expedition wintered at Fort Mandan on the Missouri River in 1804. This map for the first time traced the Missouri River accurately as far north as the Mandan villages in present-day North Dakota. The collection also contains three maps of the California gold fields drawn in 1848 by William Tecumseh Sherman, best remembered for his March to the Sea during the Civil War. Then a young army officer stationed in Monterey, Sherman drew maps that gave the government accurate, first-hand information about the sensational discovery made only a few months earlier at Sutter's Mill. Robert E. Lee, another Civil War celebrity, made surveys of the Mississippi River's harbor at St. Louis in 1837–38, as well as maps of Mexico City during the Mexican War and plans of military forts prior to his participation in the Civil War. Large-scale maps of the Civil War battles of Gettysburg and Antietam provide remarkable detail for the study of these pivotal confrontations. A map of the Shenandoah Valley captured by General George Armstrong Custer from the Confederates in 1864 is part of this series as are maps relating to his misadventure with the Sioux almost twelve years later at the Battle of the Little Big Horn.

Another significant group of maps is those relating to boundaries and territorial claims of the United States. Among these maps is the Steuben-Webster copy of the famous Mitchell map of North America, which was used in the negotiations that ended the American Revolution. The nation's oldest mapping agency, the General Land Office, had the task of surveying, delineating, managing and disposing of our public lands.

Marine surveys also resulted in important cartographic records, and one of the world's major collections of manuscript nautical charts came from the Hydrographic Office of the Navy Department, whose primary mission was to chart the waters and coasts outside the United States. Reflected in this group of records are some of our nation's most glorious seafaring accomplishments, such as the United States Exploring Expedition commanded by Lt. Charles Wilkes detailed in the next chapter.

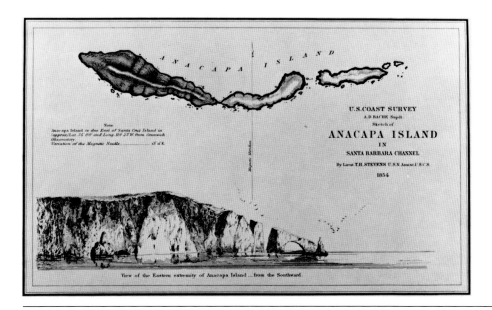

For contemporary maps a significant resource is aerial photography. Picturing the land from above gives a detailed and accurate view of the land not possible before. Contrary to the popular concept of archives, these records are neither old nor do they contain signatures of the illustrious or document great governmental decisions. Their value is in what they tell us about the changing American landscape. (Aerial photographs of other areas of the world are in the Archives' collection of World War I and World War II records.)

Architectural and related engineering drawings include complete sets of original presentation sketches and working drawings for a variety of federal structures erected across the country. As well as being visually exciting, these records give us information such as the federal government's decision in the middle of the nineteenth century to centralize control of the construction of federal buildings outside the city of Washington. Although inspired by a desire for economy while satisfying the demand for government services in a rapidly expanding nation, the decision also had the effect of bringing to many local communities their first true work of architecture. The drawings are not limited to buildings, however. The Archives also cares for ship plans, sketches for nineteenth-century military equipment, aeronautical drawings and original drawings from the Patent Office. The patent drawings are especially intriguing, for they include designs for carpets, clock fronts, cast iron stoves, silverware, playing cards and trademarks as well as diagrams for such familiar devices as Samuel Colt's revolver, Cyrus McCormick's reaper and Eli Whitney's cotton gin.

James McNeill Whistler's career as a government draftsman was cut short because of his penchant for embellishing official documents, such as adding the two flocks of seagulls on this plate of Anacapa Island issued by the Coast and Geodetic Survey.

Eli Whitney.

Cotton Gin

Fig. 1

March 14, 1794

Fig. 2

Patent office March 14th 1815

Made under the direction of the Commissioner of Patents
conformity with act of 3 March 1837

SCIENCE AND TECHNOLOGY

ew visitors to the National Archives realize that it is one of the great resources for the history of American science and technology. The files of the Patent Office, which contain some "patently absurd" ideas, contain also the accumulation of two centuries of Yankee ingenuity. The military records document more than our nation's conflicts; they tell us about men who risked their lives to explore the farthest corners of the earth. Generations of scientists have worked to harness energy; memoranda, drawings, and reports document the development of weapons from the cap-and-ball rifle to the atomic bomb.

Although the first civilian agency created by the federal government primarily for scientific purposes—the Coast and Geodetic Survey—was not established until 1816, the Founding Fathers assumed that science was the handmaiden of the new republic. The power to regulate coinage, weights, and measures entailed technical knowledge; the census, mandated for political reasons, had scientific applications; and the administration of territories required the technologies of mapping and surveying. The word "science," however, appears but once in the Constitution. Article I, Section 8, empowers the Congress to "promote the Progress of Science and useful Arts," by securing for authors and inventors exclusive rights to their writings and discoveries. The framers of the Constitution avoided the word "patent," with its suggestion of the royal prerogative to create monopolies.

No matter what these rights were called, Yankee craftsmen clamored for them as soon as the new government opened for business. Inventors bombarded Congress with ideas for wonderful gadgets, from nail-making machines to lightning-proof umbrellas. Congress could not hope to consider each petition separately if it was to get on with the work of launching a new country; by its second session it had drafted our nation's first patent law. Under this, an inventor was to present a petition (accompanied by written specifications, drawing and model) to a patent board composed of Secretary of State Thomas Jefferson, Secretary of War Henry Knox, and Attorney General Edmund Randolph. If the board members deemed the

Opposite: The National Archives has thousands of patent drawings from the nineteenth century. Although many are for "patently ridiculous" inventions, others, like Eli Whitney's cotton gin, had a dramatic impact on American life.

Opposite: Patent drawing for a submarine explorer.

invention "sufficiently useful and important," they could grant a patent.

The board's leading member was Jefferson, an inventor himself. His design for an improved plow had a significant impact on American agricultural development and earned him a medal from French admirers. A revolving chair, still on display at Monticello, also earned him recognition, but of another sort. His political enemies called it "Jefferson's whirligig" designed so that he could "look all ways at once." His inventions included a camp chair that folded into a walking stick, a pedometer, and a machine for treating hemp. Interestingly, Jefferson never patented any of his own inventions, possibly because of his aversion to monopolies in any form.

The first patent law was hard to carry out because matters of state took precedence over whirligigs and lightning-proof umbrellas. Nevertheless, "The Commissioners for the Promotion of Useful Arts," as they were called, found time to grant fifty-seven patents during the law's three-year existence. The first, granted July 31, 1790, went to Samuel Hopkins of Vermont for his improvements in making pot and pearl ash. The earliest copy of a patent grant in the National Archives is the fourth one, issued to Francis Baily in January 1791 for type punches. The first woman to obtain a patent, in 1809, was Mary Kies of Connecticut, whose invention related to "weaving straw with silk or thread."

Because of difficulties in administering the first patent law, Congress replaced it in 1793. The new legislation relieved the three cabinet members of oversight responsibility and substituted a "registration" system for the "examination" system. This reduced the patent process to little more than a clerical function. Now anyone who submitted the proper drawings and paid the fee could obtain a patent.

The new law caused trouble from the start. Whatever incentive it gave to private industry was eroded by conflicting patents, litigation over claims of originality, and, in some cases, fraud and extortion. Eli Whitney's experience with his cotton gin shows that the patent system left much to be desired. After graduating from Yale in 1792, he constructed a machine that could clean the seeds from cotton bolls. Such a machine, he reasoned,

S. SHORT & N. BRADFORD'S

Submarine Explorer.

Patented 18th Feb. 1830.

5834 x

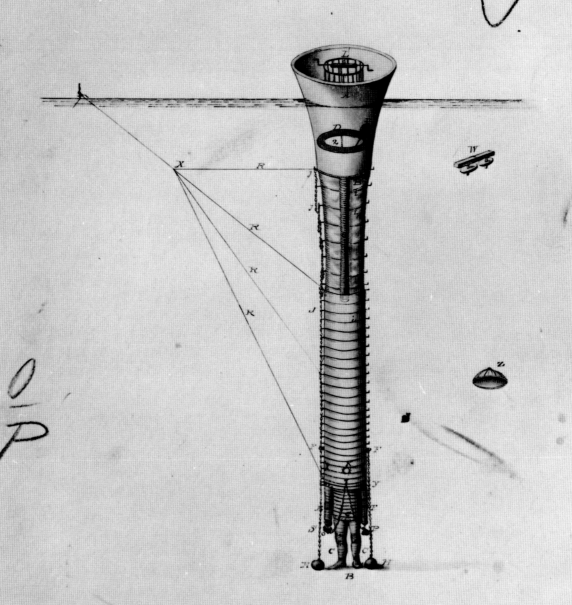

JAMES JOHNSON

FIRE LADDER

6490-4

Patented 18 April 1831.

References. *a*. the ladders. *b.b.* props. *c.c.c.c.* the wheels. *d.* platform. *e.* ropes.

Patent Office 1 Dec 1838

Made under the direction of the Commissioner

of Patents in conformity with Act 3 March 1837

Henry L. Ellsworth

Commissioner of Patents

would benefit both the South and the inventor. After perfecting his gin, he filed for a patent, which he received on March 14, 1794. Subsequent events proved him only half right. The cotton gin brought prosperity to the South, but to the inventor it brought only anguish. It could be pirated so easily that Southern planters were unwilling to pay for it. When Congress later refused to renew his patent, Whitney concluded that "an invention can be so valuable as to be worthless to the inventor."As a result, he never bothered to patent his later ideas, many of which helped to revolutionize American industry.

In 1836, a new law provided the basic principles for today's patent laws. It reaffirmed the necessity of determining an invention's "novelty" and "usefulness," authorized personnel to do this work, and established the Patent Office as a separate bureau under its own chief.

Unfortunately, a fire that same year destroyed the record of accomplishments under the first two laws—7,000 patent models, 9,000 drawings, 168 rolls of records, and 230 books. In an attempt to mitigate the loss, Congress appropriated $100,000 to restore the records as well as the most valuable and interesting models.

The efforts of some unlikely inventors appear in the patent records. One of them is Abraham Lincoln, who had a bent for gadgets. He was a firm advocate of America's patent system which, he declared, "added the fuel of interest to the fire of genius." He is the only president, in fact, to hold a patent, granted in 1849 for his "device for buoying vessels over shoals." The invention, which was never marketed, consists of a set of bellows attached to the hull of a ship just below the water line. On reaching a sand bar the bellows are filled with air and the vessel, one hopes, floats clear. Lincoln personally whittled the patent model, which is today in the Smithsonian Institution; his drawings and patent application are in the National Archives. Lincoln's interest in technology later served our nation well. It was because of his insistence that John Ericsson built the Civil War ironclad, the *Monitor*, and that the Union Army adopted the Spencer repeating rifle.

Opposite: Patent drawing for a fire ladder.

209

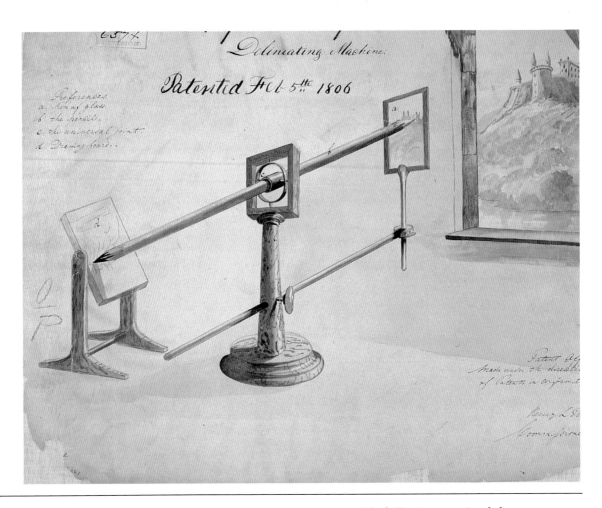

Above and opposite: Patent drawings for a delineating machine and a whiskey still.

Samuel Clemens, better known as Mark Twain, received three patents. One was for "an improvement in adjustable and detachable straps for garments," another was for a game that could help players remember important historical dates, and the third was for his famous "Mark Twain's Self-Pasting Scrapbook." Consisting of blank pages coated with a gum veneer, the scrapbook earned him a considerable profit. It sold 25,000 copies during the first royalty period, leading one of his biographers to remark that this was "well enough for a book that did not contain a single word that critics could praise or condemn." Ironically, Clemens later lost a fortune investing in the inventions of others.

The story of America's achievements in exploration begins, like the patent story, with Jefferson, who did as much for the cause of science as he did for the cause of freedom. No other president devoted a room in the White House to the study of fossil bones. It was because of his insatiable scientific curiosity that Jefferson launched the Lewis and Clark Expedition. Congress accepted Jefferson's argument that the trek across the continent would have commercial value and authorized the use of army funds for salaries and rations. By doing so, it blessed scientific exploration under military auspices and even gave tacit approval for it to take place on foreign soil. Shortly before the Expedition set out, however, the Louisiana Purchase was made. Consequently, much of the land traversed had become U.S. territory.

Patented 12 July 1843.
Vol. 3. pg. 241.

Charles F. Fisher.

Still.

Reference. a condensing tub.
b. still head. c. the beer.
d. the perpendicular tub with stop cock.
e. the still.

Patent office April 19ᵗʰ 1845.
Made under the direction of the Commissioner of Patents in conformity with act of 3ᵈ March 1837

Correct
Chs M Keller,

H L Ellsworth
Commissioner of Patents.

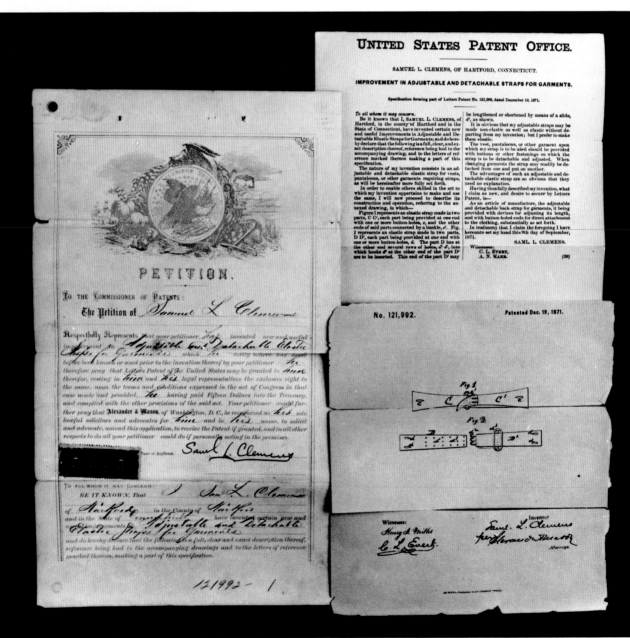

The United States Exploring Expedition of 1838–42, commonly known as the Wilkes Expedition after its commander, Charles Wilkes, was the first U.S. government-sponsored expedition to circumnavigate the globe and the only one to do it entirely under sail. Among its many accomplishments, it determined that Antarctica was a continent. It surveyed 280 islands as well as much of America's northwest coast. It prepared 200 new nautical charts, crossed the Pacific three times, and circled the globe once.

The story begins with an eccentric named John Clyves Symmes, a veteran of the War of 1812, who believed that the world was hollow and that the entrances to the interior could be found at the North and South Poles. Yankee merchants, anxious to find new sealing and whaling grounds, allied themselves with Symmes and his "holes in the poles" theory to encourage Congress to sponsor a South Seas expedition to push back the frontiers of *terra (et aqua) incognita*. The U.S. Navy welcomed an opportunity to learn more about this little-known region and to show the flag in waters where natives had killed American seamen and gone unpunished. These interests, and the enthusiasm of President John Quincy Adams, encouraged Congress in 1828 to authorize the expedition. Difficulties and bureaucratic squabbling, however, delayed the squadron ten years. In 1837, Adams, now a Congressman from Massachusetts, probably expressed the consensus of the American public when he said: "The only thing I want to hear about the exploring expedition is that it has sailed."

Six ships finally did sail on August 18, 1838, under the command of Lt. Charles Wilkes. He was not a professional scientist, but he had expertise in surveying, chartmaking, astronomy and other naval skills. He was a strict disciplinarian, often in conflict with his officers and men. He depicts himself in his five-volume official narrative of the expedition in the role of a lonely hero of the venture. He kept his orders secret, revealing only what would justify his actions.

Considerable credit for the distinction of the expedition must be given to the eight young scientists who sailed with him. These men were professionals, and they did their work well. They collected material from Latin

Opposite, top: Samuel Clemens, better known as Mark Twain.

Opposite, bottom: The patent application for an "improvement in adjustable straps for garments" filed by Samuel Clemens, who received three patents during his lifetime.

During his attempts to reach the North Pole, Commodore Robert E. Peary used the artifacts displayed here. They include a sextant, a telescope with hand-sewn canvas cover, a trail stove, and tandem watches. Shown also are sketches by James W. Davidson, who accompanied Peary on his 1893–94 expedition, and programs from banquets honoring the famous explorer.

Opposite: William Briscoe, an armorer's mate aboard the *Vincennes*, was obviously proud to be a member of the great United States Exploring Expedition of 1838–42. His diary, as well as the charts shown with it, is now part of the expedition's archival legacy.

America, Antarctica, the Central Pacific Islands, and the western coast of America. Their findings touched the sciences of anthropology, ethnology, zoology in all its major branches, botany, geology, hydrography, meteorology, and physics. Perhaps most important, the smooth collaboration of the scientists with the military in a peacetime endeavor established a precedent for cooperation that is as current as our nation's most recent efforts at space exploration.

Unlike the legacy of the Lewis and Clark journey, which was widely dispersed, that of the Wilkes Expedition was not lost to the federal government. The National Archives has the original charts, the official records, and twenty-three daily journals that Wilkes required his officers to keep. One officer noted in his that "keeping a diary is a damned bore." Some ripped out pages when they were asked to give them to Wilkes for periodic review. Still another officer kept two diaries—one for Wilkes to inspect and one for himself.

Despite accomplishments, there were numerous problems. The ships were ill-equipped for such a sustained cruise. Of the the six that set sail so confidently in 1838, only two completed the entire trip: the *Vincennes* and

PRIVATE

JOURNAL OF A CRUISE IN THE

U.S. FLAG.Ship.

VINCENNES.

CHARLES WILKS Esqurs.

COMMANDER

SOUTH SEA AND AROUND THE WORLD

the *Porpoise*. The *Relief*, a supply ship, was too slow to keep up with the squadron and returned home after only a few months at sea. The *Sea Gull* was lost off Cape Horn. The *Peacock* foundered at the mouth of the Columbia River, and the *Flying Fish* was sold at Singapore because it was no longer considered seaworthy. Native hostility also proved troublesome. It prevented the scientists from exploring the interior of several Pacific islands and cost several sailors, including Wilkes' own nephew, their lives.

The greatest achievement, the discovery of Antarctica, was almost denied. When two officers aboard the *Vincennes* thought they spotted land on January 16, 1840, their sighting was not entered in the ship's log. Three days later the vessel made another landfall just hours before a French ship claimed the discovery. Nevertheless, the American explorers can rightly claim to be the first to establish the continental proportions of Antarctica. New charts overlaid on those of Wilkes a century later show his work to have been very accurate. This is amazing considering that all the surveying work had to be done under harsh conditions and from ships standing out from shore. In 1841 a German map labeled this area Wilkesland, a name it still bears.

Another energetic naval officer whose accomplishments are recorded in the National Archives is Matthew Fontaine Maury. The careers of Wilkes and Maury intersect at several points. Both men administered the U.S. Naval Observatory (when Wilkes had charge, it was the Depot of Charts and Instruments). Maury was to have been the official astronomer for the U.S. Exploring Expedition but resigned before it sailed; Wilkes not only commanded it, but served as its astronomer. Maury had served aboard the sloop-of-war *Vincennes* when it became the first U.S. naval vessel to circle the globe in 1827; Wilkes later made it the expedition's flagship.

Although head of the Naval Observatory for much of his career, Maury found the oceans far more interesting than the skies. A deeply religious man, he credited the eighth verse of the eighth Psalm, "Whatsoever walketh through the paths of the sea . . . ," with giving him the idea to chart the highways of the oceans. "If God says the paths are there . . . I will find

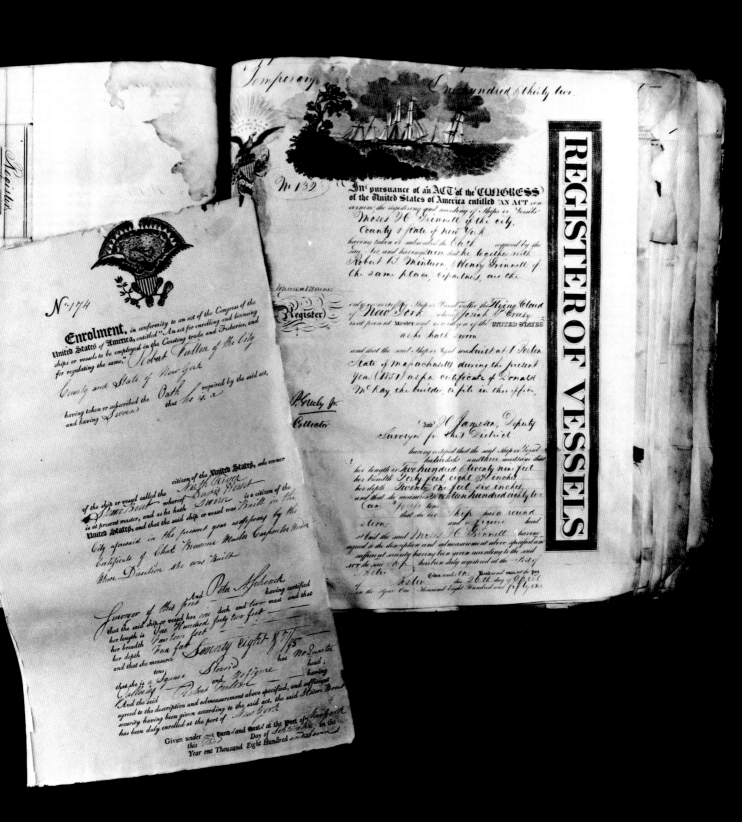

No 174

Enrolment, in conformity to an act of the Congress of the
United States of America, entitled "An act for enrolling and licensing
ships or vessels to be employed in the Coasting trade and Fisheries, and
for regulating the same." *Robert Fulton* of the City
County and State of New York
having taken or subscribed the Oath required by the said act,
and having Sworn that he is a

citizen of the United States, sole owner
of the ship or vessel called the North River
Steam Boat whereof Davis Hunt is a citizen of the
is at present master, and as he hath Sworn
United States, and that the said ship or vessel was Built in the
City aforesaid in the present year as appears by the
Certificate of Chas Browne Master Carpenter Under
Whose Direction she was Built

Surveyor of this port And Peter Ashenck
having certified
that the said ship or vessel has one deck and two mast and that
her length is One Hundred forty two feet
her breadth Fourteen feet
and that she measures Seventy eight 87/95
tons; that she is a Square Stern, No figure head; having
Galleries — Robert Fulton
And the said
agreed to the description and admeasurement above specified, and sufficient
security having been given according to the said act, the said Steam Boat
has been duly enrolled at the port of New York

Given under my Hand and Seal at the Port of New York
this Third Day of September in the
Year one Thousand Eight Hundred and Seven

No 132

Temporary

One hundred & thirty two.

Register

P. Greely Jr

Collector

IN pursuance of an ACT of the CONGRESS
of the United States of America entitled "AN ACT for
reviving the registering and recording of Ships or Vessels."
Moses H. Grinnell of the city
County & State of New York
having taken or subscribed the Oath required by the
said Act, and having Sworn that he together with
Robert B. Minturn, & Henry Grinnell of
the same place, Copartners, are the

only owners of the Ship or Vessel called the Flying Cloud
of New York whereof Josiah P. Cressy
is at present Master and is a citizen of the UNITED STATES
as he hath Sworn

and that the said Ship or Vessel was built at E Porter
State of Mapachusetts during the present
Year (1851) as per certificate of Donald
McKay the builder, on file in this office.

And H. Jameson, Deputy
Surveyor for this District
having certified that the said Ship or Vessel
hath decks and three masts and that
her length is Two hundred & twenty nine feet
her breadth Forty feet, eight inches
her depth Twenty one feet six inches,
and that she measures Eighteen hundred & eighty two
tons;
that she is a Ship has a round
stern and a figure head
And the said Moses H. Grinnell having
agreed to the description and admeasurement above specified and
sufficient security having been given according to the
Act has been duly registered at the Port of
New York
Given under our Hand and seal at the Port of
New York this 26th day of April
in the Year One Thousand Eight Hundred and fifty five

them," he exclaimed. And find them he did!

Maury began by examining the many dust-covered log books in the Naval Observatory. Dating back to the 1700s, the logs recorded the nautical observations of seamen whose ships had criss-crossed the globe. Realizing he would need even more information to complete the task he had set for himself, Maury appealed to the ship captains of the world. He had printed blank forms on which he asked mariners to record the daily course of their ships as well as data about winds, currents, and general ocean conditions. Observations on fish, bird, and whale sightings were especially welcome.

Mariners responded with such enthusiasm that completed forms sent to Washington between 1842 and 1887 filled over 500 thick volumes (of which over 300 are extant and available to Archives researchers). Maury collated this information and, over a period of seventeen years, published seven series of *Wind and Current Charts* as well as eight volumes of *Sailing Directions*, containing information on ocean meteorology and other nautical topics. These Maury distributed free to the ship masters who assisted him in compiling or updating the charts. Mariners who then used the charts to select the most favorable routes between ports often discovered that they had saved astonishing amounts of time, particularly vital during this heyday of the clipper ships, when competition for passengers and cargo was intense. Maury's name became a common word among sailors the world over. His charts, for example, chopped the average sailing time from New York to Rio de Janeiro from 55 to as few as 35 days. For the trip to San Francisco around Cape Horn, astonished ship captains saw their sailing time reduced from 180 to 133 days. Even the remarkable record of 89 days and 21 hours logged by David McKay's fabulous *Flying Cloud* was due in part to Maury's work. Maury's finest moment, however, came when Cyrus Field followed his advice when laying the transatlantic cable.

Whalers also paid homage to Maury. Whaling was big business at this time, and its commercial success was important to the United States. One purpose of the Wilkes Expedition, in fact, had been to learn more about the Pacific whaling grounds. Therefore, Maury urged ship owners to en-

Saturday 6
Latt 3°34
Long 122°48′W
122°48′W

Commences this day with strong breezes & also employd cuting at 4 finishd & stood to the N°
at 4 P.M steerd off after whales got none Commenced Boiling do End Midle & Later part strong winds
& Clear & Employd Boiling saw whales got none do Ends

Sunday 7
Latt 3°44 S

Long 123°36′
or

Commences this day with Moderate winds from
the E & ESE standing to the wind & Employd Boiling
at 2 P.M finished at 3 saw whales to the w at 3 20 Lowered
at 5 P.M took the whale Along side &
Lay by at 6 A.M commenced Cuting at 9 30 A.M finished
& stood to the N° do Ends Employd

Monday 8
Latt 4 03
Long 123° 30′

Commences this day with Moderate winds standing
to the N E & Employd Boiling Midle part strong
gales & Squaly Rainey Later part Strong gales standing
to the South & Employd do Ends Saw finbacks

Tuesday 9
Latt 3°35
Long 123°43′

Commences this day with strong winds & Squaly
standing to the SE & Employd Boiling at 4 P.M saw
whales going fast to the SE Lowered Chased caught none
wore ship & stood to the N E at 6 P.M came on board
& stood to the N.N.E at 10 P.M finished Boiling Midle
part squaly Later part Strong winds & cloudy on but
the Jibb to Repair do Ends Saw nothing more

Wednesday 10
Latt 2°45
Long 124° 28′W

Commences this day with strong gales standing
to the N.N.E Midle part a hurecane Split the
Jib All to shivers Later part More Moderate on but
the Remains & bent A New Jib do End Employd

Thursday 11
Latt 3 26′
Long 124° 15′

Commences this day with strong gales from
standing to the N.N.E at 5 P.M tacke ship to the
SSE Midle part Strong winds & Squaly with Rain
Later part Moderate & Clear Standing on & on to
the South & Employd boyling oil do Ends

Successful attempts in consequence of high wind &
sea One with 600 barrels do Ends

						69°56′S	5°S			64°56′S

五倍子

野桃

大海棠

Wu bei Tzu

Yeh Tao

Ta Hai Tong

"Five-fold seed"

"Wild peach."

"Big sea apple-fruit."

Galls on Rhus
semialata.

Amygdalus
persica

Malus sp.

(Gallnuts.)

(Crab-apple.)

"Cherry peach"

Amygdalus persica

(A small peach)

2242

courage their captains to keep accurate records about whale sightings. "I do not mean records by one or two or a dozen ships," he exhorted one owner. "I mean records by the hundreds." Although whalers tended to be inconsistent in their record keeping, Maury was able to construct a whale chart. Published in 1851, it located areas frequented by particular species of whales during their annual migrations. One captain who received a copy called it "a precious jewel," which, he told Maury, "seems to have waked up the merchants and masters to the practical utility of your researches in their behalf."

A civilian scientist hero was Frank N. Meyer (subject of a recent book by Isabel Cunningham), a government botanist who sacrificed his life for his work. Born in Amsterdam in 1875, Meyer as a boy dreamed of traveling the world to study plants, to "skim the earth for things good for man." After working under the eminent Dutch botanist Hugo de Vries, Meyer came to the United States in 1901 and was hired by the Department of Agriculture as a gardener. After he had wandered across Mexico on foot, studying the flora at his own expense, the Department of Agriculture sent him to China as an agricultural explorer. He spent the bulk of his career there, conducting four major plant surveys between 1905 and 1918.

Meyer endured many hardships and dangers on these forays into remote areas, with only an assistant and an interpreter for companionship. Walking hundreds of miles, often under the most adverse conditions, he forded swift rivers, crossed deserts, and climbed mountains; he survived snowstorms, dust storms, and bandits (he once escaped from three Siberian thugs intent on strangling him by stabbing one of them in the stomach with his bowie knife). Usually his experiences were less dramatic, but even finding a place to sleep could be an adventure. The best inn in Chiehchou, China, for instance, he described as overcrowded, "with merchants and coolies shouting and having angry disputes; with partitions between the rooms so thin as to make them almost transparent; people gambling with dice and cards all night long; others smoking opium; hawkers coming in, selling all possible sorts of things from raw carrots to straw braid hats;

Opposite: Department of Agriculture materials relating to Frank N. Meyer, a government botanist who died in China in 1918. These include a photograph of him (holding a walking stick), photographs he took, and his log book containing the Chinese, Latin, and English names for plants recorded during his field work.

The Observers' School of Aerial Gunnery, where army officers during World War I learned how to shoot at airplanes by using a small model.

and odors hanging about to make angels even procure handkerchiefs." Yet Meyer considered any hardship worthwhile. "When the sun comes out and I see the beautiful bluish mountains in the distance, I feel it isn't so bad after all," he once wrote. "There goes nothing above fresh air, a blue sky above one's head, some mountains in the distance, and a rippling brook or foaming sea close by. . . . I love better exploring than anything else."

On his last expedition to China, Meyer ventured far up the Yangtze in search of blight-resistant pears and blundered into fighting between government troops and revolutionaries. After breaking through the battle lines, he and his guide boarded a river boat and started back down the Yangtze, but on June 1, 1918, he disappeared. A week later his body was recovered from the river.

Meyer had promised to "skim the earth for things good for man," and he kept that promise. He introduced more than 2,500 plants to American horticulture including drought-resistant trees like the Siberian elm (*Ulmus pumila*) that now shades formerly treeless prairies from Canada to Texas, the Manchurian spinach that saved the American spinach industry when it was threatened with wilt and blight, and a fire-blight-resistant pear stock that saved American orchards threatened by this disease. His greatness lies not in individual introductions, however, but in the pioneering nature of his work, for he opened the field of agricultural exploration in Asia.

For all his accomplishments, Meyer is little known in America today, although a Meyer medal is awarded annually to the person who has done the most for the cause of plant exploration and introduction. Ironically, Meyer financed it himself through a bequest in his will. He left money to the USDA Plant Introduction Section for an outing or similar activity that his colleagues would enjoy. Instead, they voted to use the money to establish the medal.

His colleagues did one more useful thing in his memory. They gathered more than 2,500 pages of correspondence that he had sent during his travels and prepared a typescript account of his career that tells where he went, whom he saw, the problems he faced, and the circumstances that sur-

American aviators during World War I learning how to drop bombs on enemy targets. Note bomb sight on the side of the cockpit and the moving carpet under the fuselage.

Below: With the advent of the airplane as a weapon of war came the need for detection devices. One of the first was the Perrin Telesitemeter, an early form of radar developed in France during World War I that located approaching airplanes by the sound of their engines. The study pictured here, prepared by American observers, discusses the telesitemeter's utility and effectiveness.

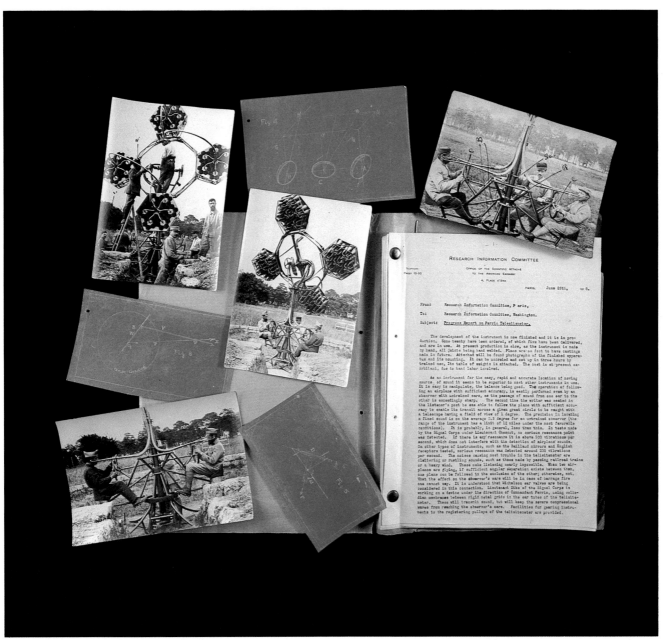

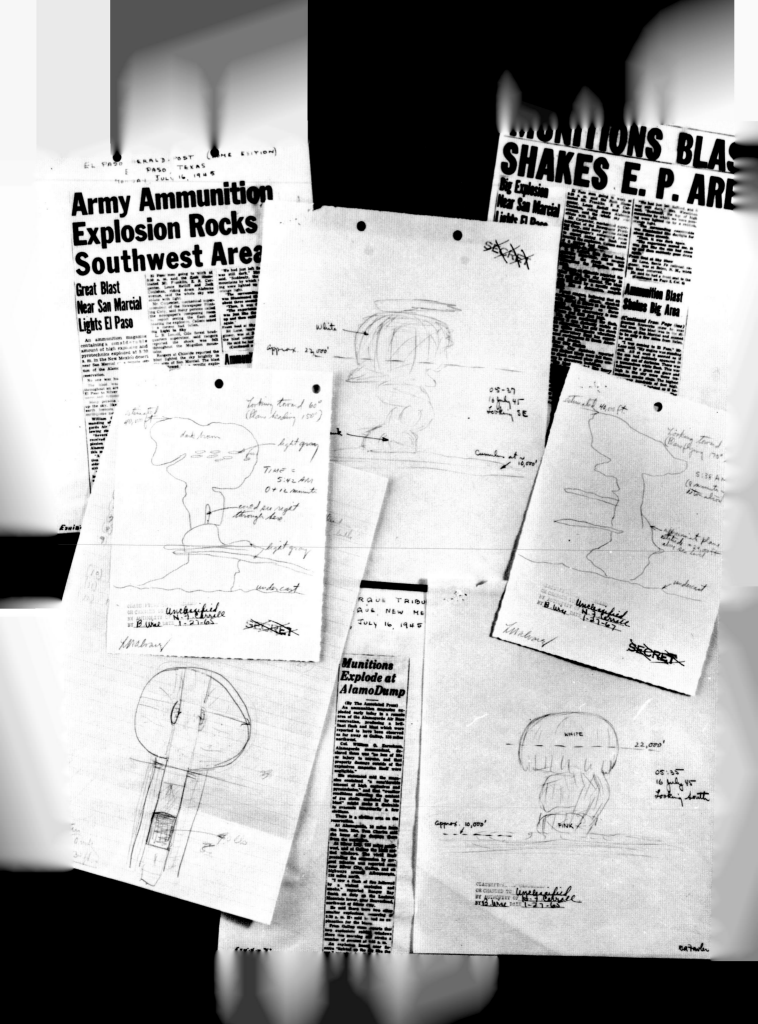

rounded his collection of plants. A copy of this typescript, along with Meyer's itinerary reports, letters written to him, clippings, photographs, and the consular report of his death, has been given to the National Archives and is to be found in the Department of Agriculture records.

Another civilian scientist who may be tracked in Archives records is James B. Conant, a major figure in the development of the atomic bomb. Conant had significant scientific roles in both World Wars. After receiving a Harvard Ph.D. in organic chemistry in 1916, he offered his services to a chemical research team working under the direction of the Bureau of Mines. During World War I he was a major in the Chemical Warfare Service Branch of the Army, trying to perfect a poison gas called Lewisite. Writing years later, Conant discussed the morality of poison gas as a weapon of war. "To me," he declared, "the development of new and effective gases seemed no more immoral than the manufacture of explosives and guns. . . . All war is immoral."

Conant was released when the Armistice ended the need for Lewisite. He gave up his work in applied chemistry and returned to academe, becom-

Records do not have to be old to be found in the National Archives. Shown here is a collection of photographs taken in March and April 1979 for the Department of Energy that document events surrounding the accident at the Three Mile Island Nuclear Power Plant.

Opposite: Eyewitness drawings of the first atomic test at Alamogordo, New Mexico, with copies of news stories reporting the test as an accident at a military arsenal.

to your attention the following facts and recommendations:

In the course of the last four months it has been made probable - through the work of Joliot in France as well as Fermi and Szilard in America - that it may become possible to set up a nuclear chain reaction in a large mass of uranium,by which vast amounts of power and large quantities of new radium-like elements would be generated. Now it appears almost certain that this could be achieved in the immediate future.

This new phenomenon would also lead to the construction of bombs, and it is conceivable - though much less certain - that extremely powerful bombs of a new type may thus be constructed. A single bomb of this type, carried by boat and exploded in a port, might very well destroy the whole port together with some of the surrounding territory. However, such bombs might very well prove to be too heavy for transportation by

This letter (here shown in extract) from Albert Einstein to Franklin D. Roosevelt was instrumental in the American race to build an atomic bomb before the Germans did.

ing a professor at Harvard, then chairman of the Department of Chemistry, and finally, in 1933, President of the University. Although only forty, he had already gained international recognition for his studies on chlorophyl and hemoglobin. In 1941, the course of Conant's life was again changed by war. Summoned to Washington, he joined with Vannevar Bush and other distinguished scientists whose task it was to organize scientific research for the war effort. He chaired the National Defense Research Committee, and was picked to head the committee charged with planning the construction of the atom bomb. The result is well known to history. Now in the National Archives is a report of 1943 in Conant's hand that clearly reveals the turmoil felt by the scientists working on the atomic bomb. "I suppose every one concerned with the project would feel greatly relieved and thoroughly delighted if something would develop to *prove* the impossibility of such an atomic explosive," he wrote. Conant already knew that mastery of nuclear energy would be a reality. His only doubt concerned its practicality as a weapon of war. A failure of the military test would be desirable, he thought. "Civilization would then, indeed, be fortunate —atomic energy for power a reality, for destruction an impossibility."

Conant's hopes disappeared with the first atomic explosion at the New Mexico proving ground on July 16, 1945. He was one of the few witnesses to the first atomic test, a test so secret the Army reported it as an accident at a military arsenal. Less than a month later, the bomb was used on the cities of Hiroshima and Nagasaki.

Another story of scientific development from World War II is available in the Archives. Although Alexander Fleming, a Scotsman, discovered penicillin in 1928, it was not until early 1941 that British scientists established the drug's anti-bacterial value and its safety for humans. With British industry over-extended by the war, England turned to the United States for help. Two Oxford scientists were sent to work on the drug at the Agriculture Department's Northern Regional Research Laboratory in Peoria, Illinois. As was usual during the war, the British shared their secrets with no thought of patent protection; they were anxious to hasten production for the war effort. Records show that the American drug industry joined with the federal government in a cooperative venture of titanic proportions. Twenty-one penicillin plants were built in 1943; within a year production of the wonder drug had been increased one hundred fold. By the time of the Normandy Invasion, penicillin was available in sufficient amount to treat all the Allied forces.

This twentieth-century miracle is well chronicled in Department of Agriculture records, thanks to the careful documentation by the original research team. As one of them wrote at the time, "I want future generations to share in the excitement, disappointments, and ultimate success of a group fortunate enough to devote wartime effort to the preservation of life rather than its destruction."

Additional documentation of the remarkable story of the distribution of penicillin can be found in the Archives among records of the Committee on Medical Research of the Office of Scientific Research and Development.

The stories told above are merely sketches that can be, as some have been, expanded into definitive histories largely from National Archives holdings. They give only a glimpse of the scope of these holdings.

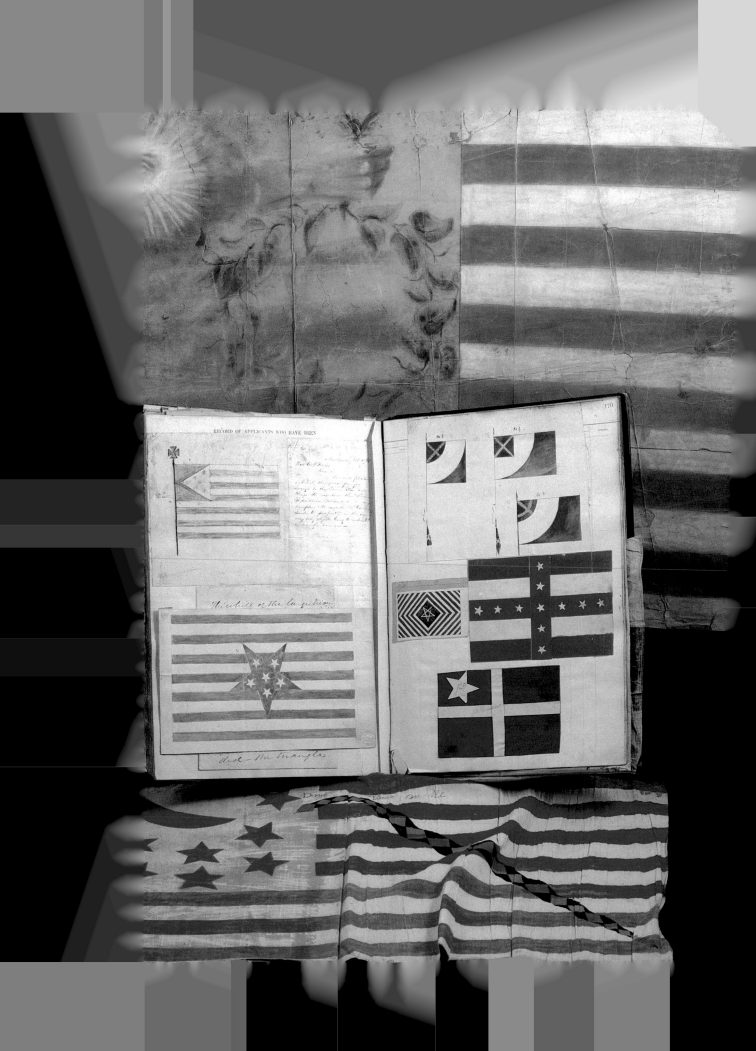

TO PROVIDE FOR THE
COMMON DEFENSE

*O*f the 1.4 million cubic feet of permanently valuable records of the federal government stored in the National Archives, well over half, some 700,000 cubic feet, relate to military affairs. Some are as old as the 1775 appeal of Massachusetts to the Continental Congress for help after the battles of Lexington and Concord, but about a fourth concern World War II.

Not all the records are about combat, of course. Some have to do with military education, with West Point and Annapolis, as well as with G.I. Basic Training. Some attest the role of the U.S. Army Engineers in exploring and surveying the land and in developing civil works projects. Some reflect the military's interest in applied science: ordnance development, ship building, and aeronautics. Some trace the development of logistics (servicemen have to be housed, fed, clothed, transported and equipped); other holdings describe the improvisations needed to field a citizen army in the Revolutionary War and the bureaucratic juggernaut that is military logistics today.

One particularly interesting group of records is the "Quartermaster Consolidated File," containing information on civilian contracts issued during the nineteenth century. Rather surprising things can be found there, such as a broken spur sent to the War Department by a disgruntled Civil War cavalryman, who wanted the army to know what shoddy equipment was being furnished the Northern troops.

Many military records, of course, relate to America's wars. The holdings of the Archives for the Revolutionary War are incomplete for many reasons. Nonetheless, treasures survive. There are copies of logs and journals of famous warships of the period: the *Wasp, Ranger,* and *Bonhomme Richard*. There are Papers of the Continental Congress, which contain much information about the operations and command of the Continental Army. There is the War Department Collection of Revolutionary War Records, containing muster and pay rolls, orderly books, and pension files.

The orderly books kept by George Washington are especially revealing. They show that he spent as much time worrying about the morale and

Opposite: These designs were among those submitted to a committee charged with selecting the flag for the Confederate States of America.

I **Benedict Arnold Major General**
do acknowledge the UNITED STATES of AME-
RICA to be Free, Independent and Sovereign States, and
declare that the people thereof owe no allegiance or obedience to George the Third, King of Great-Britain; and I
renounce, refuse and abjure any allegiance or obedience to
him; and I do *Swear* that I will, to the utmost of my power, support, maintain and defend the said
United States against the said King George the Third, his
heirs and successors, and his or their abettors, assistants and
adherents, and will serve the said United States in the office of
Major General which I now hold, with
fidelity, according to the best of my skill and understanding.

*Sworn before me this B Arnold
30th May 1778 at the
Artillery Park Valley Forge*

The Oath of Allegiance to the United States signed by General Benedict Arnold on May 30, 1778. Despite his important victory over the British at the Battle of Saratoga the previous October, Arnold's name still is synonymous with the word "traitor."

discipline of his rag-tag army as he did planning and directing military campaigns. He condemned the troops' practices of strolling about late at night, of dancing and reveling in civilian houses, and of making free with the produce of citizens' gardens. He forbade card and dice playing, as well as cursing, swearing, and drunkenness. The General ordered his officers to keep their men neat and clean and to provide fresh straw, "if it be had," for their beds; and he urged "punctual attendance on divine services . . . to implore the blessings of heaven."

The Father of Our Country also had to deal with a problem that still plagues guardians of high-spirited youngsters, as this entry indicates:

> The General does not mean to discourage the practice of bathing while the weather is warm enough to continue it, but he expressly forbids any person doing it near the bridge at or in Cambridge where it has been observed and complained of that many men [have] lost all sense of decency and common modesty . . . running about naked upon the bridge whilst passengers and even Ladies of the First Fashion [are] passing over it as if they meant to glory in their shame. The Guards and Sentries are to put a stop [to it].

From the War of 1812, our "Second War for Independence," the National Archives has a variety of treasures, from maps to recruiting posters. These document our successes and failure in that conflict, which we lost on the battlefield but won at the negotiating table. Our worst humiliation was the burning of Washington by a British expeditionary force. Congressman Israel Pickens of North Carolina called it a "disgraceful injury." The Archives has papers from the Congressional Committee that investigated the sad affair. It has also an unusual memento. A descendant of one of the British raiders returned a medicine chest looted from the White House before it was set afire. The chest is now in the Roosevelt Presidential Library.

The National Archives holds a wealth of material about the Civil War. Mathew Brady's photographs are world famous, and maps and drawings

George N. Barnard, a veteran photographer who accompanied General William T. Sherman on his March to the Sea during the Civil War, captured this scene of the defense of Atlanta. Atlanta fell to Sherman and Barnard's photographs are superb resources for military historians.

Below: In this photograph taken by Alexander Gardner after the Battle of Gettysburg, July 1863, a dead southern soldier lies behind a stone breastwork. Gardner actually composed this famous scene by bringing the body from elsewhere and supplying the musket.

from the conflict number in the thousands. Inventions that ushered in the era of modern warfare—the Gatling Gun, the iron-clad *Monitor*, and the breech-loading rifle—are documented in the patent application files. There are relics of both the Confederacy and the Union: a volume of original drawings submitted to the Confederate government suggesting designs for the new country's flag; the amnesty oath Robert E. Lee took after the war, by which he renewed his allegiance to the United States; original watercolors by Civil War artists. There are even letters written by Confederate officers on wallpaper and on pages torn from books. These reflect the severe paper shortage in the South and, by implication, the deterioration of the Confederate economy.

One aspect of the conflict too often overlooked is the role played by women. Nevertheless, according to a British journalist visiting America at the time, no conflict in history was as much "a woman's war" as the Civil War. Although its total effects on the fifteen million women in the embattled states and territories will probably remain forever unknown, some particulars can be found in the National Archives, in pension records, correspondence, Congressional records, and photographs.

Documents from the "rebel archives," confiscated by the federal government after the Civil War. These archives say much about the short-lived Confederacy, including that paper itself was in short supply. When writing letters, Confederate officers often used wrapping paper, canceled envelopes, and wallpaper.

Opposite: William McIlvaine (1813–67), a private in the 5th New York Volunteers—better known as Duryee's Zouaves because of their colorful uniforms—was almost fifty years old when the Civil War began. Although not a trained artist, his twenty-seven watercolors are important for the information they provide on camp life, uniforms, and engagements. Top: *Burning of the* Cataline, *Fortress Monroe*. Bottom: Three Zouaves lounging before a medical dispensary tent.

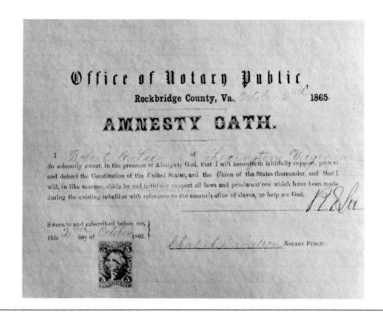

For more than a century historians believed that Robert E. Lee had not taken the oath of allegiance to the United States required to regain his citizenship after the Civil War. However, this amnesty oath signed by Lee was found among State Department records in the National Archives in 1970. On the basis of this document, Congress restored Lee's citizenship posthumously.

A few women posing as men fought in the Revolution, but as many as four hundred so disguised saw service as soldiers in the War Between the States. These latter-day Joan of Arcs faced the dangers of battle, the threat of disease, and the hardships of camp life only to risk ridicule and censure if their charades were discovered. It was no great feat for a woman to enlist undetected, however. The physical examination simply estimated the recruit's height and ensured that he could see and hear, had sound arms and legs, and possessed the four front teeth necessary for biting the paper cartridges used in muzzle-loading rifles. Once in the army, a female soldier might well escape detection until severely wounded or incapacitated by illness.

Although women soldiers usually enlisted under assumed names, the service records of some of them have been identified. Sarah Emma Edmonds used the name of Franklin Thompson. During her twenty-three months of active duty as a private in Company F, Second Regiment, Michigan Volunteer Infantry, she participated in the First and Second Battles of Bull Run, the Peninsula Campaign, and the Battle of Fredericksburg. Because of recurring bouts with malaria, she deserted rather than risk having her sex discovered at a hospital. Once out of the army, she resumed woman's garb and wrote *Nurse and Spy in the Union Army*, based to some degree on her own experiences. In 1884, armed with appropriate affidavits verifying that she and Franklin Thompson were one and the same, she applied for a pension. A special act of Congress removed the charge of desertion and placed her, now Mrs. Sarah Seelye, on the pension rolls at a rate of twelve dollars a month.

When Albert D. J. Cashier mustered out with his regiment on August 17, 1865, he had served three years and twelve days in the Union Army as a private in Company G of the 95th Illinois Infantry. In 1910 he gained admittance to the Soldier's and Sailor's Home in Quincy, Illinois. Not until 1913, when he was hospitalized for a broken leg, did officials discover that "Albert" was in reality Jennie Hodgers, an Irish immigrant. The news did not shock her former comrades-in-arms, however. At the fiftieth reunion

of her regiment in 1915, several members of Company G recalled that "Albert" had been the shortest man in the outfit and never had to shave.

Of several female doctors, the most notable is Mary E. Walker. The twenty-eight-year-old physician accepted a position as a contract surgeon with the 52nd Ohio Volunteer Infantry and was soon captured at Gordon's Mill, Georgia. Before being exchanged for a Confederate surgeon, she spent four months in Richmond's notorious Castle Thunder, where she caused quite a stir in her military uniform. One Confederate officer wrote his wife that everyone was "disgusted . . . at the sight of a *thing* that nothing but the debased and depraved Yankee nation could produce." He also reported that she had "tongue enough for a regiment of men."

Controversy seemed to be Walker's constant companion. When she applied for a pension based on medical disability, the government claimed she had been a nurse, which meant that she qualified for less money. "This is false," she retorted, "as I never had a position as a 'nurse' and would not accept one as either nurse or bootblack any more than would any other officer." President Andrew Johnson thought enough of her services to award her the Congressional Medal of Honor. Years later, however, a review board withdrew the award. President Lyndon Johnson finally and officially restored it, long after her death.

Women doctors in the Civil War were rare, but not women nurses. When the war began, the only trained women nurses were Catholic nuns, the Sisters of Charity and the Sisters of Mercy, who administered to both armies. Before the war ended, at least 3,200 women held paying positions in military hospitals for both North and South, while thousands more volunteered their services. The most famous was Clara Barton, a former government clerk who believed she could be more effective on the battlefield. When discussing her experiences after the war, she told audiences that if her work appeared to be "rough and unseemly for a *woman*," they should remember that combat was equally "rough and unseemly for *men*."

Outside the war zones the most dangerous employment for women was arsenal work, which claimed scores of lives in accidents from Connecticut

In this photograph of Dr. Mary E. Walker, a Civil War surgeon, Mathew Brady captured some of the pride and determination that marked so much of her life.

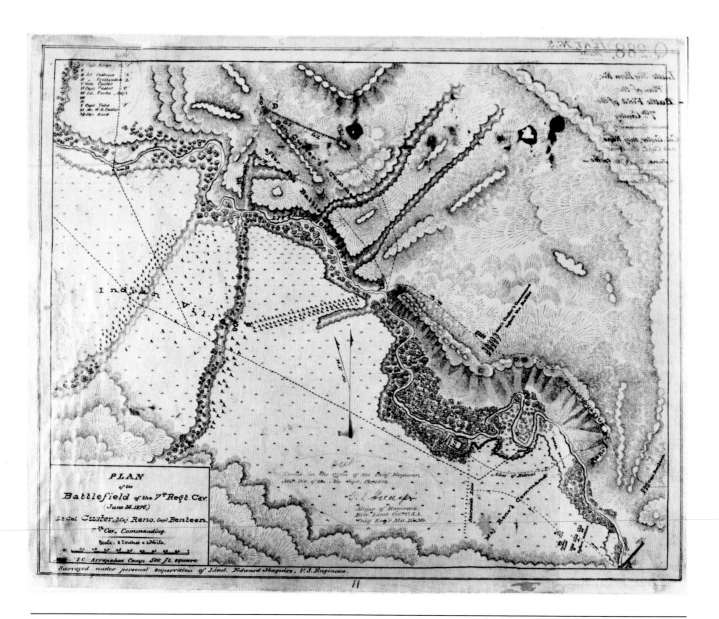

PLAN
of the
Battlefield of the 7th Reg.t Cav.
(June 26.1876)
Lt. Col. Custer, Maj. Reno, Capt. Benteen.
7th Cav. Commanding.
Scale: 3 Inches = 1 Mile.

Surveyed under personal supervision of Lieut. Edward Maguire, U.S. Engineer.

Known as Custer's Last Stand, the Battle of the Little Big Horn was actually the last stand of the Plains Indians; the Army retaliated with such vengeance that most of Sitting Bull's followers fled to Canada or sought refuge on reservations. Here is the map of the Little Big Horn battlefield made by the U.S. Army Corps of Engineers in September 1876.

Opposite: A letter written by the mother of Lt. William Van Wyck Reilly seeking return of the heirloom ring he was wearing when killed in the Battle of the Little Big Horn. The photograph, taken shortly before the Sioux campaign, shows the young officer in the dress uniform of the Seventh Cavalry.

to Mississippi. The worst occurred in the Confederate States Laboratory in Richmond where forty-two women died. A similar explosion at the Washington Arsenal late in the war killed nineteen, most of them Irish immigrants. They were buried in a mass grave in Congressional Cemetery, their funeral cortege led by President Lincoln.

The Indian Wars are also well documented in the Archives. Although many books have been written about this clash of cultures, never-told tales are still be to be found in the files. One from the Seminole Wars concerns the capture of a traveling company of Shakespearean actors, ambushed in May 1840 on a road outside St. Augustine, Florida, by Chief Wild Cat and his warriors. The Indians killed three actors and captured all their possessions, including eighteen trunks of costumes and props. Later the Seminoles, now fantastically arrayed in the marvelous garments, stopped for food and rest with the slaves of a nearby plantation. Wild Cat looked especially splendid in the turban and costume of Othello, made of richly trimmed black velvet. It pleased him so much that he would not take one

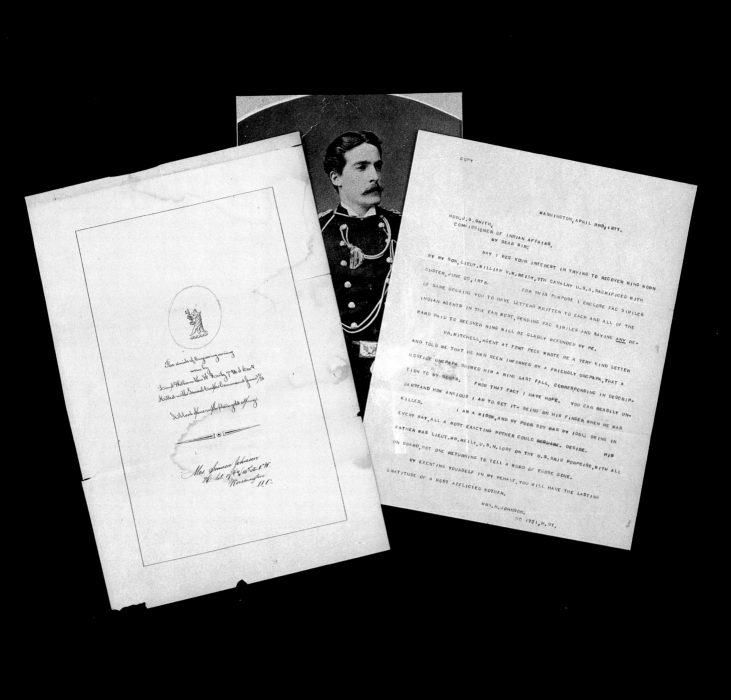

For similie of Engraving or ring
worn by
Lieut William Van W Reily 7th U.S Cav.y
Killed with Genal Custer Command June 25/76

Will and Fame with the simple of ring:

Mrs Simeon Johnson
No. 1721 of H St. N. W.
Washington
D.C.

COPY

WASHINGTON, APRIL 3RD, 1877.

HON. J.Q. SMITH,
COMMISSIONER OF INDIAN AFFAIRS,
MY DEAR SIR:

MAY I BEG YOUR INTEREST IN TRYING TO RECOVER RING WORN BY MY SON, LIEUT. WILLIAM V.W. REILY, 7TH CAVALRY U.S.A. SACRIFICED WITH CUSTER, JUNE 25, 1876.   FOR THIS PURPOSE I ENCLOSE FAC SIMILES OF SAME BEGGING YOU TO HAVE LETTERS WRITTEN TO EACH AND ALL OF THE INDIAN AGENTS IN THE FAR WEST, SENDING FAC SIMILES AND SAYING <u>ANY</u> RE- WARD PAID TO RECOVER RING WILL BE GLADLY REFUNDED BY ME.

MR. MITCHELL, AGENT AT FORT PECK WROTE ME A VERY KIND LETTER AND TOLD ME THAT HE HAD BEEN INFORMED BY A FRIENDLY UNCPAPA, THAT A HOSTILE UNCPAPA SHOWED HIM A RING LAST FALL, CORRESPONDING IN DESCRIP- TION TO MY SON'S.   FROM THAT FACT I HAVE HOPE.   YOU CAN READILY UN- DERSTAND HOW ANXIOUS I AM TO GET IT- BEING ON HIS FINGER WHEN HE WAS KILLED.

I AM A WIDOW, AND MY POOR BOY WAS MY IDOL: BEING IN EVERY WAY, ALL A MOST EXACTING MOTHER COULD REQUIRE. DESIRE.   HIS FATHER WAS LIEUT. WM. REILY, U.S.N. LOST ON THE U.S. BRIG PORPOISE, WITH ALL ON BOARD. NOT ONE RETURNING TO TELL A WORD OF THOSE GONE.

BY EXERTING YOURSELF IN MY BEHALF, YOU WILL HAVE THE LASTING GRATITUDE OF A MOST AFFLICTED MOTHER.

MRS. H. JOHNSON,
NO. 1721, H. ST.

Above and opposite: The story of the United States military role in World War I is to be found largely in the records of the American Expeditionary Forces, which include a variety of documents from unit histories to battlefield messages, like the one shown *opposite* announcing the victory at Belleau Wood. *Above:* U.S. Marines of the 5th Regiment entering Menacourt, France, in January 1918. Less than six months later, they earned a major victory at Belleau Wood.

hundred cows for it, he swore. While bragging to the slaves, he ignored a passing mail wagon. His men had already killed two mail men, he claimed, and all they got for their pains were "bundles of paper."

Few episodes in American history have captured the popular imagination more than Custer's "Last Stand." Of the many details of that brutal encounter documented in federal records, one of the strangest coincidences concerns Lt. William Van Wyck Reilly. The strikingly handsome young man joined the Seventh Cavalry shortly before the campaign against Sitting Bull and his Sioux and Cheyenne followers. Reilly was the pride of a widowed mother whose husband, a naval officer, had died at sea in the boy's infancy. When Reilly rode into battle on the fateful day in June 1876, he was wearing an heirloom ring. Because the ring was not recovered with his body, his mother appealed to the Commissioner of Indian Affairs for help in finding it: "You can readily understand how anxious I am to get it, being attached on his finger when he was killed. I am a widow and my poor boy was my idol." With her letter she included a drawing of the ring with its distinctive crest.

The chance of recovering the heirloom seemed remote. Nevertheless, the Bureau of Indian Affairs and the War Department dutifully sent copies of the drawing and the letter to Indian agencies and military posts in the Northern Plains. In less than three weeks, a soldier at Fort Robinson, Nebraska, obtained the ring from a recently surrendered Sioux warrior and returned it to Reilly's grateful mother. Today the ring is in the Smithsonian Institution; her letter is in the National Archives.

Personal anecdotes from all our wars abound in the Archives files. Records of collective achievement abound also, like the victory at Belleau Wood in World War I by the Marines attached to the Second Division of the American Expeditionary Force. Fought in June 1918, this confrontation with the Germans was the first major engagement for America's soldiers in that terrible war.

The Germans were within forty miles of the French capital, almost within shelling distance. French Marshal Foch, commander of all Allied forces,

Secretaries enlisting in the Marine Corps in 1918. The "marinettes" worked in Washington offices, thereby freeing the marines in those jobs for the fight overseas.

Below: Draft registration cards and photographs of baseball player Ty Cobb and Sergeant Alvin York, the conscientious objector who went on to become America's most celebrated combat hero of World War I.

Women of Boston helping in the campaign to save peach stones, which were used in the production of the filters for World War I gas masks.

called upon the 27,000 men of the U.S. Second Division to blunt the German advance. The Americans were convoyed to the front by three thousand trucks, taxicabs, and cars, most of them driven by Frenchmen too old to fight. By June 1 they had reached Belleau Wood, one square mile of forest between two hills that the Germans had just captured.

The fighting began in earnest on June 4, 1918. By then the Second Division had taken over from the French a twelve-mile stretch across the Paris-Metz highway in front of Belleau Wood. The Germans had the advantage of terrain: they held the high ground and rocky ledges. When several German attacks had been driven back, the Marines of the Fourth Brigade counter-attacked. In a move reminiscent of Pickett's desperate charge at Gettysburg, the Marines rose from their trenches and started across a field of green, knee-high wheat.

A tattered copy of *Marines Magazine* from March 1921, preserved in the National Archives, tells what happened next. As the Marines advanced, a hush fell over the battlefield. Even the enemy appeared paralyzed. When the silence broke, the crash ripped the sunny afternoon apart. High explosives, shrapnel, and machine gun bullets in whistling sheets tore at the advancing Americans. Although German snipers searched out officers and non-coms first, a few eluded death. One was Gunnery Sergeant Dan Daly. Turning his back to the Germans, he yelled to the men who remained alive behind him: "Come on you bastards, do you want to live forever?" But the impossible had been asked. When the survivors fell back, they left more than two hundred of their comrades behind.

For three weeks the two armies faced each other across the tight square mile of Belleau Wood. Every yard of this blood-drenched soil was contested, for it had become a symbol to both armies that exceeded its tactical importance. The Americans, who had taken the southern half of the forest, were determined to get the rest. The veteran Twenty-eighth German Division, which occupied the northern half, was ordered to hold it at all costs.

On June 25, following an intense artillery barrage, a battalion of Marines made a final assault, driving the Germans from Belleau Wood. It was a

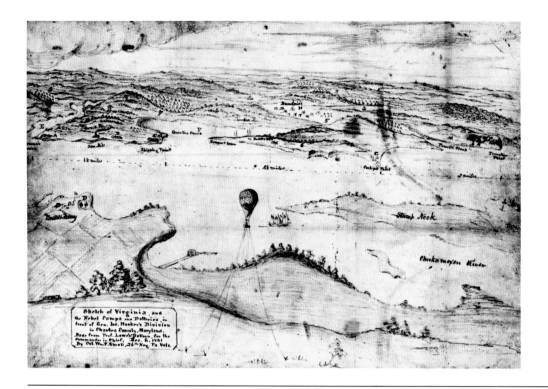

During the Civil War, inventor and meteorologist Thaddeus S.C. Lowe organized and directed a balloon corps for the Union Army, which used balloons to direct artillery fire and report on Confederate troop movements. Here is a sketch of Confederate camps and artillery batteries drawn by a Union officer from Lowe's balloon, December 8, 1861. The balloon was tethered on the Maryland side of the Potomac River and the observations were made of Confederate positions in the present area of Quantico, Virginia.

Opposite: Lt. Donald Toye, an American pilot who avoided capture by the Germans after his bomber was shot down over Luxembourg during World War II, is represented by documents known as "escape and evasion" reports. These once-secret files normally contain a variety of questionnaires that describe the adventures of downed airmen and provide information about the people who assisted them.

great victory for which the Americans had paid dearly. Casualties during the three-week battle totaled 9,777, including 1,650 dead.

Did Belleau Wood save Paris? Some historians doubt it. The Allies, even in that fateful hour, might have found a way to halt the German offensive. Perhaps the battle's greater significance lies in the respect Americans gained in world opinion as a fighting force. According to a report confiscated after the battle, a German intelligence officer admitted the Americans had been underestimated. He classified the Second Division as very good, perhaps on the level of assault troops, for they had carried out their attacks on Belleau Wood "with dash and recklessness." Individually, the American soldiers seemed fresh and confident, lacking only adequate training to make them "redoubtable opponents." Typical of their spirit, he thought, was the remark of one prisoner: "We kill or get killed."

The officer could appreciate and understand good soldiers. What puzzled him was the moralistic fervor that seemed to imbue the Americans. "They . . . regard the war from the point of view of the 'Big Brother,' who comes to help his hard pressed brethren." Furthermore, by fighting in Europe, they seemed to think they were somehow defending their homeland. Their intense patriotism also seemed inexplicable, since only a few were "pure" Americans. Most were actually of German, Dutch, and Italian parentage. Nonetheless, the officer reported, "these semi-Americans . . . fully feel themselves to be true-born sons of their country."

The history of military aviation, as recorded in Archives files, dates from the Civil War and the achievements of Professor Thaddeus Lowe's balloon corps as an observation arm of the Union Army. Among the relics of his pioneering effort is a sketch of Confederate positions in the area of what is now Quantico, Virginia, that he made on December 9, 1861, from a balloon

Left document

2327

Toye, Donald C.   2nd Lt O-691319   703rd Sqdn 445 Gp. 8th AF
Rank & Serial No.   Organization & Air Force.

Shot down: April 13 1944   Northern Luxemburg (Duchy)
Date & Approximate location.

Experiences after being shot down: Lived with Belgian partisans
for one month. Walked for 18 days into Suisse.

Status: Escapee - Evadee - Internee

Date of Escape: May 31, 1944

Date of Arrival at Annecy: Sept 13, 1944

Physical Condition: Good

Remarks: Internees should be told of Suisse
border customs regulations. Suisse merchants
sell ladies' watches, films, etc, without informing
of border restrictions. Our baggage inspection very lenient.

Home Address: Route 1, Box 335, Lake Grove, Oregon

Departed MAAF

Middle document

HEADQUARTERS
EUROPEAN THEATER OF OPERATIONS
P/W and X Detachment
Military Intelligence Service

QUESTIONNAIRE FOR SERVICE PERSONNEL
EVADING OR ESCAPING FROM ENEMY OCCUPIED COUNTRIES

Toye, Donald C.   2nd Lt   O-691319   TARGET:
(Name)   (Rank)   (ASN)   Date mission in action: 4/13/44

7 (No. of missions)   Date arrived in UK: 9/29/44

703 (Squadron)   445 Bomb (Group)

MEMBERS OF CREW: (Please list names next to positions)   Indicate what happened to each man and how you know.

PILOT Farmer, Jack - German Prisoner I.R.C.
CO-PILOT (myself)
NAVIGATOR Korth, Robert - Situation unknown. Left him in France 5/13/44
BOMBARDIER Carey, Leo - Probably dead - Advised by Patriots
RADIO OPERATOR (name unknown - Substitute) - German Prisoner
TOP TURRET GUNNER Standridge - German Prisoner I.R.C.
BALL TURRET GUNNER ~~Kerpan~~, Butler, Harold - German Prisoner IRC
WAIST GUNNER Suber, Talmadge - German Prisoner IRC
WAIST GUNNER Kerpan, Joseph - With Korth
TAIL GUNNER Beckham - German Prisoner - I.R.C.

SECRET

APPENDIX "B" TO E AND E REPORT NO.

No., Rank, Name: 2nd Lt Donald C. Toye

Units: 445th Bomb Gp 703rd Sqdn

Suggestions for improvement of escape equipment and training come largely from those who make use of them. Your report and comments will help others to evade capture or to escape.

AIDS BOX

a. Did you use your aids box? No. Used box of other chutists.

b. If not, why? Lost in parachuting.

c. If you used it, state briefly the circumstances in which you used each item, for example, "While hiding in woods for two nights".

Horlicks tablets. No

Chocolate or Peanut Bar. No

Milk (tube). No

Benzedrine tablets (fatigue). No

Halazone tablets (water purifier). No

Matches. Yes - fires for warmth and cooking

Adhesive tape. Foot blisters - Not nearly enough for needs

Chewing gum.

Water bottle. No

Compass. Yes - Used for 18 days for navigation

Sewing kit. Yes - darning socks, etc.

d. Did any of the above items prove unsatisfactory? No

e. How did you finally dispose of the box?

f. Can you suggest any way in which the contents of the aids box might be changed to make it of greater use, bearing in mind that the size of it cannot be larger?
A small knife is of unlimited importance.

2. PURSE

a. Did you carry a purse? - A wallet. No
State color of stripes and letters. - None engraved on. Brown
If NOT, state why not.

b. Did you use the purse?

(over)

Right document

"G" Report   2327

2nd Lt. Donald C. Toye   O-691319
703/445   3r Sept 44

On the 13th APRIL 1944 our plane was hit by enemy fighters and we crashed near Hipperdang (Luxembourg). I was picked up by Partisans and taken to Heldhausen where I stayed at the house of Joseph Fatron whose brother was one of the Partisans who picked me up. A Pierre brought me clothes.
On the 5th day of my stay there Lt. Korth and Sgt. Kerpan were brought to the farm of Mr. Hirsch. We were given more clothes, and, after staying here for 2 days, we crossed the border into Limerle(Belgium) accompanied by about 40 Luxembourgers. In Limerle we got a train for Bastogne(Belgium) where we spent the day at a Beer Hall which was the meeting place of members of the White Army. That evening we were taken to MarvA by the Priest of that village and we stayed at his house for 5 days. We were given identity cards. The Priest was the leader of a Resistance group...
There was very little discipline and unity among the men of the "White Army", so on the 13th May we left the camp. In the early morning of the 14th we crossed into France at Sedan(Ardennes).
On the 15th we reached ... We split up into pairs. Korth and Kerpan intending to reach Spain. We two kept walking toward Switzerland and passed through Verdun, St. Michel, Autreville, Sonal and Rombleres les Baies. We reached Champagnole (L. Donna) on the 28th day. Here we met a farmer who fed us and directed us to the Resistance. We were sheltered overnight by the Resistance and then escorted to Mericourt(Vienne) where we spent 1 night. We were then taken to Mandeure (Laval) where we were sheltered until the 31st May when 2 guides took us to the border at Baavan(Doubs). One of the guides was caught by the Germans. The other guide gave us instruction and left us. We crossed into Switzerland late in the afternoon and were taken to Porrentruy by the Police. We were interned at Glion until the 13th September when we were evacuated.

R. Durant
2nd Lt. AUS

Casualty information: According to information received by Lt. Korth from Patriots, those members of our crew who were killed when our plane crashed have been buried in Hipperdang.

Date, time and approximate location of plane crash or landing: Hipperdang - Northern tip of Luxemburg - 4/13/44 1600 Hrs

Nature and extent of damage to plane when source bailed out. Was it on fire, etc? On fire, Controls shot out, oxygen out, Tail Turret shot off, Ship exploded

At approximately what altitude did source bail out? 17000

Were any of the crew injured or killed before the plane crashed?
Tail Turret Gunner - Beckham - Fatal (lacerations) } not certain
Rt Waist Gunner - Suber - Shrapnel in one leg

What members of the crew bailed out? Did their parachutes open?
All members - Counted 9 chutes including mine

Did the plane explode on striking the ground? Exploded in Air

Did source see any other members of the crew dead or alive after reaching the ground?
Yes - Claimed 2 dead - Buried Hipperdang. Only Korth confirmed.

Did he receive any information from others as to whether any other members of the crew were dead or alive? If so, give details furnished by his informant and whether the other crew members were identified by name or otherwise.
As above.

Did source examine the wreckage of the plane? If so, what was its condition?
Completely destroyed

If the plane crashed in water how far was the plane from land and by what means was source rescued and what life rafts, wreckage, etc., remained on the surface that would have assisted other personnel to keep afloat?

What is source's opinion as to the fate of the other crew members and his reason for his opinion?
All prisoners except Carey killed. Korth & Kerpan still not located.

During World War II, Edward Steichen had charge of the Naval Aviation Photographic Unit. Responsible for documenting the combat role of aircraft carriers, he directed a hand-picked crew of professional photographers—Victor Jorgensen, Wayne Miller, Charles Kerlee, and others—who lived aboard the carriers and compiled a monumental visual record of the war against Japan. Some of the finest shots are by Steichen himself, who served aboard the U.S.S. *Lexington* even though he was over sixty years old when the war began. *Above, left:* Steichen produced this unusual shot of an F6F Hellcat torpedo bomber taking off from the *Lexington* in November 1943. *Above, right.* Steichen took this shot of jubilant pilots celebrating their safe return to the *Lexington* from a bombing mission in which they shot down seventeen of twenty Japanese planes that had tried to intercept them.

Opposite: A sampling of cartographic records from World War II, including a roll of aerial film, aerial photographs, a 3-D relief map of Japan, maps made of paper, cloth, and rice paper (for easy eating) all for use by American pilots, as well as maps captured from the Germans.

tethered on the Maryland side of the Potomac River.

Combat aircraft was first used by the U.S. Army in early 1917 during the Mexican Punitive Expedition against Pancho Villa. Among the records that document this episode is the operational diary of the First Aero Squadron, which later that same year was merged into the Lafayette Escadrille to serve for the duration of World War I as part of the U.S. Army.

Among the most popular of the military aviation records are the "mission and combat" reports from World War II and the Korean War. Each usually consists of a brief description of a mission and its encounters with the enemy. Closely related are "missing aircrew" reports, especially those which cover flyers downed in enemy territory. These files furnish information about airmen who were killed or captured, as well as those who escaped capture and those who benefited from assistance from civilians in combat zones.

A typical story is that of Lt. Donald Toye, shot down as his plane approached Germany just three days short of his thirtieth birthday. He was co-pilot of a B-24 in the 445th Bombardment Group, Eighth Air Force. The plane suffered a direct hit from anti-aircraft fire, but its eight crewmen managed to bail out before it exploded in mid-air. Toye landed unhurt near Hipperdome, a small town in Luxembourg, and was spotted immediately by a farmer, Robert Fairon, a member of the anti-German partisans. Fairon took the airman to the home of Joseph Fairon, his brother, where two other crew members soon joined Toye. After five days, the three aviators, outfitted with new clothes and identities, set out to rejoin the Allied forces. Mingling with a group of Europeans, they took a train to Bastogne. Here they remained several days in the home of a Roman Catholic priest before crossing into France. Told that a threesome was too large a group to avoid capture, the airmen went their separate ways. Toye, equipped with French money, maps, and advice, finally reached the Swiss border. There two French guides met him and helped him across. One, scouting ahead, was captured by German guards; the other was shot shortly after Toye crossed into Switzerland. Toye was the only one of the eight crewmen to escape.

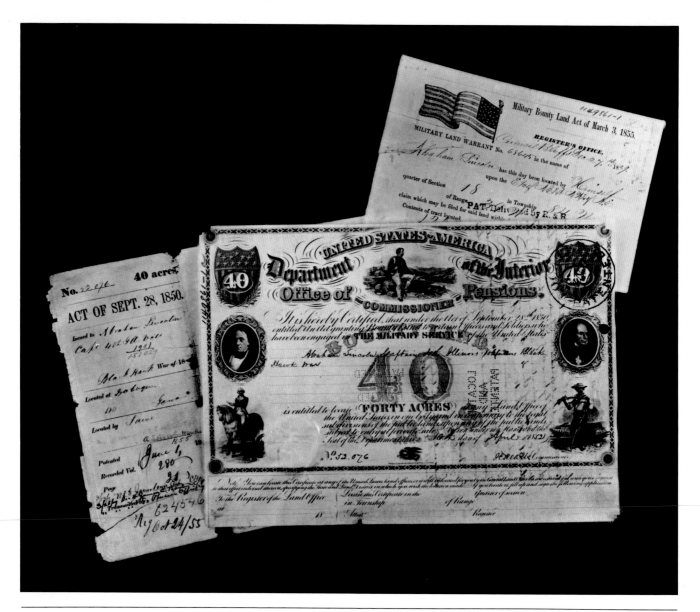

Veterans of our early wars were entitled to grants of bounty lands as reward for service. Abraham Lincoln, who served in the Black Hawk War as a captain received two grants.

Opposite: Although a number of women were soldiers, only Ella G. Hobart served as a commissioned chaplain during the Civil War. Her concern for Wisconsin soldiers so impressed the Governor that he offered her a commission if any state unit would elect her its regimental chaplain. The 1st Wisconsin Heavy Artillery did so, and the Governor honored his pledge. The photograph is from Mrs. Hobart's pension file and was sent by her to the Adjutant General after learning that an imposter planned to apply for her pension.

Six were captured; one was killed.

Toye did not forget the Fairons. ''I will always be indebted to you for your kindness to me and can never do enough to repay you in full, for actually I owe my life to you,'' he wrote to them from his home in Oregon on January 15, 1946. The Luxembourg farmer eventually gave the letter to American military authorities to document the help his family had given to Allied airmen. This enabled the Fairons, like hundreds of others who aided American servicemen at the risk of their own lives, to qualify for an award and letter of appreciation from the United States government. Many of these letters today adorn the walls of European homes. The stories behind them, however, are in a branch of the National Archives.

The gratitude of the nation to those who aided its servicemen is great. Even greater is its gratitude to those servicemen who gave their lives or their future health to defend their country. As early as 1636, Plymouth Colony provided that any man disabled in conflict with the Pequot Indians should be cared for by the colony as long as he lived. Other colonies passed

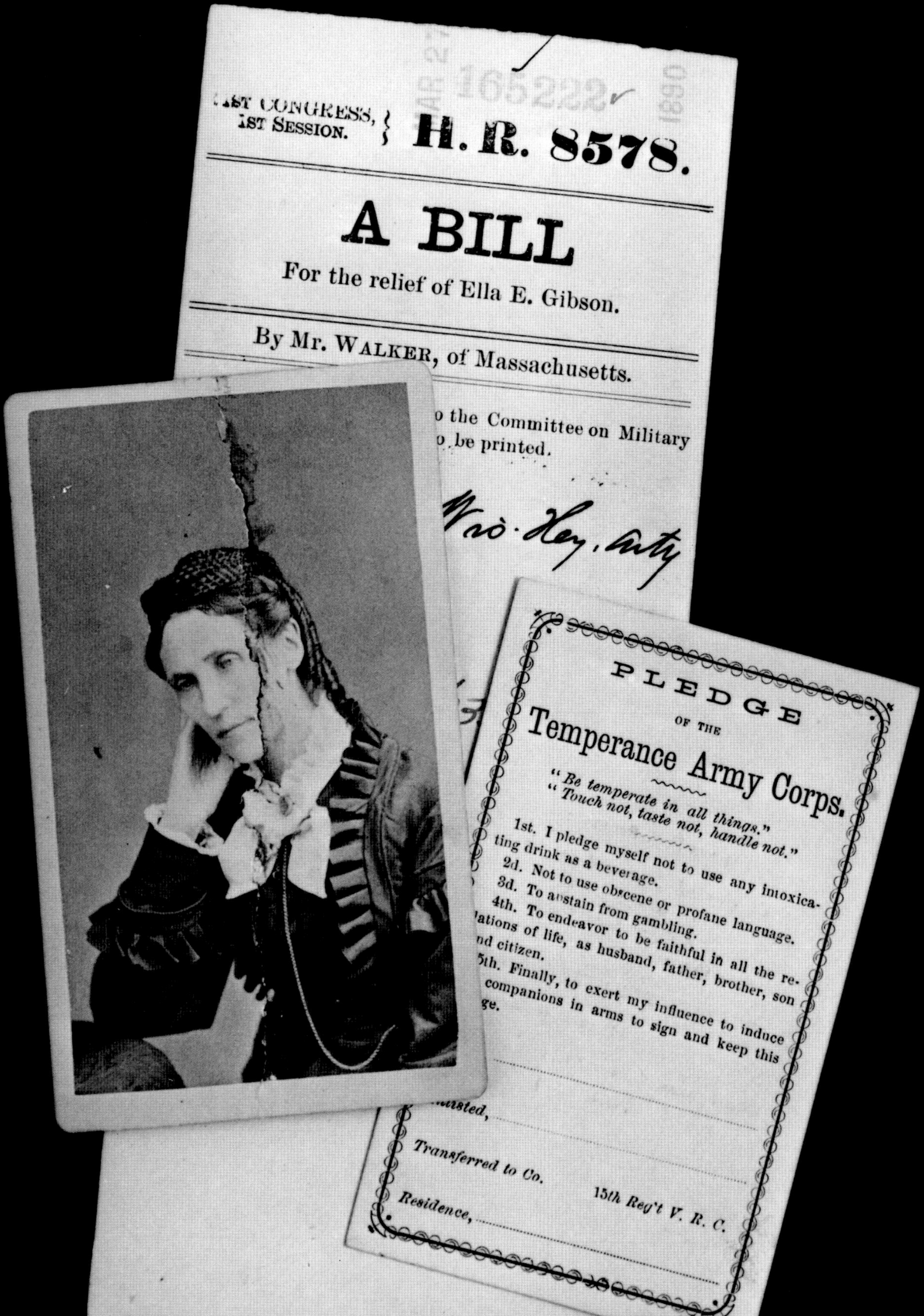

51ST CONGRESS, **1ST SESSION.** } **H. R. 8578.**

MAR 27 1890

165222

A BILL

For the relief of Ella E. Gibson.

By Mr. WALKER, of Massachusetts.

to the Committee on Military
to be printed.

W.o. Hey, anty

PLEDGE

OF THE

Temperance Army Corps.

" Be temperate in all things."
" Touch not, taste not, handle not."

1st. I pledge myself not to use any intoxicating drink as a beverage.
2d. Not to use obscene or profane language.
3d. To abstain from gambling.
4th. To endeavor to be faithful in all the relations of life, as husband, father, brother, son
and citizen.
5th. Finally, to exert my influence to induce
companions in arms to sign and keep this
ge.

listed, _____

Transferred to Co. _____ 15th Reg't V. R. C.

Residence, _____

The National Archives has more than three thousand posters, most of them from World Wars I and II, which cover a wide range of themes and images. Most are graphically striking and many are true works of art.

similar legislation. By the time of the Revolutionary War, veterans' rights to benefits were taken for granted. At first these were limited to pensions in money or bounties paid in land, but now they include everything from hospital care to vocational training.

Although the Continental Congress established half-pay for disabled men in 1776 and added half-pay for widows and orphans of line officers in 1780, it was not until 1832 that the dependents of enlisted men were eligible. Ordinary citizens like Cornelia Anderson of Boston had to petition Congress for assistance. Having lost her husband, son, and home (it was burned by the British) in the Revolutionary War, she was assessed taxes for building a road in front of her now vacant lot. In 1785, full of frustration and desperate, she appealed to the Continental Congress for assistance, praying that the members would be moved to "generosity" in her behalf. Hers is but one of two thousand petitions and memorials sent to the Continental and Confederation Congresses.

Another of these petitions was filed by Benjamin Gannett on behalf of his wife, Deborah Sampson Gannett, who sought compensation for wounds received while serving in a Massachusetts regiment as a private with the name of Robert Shurtleff. When Deborah died in 1827, her husband embarked on a ten-year campaign to convince Congress that the husband of a soldier was entitled to benefits under the law. With the aid of John Quincy Adams, then a Representative from Massachusetts, a special act was

PLANT MORE SUGAR BEETS
SUGAR IS ENERGY —
LET'S GIVE 'EM PLENTY

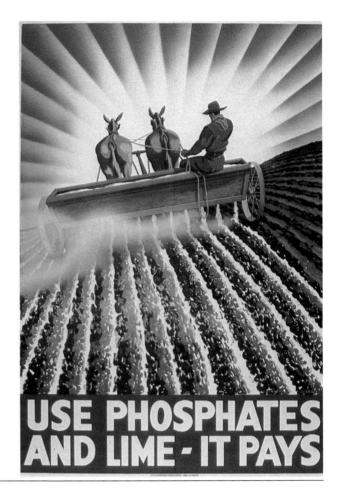

USE PHOSPHATES AND LIME — IT PAYS

passed to meet the peculiar circumstances of this 83-year-old widower and his two indigent daughters. Not for another 130 years would a widower again receive a pension based on his wife's military service.

During the War with Mexico, a new type of benefit emerged: hospital care. Congress and General Winfield Scott cooperated to establish a military "asylum" for soldiers in Washington, D.C. Later known as the U.S. Soldiers Home, it was funded in part by the wartime tribute Scott levied on Mexico City. After the Civil War, disabled veterans were welcome at the National Home for Disabled Volunteer Soldiers, actually several "homes" across the country, each a self-sufficient community.

The tremendous increase in the veteran population and its dependents after the Civil War prompted Congress to authorize construction of a building to house the Pension Bureau. Completed in the 1880s, the Pension Building served also as a monument to the veterans. A three-foot-high frieze circles the building depicting the Union Army in action: soldiers, sailors, and wounded march in bold relief between the building's first and second floors. Although the Pension Bureau has long been merged into the Veterans Administration, its retired records are now in the Archives where they are among the documentary treasures most meaningful to American citizens today. Pension files demonstrate the impact of war on ordinary Americans, as we have seen in the correspondence of Benjamin Chase, the young Union volunteer who died at Fredericksburg.

It was because of the enormous number of casualties in the Civil War that the federal government established the first military cemeteries in 1862. One of the most poignant, at the site of the infamous Confederate prisoner-of-war camp in Andersonville, Georgia, owes much to the efforts of Clara Barton. After the war, she worked with Pvt. Dorence Atwater to identify the graves from a "Book of the Dead" that he had kept while imprisoned there. They used this book, a copy of which is in the National Archives, to mark the graves of 12,290 Union war prisoners, providing for each his name, company, regiment, and date of death.

During World War I, it became necessary to establish cemeteries overseas as well. Not all Americans liked the idea of leaving the bodies of our servicemen in Europe, however, and opponents formed organizations such as the "Bring Home the Soldier Dead League." Their efforts succeeded in bringing back fifty thousand bodies, but thirty-one thousand remained behind. Most of these are buried in cemeteries modeled after the Civil War section of Arlington, their graves marked by tombstones designed by Charles Platt, architect of the Freer Gallery in Washington.

In 1944 during World War II, a significant shift in attitude to veterans' benefits was reflected in the Serviceman's Readjustment Act, popularly known as the G.I. Bill of Rights. This made higher education possible for many men and women who otherwise would have been unable to afford it. Honorably discharged G.I.s from World War II could earn up to a maximum of four years tuition-free college or technical training with a monthly subsistence payment. Some twelve million men and women took advantage of the G.I. Bill.

No army can fight successfully without the support of the people on the home front. Their individual sacrifices may not be so great as those of the combat forces, but they are vitally important nonetheless. Goods and services taken for granted in peace time suddenly become scarce. Priorities change. Production facilities, transportation, food, and money must now serve the war effort.

To remind the citizenry of its role, as well as to bolster the general morale,

governments use whatever techniques are effective. Among these are slogans and their graphic counterparts, posters. The National Archives has a collection of more than three thousand posters from World Wars I and II.

The art of poster making came into its own in France in the late nineteenth century. By the outbreak of war in 1914, most countries were using posters for educational and propaganda purposes and the United States was no exception. President Wilson set up a Committee on Public Information to build public support for the war. Newspaperman George Creel, its head, declared later: "The poster must play a great part in the fight for public opinion. The printed word might not be read . . . but the billboard was something that caught even the most indifferent eye."

On April 17, 1917, artist Charles Dana Gibson was appointed Chairman of the Division of Pictorial Publicity and assigned that task of enlisting American illustrators, cartoonists, and artists in the poster campaign. He succeeded admirably. Among those who donated their talents were Howard Chandler Christy, Joseph Pennell, and James Montgomery Flagg, whose "Uncle Sam Wants You" became the best-known poster, not only of World War I but of all time. Originally a magazine cover, Flagg's Uncle Sam, actually a self-portrait, was quickly adopted by the army for recruiting purposes. A record four million copies were printed during the war and several million more afterward.

Although new communications techniques existed in World War II, posters were once again featured in the American government's war effort. This time the Office of War Information was responsible for their production and distribution. A few older artists, like Gibson and Flagg, joined newcomers like Norman Rockwell, Ben Shahn, and Walt Disney in this endeavor. Today, their posters give later generations of Americans a sense of the time when, in the words of poet Wallace Irwin, "art put on khaki and went into action."

Many artists did, in fact, put on khaki. The sculptor and painter Samuel Bookatz became the first artist-in-residence at the White House. As a Lieutenant, j.g., in World War II, his first task was to furnish artwork for a

In 1907, President Theodore Roosevelt sent sixteen battleships on a goodwill tour around the world. Known as "The Great White Fleet" (all U.S. battleships were painted white at that time), it dramatically demonstrated to the world that America had come of age. Shown here is the fleet in San Francisco harbor, with the U.S.S. *Connecticut*, the flagship, in the foreground.

A sampling of propaganda leaflets aimed at Japanese soldiers during World War II. *Above:* This leaflet appeals to a popular superstition that northeast is an unlucky direction and warns the Japanese of bombers flying from Alaska through the "Kimon," or Devil's Gate, to attack their industrial centers. The octagon in the lower right-hand corner of the leaflet is an astrological device showing Kimon. *Above, right:* If anyone missed the pictorial point that the Nazis treated their Japanese allies like cormorants—birds that fished for their masters but could not keep what they caught—the message was fully explained in the accompanying text.

Opposite: These leaflets also suggest that the Japanese were being exploited by their Axis partners and include one of the surrender passes that were dropped on Japanese positions. The leaflets were prepared in Australia by the Office of War Information.

history of the Naval Medical Corps. Since the admiral to whom he was assigned was F.D.R.'s personal physician, Bookatz was quartered during duty hours in the Executive Mansion. His studio was the Lincoln Bedroom, which had the best light. Later he worked closely with plastic surgeons in navy hospitals as they attempted to reconstruct the features of disfigured sailors and marines.

Photographers, too, played a major role in the Great Wars. One of the best was Edward Steichen. In World War I, as a lieutenant assigned to the photographic section of the Army Signal Corps Air Service, he gained experience that served him well during World War II. Then, as a lieutenant commander, he was in charge of taking countless photographs of naval aviation in the Pacific. He later had command of all navy combat photography. Along the way, he supervised filming of the navy's popular motion picture, *The Fighting Lady*, and organized two wartime exhibitions for the Museum of Modern Art: "Road to Victory" and "Power in the Pacific."

This section has barely skimmed the surface of the rich resources open to researchers in military records. Left unexplored here are logs of Teddy Roosevelt's Great White Fleet of warships sent around the world in 1908 to demonstrate the naval power of the United States and its will to keep the peace; journals of the Black Eagles, distinguished Black pilots of World War II; the extensive files reflecting the development of the Nazi Party and the Third Reich in German documents captured at the end of the war; and countless others.

Additional incidents of heroism and valor can be traced in the records of

the U.S. Coast Guard, an agency now within the Department of Transportation but nevertheless part of the Armed Forces of the United States in time of war. Indeed, arms were often necessary in maritime law enforcement, especially during the Prohibition Era. The logs of Coast Guard cutters are filled with dramatic accounts of their attempts to stop the traffic in liquor. A favorite tactic of the rum-runners was to transport their contraband from foreign vessels standing outside the three-mile limit by speedboats to sheltering coves and inlets along the Pacific and Atlantic coasts.

The stakes were high and so were the risks as four rum-runners discovered in June 1928. At ten minutes past midnight, the captain of the *Arcata*, an 85-foot harbor cutter operating out of Seattle, met a speedboat running without lights in Puget Sound. The cutter signaled it to heave to and fired a blank warning shot. During a thirty-minute chase, the revenuers fired at the speedboat with rifles and their deck cannon, which scored a direct hit and set it afire. Although the four wounded crewmen were rescued and taken into custody, they had managed to throw their illegal cargo overboard during the chase. A month later the *Arcata* captured a fleeing boat when the crew ran it aground. This time the rum-runners escaped, but they left behind 948 quarts of whiskey and 72 quarts of gin.

The records of the U.S. Life Saving Service, which highlight another role of the Coast Guard, contain exciting stories of their own, like the one behind the wreck of the *M & E Henderson*, a 387-ton schooner out of Philadelphia that foundered on the Outer Banks of North Carolina on the morning of November 30, 1879. Although the Banks—"The Graveyard of the At-

Form 1800.

Application for, and Certificate of, Medical Inspection of Surfman.

Pea Island Life-Saving Station,

6th District,

J. E. Wood   August 16th, 1886.

Surgeon Marine-Hospital Service,

or (c), as the case   (b) That he is not as for duty for the following reasons:
may be.   (c) That he is not physically sound, but is fit for duty. His physical defects are:

Not Color Blind

J. E. Wood

Surgeon U. S.-M. H. Service.

To the

[Ed. 5-14-'83—5,000.]

LR 23495. Vol. 15 255

Form 1800.

APPLICATION FOR, AND CERTIFICATE

OF,

MEDICAL INSPECTION OF SURFMAN.

NAME OF SURFMAN INSPECTED:

Lewis S Wescott

INSPECTED BY

W H Griggs M D

Surgeon U. S.-M. H. Service,

UPON APPLICATION OF

Richard Etheridge

Keeper of Pea

Port of Island Station

U.S. LIFE SAVING SERVICE
1848—1871

UNITED STATES
OCT 10 1884
LIFE SAVING SERVICE

APPLICATION FOR,

MEDICAL INSPECT

NAME OF SURFM

Geo W. Bo

238   INSPEC

J B Hatte

UPON APP

Richar

Keeper Pea

one at

Port of Roa

August

U. S. LIFE S

DEC

LIFE SA

---

proportions
It is further agreed, that
beyond the present fiscal year, and

NAMES.	Date of Entry.	Term.	Capacity.	Dolls.	Cts.			
L. S. Wescott	Sept 1st 1882	one Year	Surfman	$50.	00	$3.	00	Colored age 29
R. F. Toler	Sept 1st 1882	one Year	Surfman	$50.	00	$3.	00	Colored age 28
B. B. Bowser	Sept 1st 1882	one Year	Surfman	$50.	00	$3.	00	Colored age 24
W. B. Davis	Sept 1st 1882	one Year	Surfman	$50.	00	$3.	00	Colored age 50
W. C. Bowser	Sept 1st 1882	one Year	Surfman	$50.	00	$3.	00	Colored age 32
Henry Daniel his mark	Sept 1st 1882	one Year	Surfman	$50.	00	$3.	00	Colored age 29

Witness by
Richard Etheridge
Keeper

Richard Etheridge
Keeper Station No. 17, District No. 6

[Ed. 3-10-'81—2,000.]

lantic''—have claimed more than two thousand vessels since the days of the Spanish galleons, this one turned out to have all the mystifying elements a novelist could hope for.

The incident immediately attracted attention. The government wanted to know how the *Henderson*, carrying a crew of seven and 425 tons of phosphate rock, could run aground on a clear, moonlit morning marked by running surf and a fresh breeze. Furthermore, she broke up within three hundred yards of shore, virtually in front of Life Saving Station No. Seventeen, yet the only survivors were three Spanish-speaking Blacks. The victims, including the captain and two mates, were White. The owners claimed that the Blacks had murdered their White shipmates and inadvertently wrecked the ship. A government investigator, however, suspected a bungled insurance scam. ''Either the vessel was wrecked as the result of gross carelessness and mismanagement of those in charge,'' he said, ''or . . . she was purposely run ashore.''

This still did not explain the loss of life. The men at the Pea Island Station must have been negligent. Since a surfman from the station should have passed the vessel during his beach patrol, his failure to see it could be accounted for in only two ways: either he did not make his required rounds, or he had been inattentive because of the ''clear, beautiful state of the weather.'' The surfman was dismissed, the station keeper resigned, and the government completely overhauled the station staff.

Neither murder nor insurance fraud was ever proved, but the *Henderson* affair had an unexpected sequel. In the shake-up of Station Seventeen the Life Saving Service appointed Richard Etheridge, a surfman at a neighboring station, to be the new keeper. Only thirty-eight years old, and reputed to be ''one of the best surfmen . . . on the coast of North Carolina,'' he was also Black: the first Black keeper in the Life Saving Service. To offset possible racial difficulties with the men under his command, he was given an all-Black crew. Prior to his appointment, Blacks generally performed menial duties in the Service. They tended horses, cleaned stables, hauled boats. Only a few actually served as surfmen. Thanks to Etheridge, this changed.

Opposite: Documents recording the career of Richard Etheridge, the first Black station keeper in the Life-Saving Service (a forerunner of the U.S. Coast Guard).

Within six months of the shake-up, persons unknown set fire to the station, destroying it completely. Etheridge was not intimidated. He supervised the rebuilding and quickly earned a reputation for running one of the best and "tautest" stations on the Outer Banks. For twenty years he served as keeper at Pea Island, becoming a legend in the process. When he died in 1900, another Black keeper was appointed in his place. Blacks continued to man the station until it was deactivated in 1947.

The Lighthouse Service also has its heroes and heroines. In fact, as many as one hundred keepers have died in the line of duty. Some perished trying to rescue others; others were caught by squalls as they traveled between their stations and shore; a few died when storms demolished their towers.

A case file documents the exploits of Ida Lewis-Wilson, a keeper of the Lime Rock Light Station at Newport, Rhode Island. Between 1854 and 1881, she saved thirteen people from drowning. Ida, whose parents kept the Lime Rock Station before her, was only twelve years old when she rescued four men whose sailboat had capsized. Later, she saved three men and a sheep that they had been trying to pull from the water before falling in themselves. Her last rescue was of two soldiers who had fallen through weak ice near the lighthouse. The Treasury Department in 1881 awarded her a life-saving medal of the first class. As the investigator noted in his official report, "one woman . . . rescued from imminent peril thirteen persons under circumstances requiring the highest courage and in most cases very great exertion and skill."

As we see, tactics and technology are only a small part of America's military legacy that is reflected in the National Archives. The larger story is what the records tell us about the people behind military events of peacetime and wartime over the past two centuries. The National Archives bear tribute to millions of Americans whose sacrifice and service answered the call of the Founding Fathers to "provide for the common defense," as they expressed it in the Constitution, "to secure the blessings of liberty to ourselves and our posterity."

Clem Albers photographed this young Japanese-American during relocation.

Opposite: Because of alleged military necessity, President Franklin D. Roosevelt issued Executive Order 9066 authorizing the relocation of Japanese Americans from strategic areas on the West Coast to camps located elsewhere, like the one at Heart Mountain, Wyoming. There, Estelle Ishigo, wife of one of the internees, illustrated the camp's quarterly reports with watercolors like those shown here.

PASSENGER'S INSTRUMENT BOARD
PILOTS INSTRUMENT BOARD
FIRE WALL
GAS TANK
PASSENGER'S FORWARD BULKHEAD
U.S. MAIL - K
LKHART
LAGRANGE
NOBLE
STEUBEN
DEKALB
AUBURN
ALBION
Scale 7 miles = one inch
MACOUPIN
CARROLLTON
WAUSEON

TO PROMOTE THE
GENERAL WELFARE

*T*he component parts of the National Archives contain mountains of paper that document the many forces of social change. Two centuries of industrialization, immigration, and political action transformed America from the agrarian and mercantile society of the Founding Fathers to the complex, economically diverse, multicultural society of the 1980s. The records testify to the federal government's role in American social history, sometimes initiating change, usually responding. Often the basis for the federal role has been the purpose of government set forth in the Preamble of the Constitution, "to promote the general welfare."

One of the most controversial changes was the extension of the suffrage to Blacks, women, and eighteen-year-olds. Indeed, the Founding Fathers would be astonished at the voting standards of our day. Free White males, twenty-one or over, constituted their electorate. A Civil War was necessary before most Black males got the right to vote. More than a century of agitation was necessary before women got it.

Three amendments ratified between 1865 and 1870 were expected to guarantee the civil rights of Blacks. Freed by the Thirteenth Amendment, guaranteed citizenship by the Fourteenth, they were given the franchise by the Fifteenth. These amendments, however, were merely the beginning of a century-long struggle for racial equality.

In the Archives are copies of Supreme Court decisions that affected Black Americans in their struggle for social justice. In 1896 the controversial *Plessy v. Ferguson* decision legalized "separate but equal" facilities for the races. This was a crushing blow to Blacks throughout the South, many of whom had lost the franchise because of actions taken by Southern communities to ensure White supremacy. Not until 1954, in *Brown v. The Board of Education of Topeka*, did the Court strike down the principle of "separate but equal."

No positive effort to ensure equality of citizenship was made until the Civil Rights Act of 1957. Even then, continuing discriminatory voting practices in many Southern states prompted President Lyndon B. Johnson, himself a Southerner, to urge Congress on March 15, 1965, to pass legisla-

Opposite: Pilots like William C. Hobson, shown here, relied primarily on their wits, the weather, and their flimsy World War I surplus De Havilland DH 4B's to carry the mail. Their navigation charts were little more than ordinary road maps cut into long strips.

Members of the National Womans Party picketing for voting rights in front of the White House, July 14, 1917. When arrested, the women refused to pay their $25 fines, and they were sent to a workhouse on July 17; but they were pardoned two days later.

Opposite, top: Opposition to voting rights for women came from many quarters. The Woman Suffrage Party of New York ridiculed them all in this 1912 folding postcard which shows Ida Tarbell, the Reverend Lyman Abbott, and the *New York Times* chained along with anti-suffrage brewers, bosses, socialites, senators, and standpatters.

Opposite, middle: Suffragettes registering to work as volunteers during World War I.

Opposite, bottom: Officers of the National American Woman Suffrage Association, about 1900.

Opposite, left: Voting rights petition to the Senate and the House of Representatives signed by Susan B. Anthony, Elizabeth Cady Stanton, and other suffragists, 1871.

tion "which will make it impossible to thwart the Fifteenth Amendment." The Voting Rights Act, extended in 1975 and 1982, abolished remaining restrictions to the free exercise of the franchise.

Although the intensive campaign to enfranchise women did not begin until after the Civil War, sparked largely by Black suffrage, its roots go back much farther. During the 1780s, Abigail Adams warned her husband John "to remember the laidies" when he and his colleagues in the Continental Congress drafted laws for the nation. "Be more generous and favorable to them than your ancestors," she cautioned. "We are determined to foment a rebellion and will not hold ourselves bound by any laws in which we have no representation." A century later women of America organized, petitioned, picketed, and even went to jail in their attempt to correct the imbalance in the democratic system.

Only through the ballot, they believed, could women establish the legal right to own property, have custody of their children, and demand equal pay. The American Woman Suffrage Association sought state legislation; the rival National Woman Suffrage Association sought a Constitutional amendment. In 1890, the two groups merged into the National American Woman Suffrage Association, with Elizabeth Cady Stanton as its first president.

The suffragists ran headlong into equally determined opposition. When the National Association Opposed to Woman Suffrage published a newspaper and other literature, the suffragists countered with their own paper barrage.

Strangely enough, woman suffrage enjoyed one early success, though not for egalitarian reasons. Wyoming in 1868 became the first territory (or state, for that matter) to grant women the right to vote. This came about because it wanted to change its rough-and-tumble image. What better way to create respect for law and order than by doubling the electoral power of families trying to establish communities? In fact, six of the fourteen members of the first grand jury in Laramie were female; an associate justice of the territorial Supreme Court said these women jurors posed "such a ter-

To the Honorable the Senate and House of Representatives of the United States in Congress assembled.

The undersigned, Citizens of the United States, believing that under the present Federal Constitution all women who are citizens of the United States have the right to vote, pray your Honorable Body to enact a law during the present Session that shall assist and protect them in the exercise of that right.

And they pray further that they may be permitted in person, and in behalf of the thousands of other women who are petitioning Congress to the same effect, to be heard upon this Memorial before the Senate and House at an early day in the present Session.

We ask your Honorable Body to bear in mind that while men are represented on the floor of Congress and so may be said to be heard there, women who are allowed no vote and therefore no representation cannot truly be heard except as Congress shall open its doors to us in person.

Elizabeth Cady Stanton
Isabella Beecher Hooker
Elizabeth S. Bladen
Olympia Brown
Susan B. Anthony
Josephine S. Griffing

Hartford Conn.
Dec. 1871.

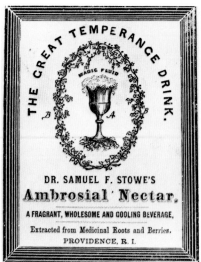

Los Angeles authorities emptying barrels of rum seized during Prohibition.

Above, right: Patented labels, like this one for Dr. Stowe's Ambrosial Nectar, obviously a product of the Temperance Movement, can be fascinating nuggets of social history.

Opposite, top: Design for barrel labels, patented in 1864.

Opposite, bottom: Pills and elixirs produced by the Lydia E. Pinkham Medicine Company held out the promise of relief for female ailments. In the case of the elixirs, the promise was probably not hard to keep, thanks to the high alcoholic content. Nonetheless, such claims made in ads like these, which ran from 1933 to 1936, were challenged by government regulatory agencies several times over a score of years.

ror to evil-doers that a stampede began among them and very many left town forever." Because it permitted women to vote, Wyoming had a difficult time attaining statehood. Aware of the opposition on Capitol Hill, Wyoming legislators wired Congress: "We may stay out of the Union for 100 years, but we will come in with our women." By a narrow margin, they did, in 1890.

The first resolution to permit women to vote was introduced in Congress in 1870. Ten years later Senator A. A. Sargent of California introduced another, which declared: "The rights of citizens of the United States to vote shall not be denied or abridged by the United States on account of sex." Not until 1920, however, was an amendment to the Constitution enabling women to vote ratified. Abigail Adams would finally have been satisfied.

Even before gaining the vote for themselves, women often led campaigns against social evils that affected other individuals. Industrial labor by children was a pervasive one. Failing to secure state laws that addressed the problem, the reformers turned to Congress. At first the federal government limited itself to documenting the economic exploitation of children. There are no more graphic documents in the National Archives than the photographs of child workers by Lewis Hine. The first federal Child Labor Law, signed by Woodrow Wilson in 1916, outlawed the employment of workers under age fourteen in any factory and limited those aged fourteen to sixteen to an eight-hour day. When the law was struck down as unconstitutional, reformers sought to amend the Constitution. An amendment that would have given Congress the power to limit, regulate, and prohibit the labor of persons under eighteen was passed in 1924, but the requisite number of states did not ratify it.

The reformers, however, enjoyed some success. President Taft in 1912 established the Children's Bureau, headed by Julia Lathrop, the first woman to hold a statutory federal position. The Bureau conducted nation-wide investigations of child labor abuses and issued reports and regulations. It also prepared publications on a variety of subjects, such as the care and

To document child labor conditions in the United States, Lewis W. Hine took hundreds of photographs for the National Child Labor Committee between 1908 and 1912. This group of boys labored in a Pennsylvania mine as "breakers," pounding large chunks of coal into small ones. At times the dust was so thick it obscured their vision and penetrated "the innermost recesses" of their lungs. To keep the boys working, Hine reported, "a kind of slave driver stands over them and prods or kicks them into obedience."

Opposite, top left: Some of the children working at Bibb Mill No. 1 in Macon, Georgia, were so small that they had to climb onto their spinning machines to mend broken threads or replace empty bobbins.

Opposite, top right: Doffers—bobbin removers—at the Elk Cotton Mill in Fayetteville, Tennessee.

Opposite: Hine found very young children working in southern cotton mills. According to a South Carolina overseer, this little girl "just happened in." Hine found that the mills were full of youngsters like her who "just happened in to help an older sister."

feeding of babies, preserving foods, and running households.

Some attempts to affect the general welfare seem today to have been misguided. Reformers, sincerely concerned about their fellow man, tried zealously to impose their own concepts of right behavior on everyone else. One such social crusade well documented in the National Archives is the Temperance Movement. Born in the ideas of men like Benjamin Rush, Surgeon General of the Continental Army, who condemned the excessive use of alcohol, the anti-liquor crusade gained momentum through the 1880s as temperance societies proliferated.

Although Maine, in 1851, became the nation's first "dry" state, Demon Rum thrived until the early 1900s, when the Anti-Saloon League of America adopted a successful state-by-state approach for solving the liquor problem. The League and the Woman's Christian Temperance Union mounted a massive campaign for Prohibition through a Constitutional amendment. Backed for the first time by the national business community, the drive achieved success in 1919 with ratification of the Eighteenth Amendment only two years after Congress had proposed it. Andrew Volstead, a Congressman from Minnesota, introduced the implementing legislation that made Prohibition a reality on January 16, 1920.

The reformers' success was short-lived, however. Prohibition simply shifted drinking from saloons to homes and speakeasies. Total enforcement proved impossible. Furthermore, gangsters flourished on the sale of illegal spirits. By the late 1920s, enthusiasm for Prohibition was all but gone, and F.D.R. swept to the presidency in 1932 on a platform that included a Prohibition Repeal plank. Following his election, the Congress passed and the states ratified the Twenty-first Amendment ending national Prohibition. This is the only amendment that repealed another.

A similar attempt to control personal behavior in the name of morality was a law passed in 1873 at the behest of Anthony Comstock and the Society for the Suppression of Vice. This required postal officials to scrutinize the mails for obscene materials. Because information on birth control was considered obscene, the eminent feminist Margaret Sanger had difficulties

Leviathan at Southampton.

UNITED STATES LINES
Europe – America

Hamburg
Emigrant Halls.
Types of emigrants.

with the Comstock Law. Post Office records in the National Archives include Volume I, Number 1, of the *Woman Rebel*, in which Sanger announced, "It will also be the aim of the WOMAN REBEL to advocate the prevention of conception and to impart such knowledge in the columns of this paper." In answer to an inquiry from the Postmaster of New York City, the Attorney General ruled that the *Woman Rebel* for March 1914 was unmailable and Sanger was indicted. The government, however, later dropped its indictment against her.

Efforts to regulate the food and drug industries enjoyed greater success than reforms aimed at policing morals. Upton Sinclair's exposé, *The Jungle*, like the works of other muckrakers, which called attention to the problem of the adulteration of food and medicine by unscrupulous purveyors, inspired the creation of the Bureau of Chemistry, a branch of the Agriculture Department and forerunner of the present Food and Drug Administration. One of its purposes was to make manufacturers of over-the-counter drugs toe the line.

One manufacturer with more than her share of stubbed toes was Lydia E. Pinkham, who made ends meet during the Panic of 1873 by providing a home remedy to Victorian ladies too embarrassed to discuss their personal problems with the predominantly male medical profession. In time, she

Hamburg was once known as the "Ellis Island of Europe" because an emigrant village that could process four thousand people at one time was established there in 1901 by the Hamburg-American Line–North German Lloyd. The village became the embarkation point for millions of Europeans in a massive migration that is documented in photographs like this one which the United States confiscated during World War I.

Opposite: A poster advertising the United States Lines, a steamship company owned and operated by the U.S. Shipping Board, established in 1917 to develop a naval auxiliary and merchant marine for this country.

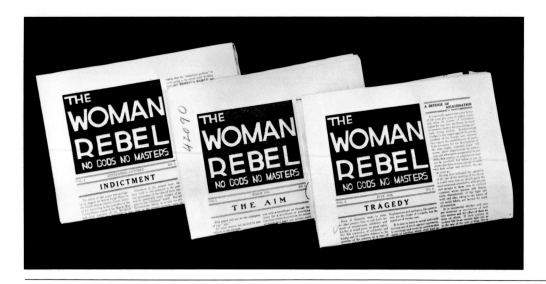

These copies of *The Woman Rebel*, edited and published by birth control advocate Margaret Sanger, are found in records of the Post Office Department, which used them in 1914 to support its charge that the periodical contained questionable material that could not be sent through the mails.

developed a national market for a compound in liquid and tablet form that promised to carry a woman "smiling through" her monthly travails, a promise easy to keep because the elixir contained eighteen percent alcohol. When the Bureau of Chemistry cited it for violating the Food and Drug Act by falsely claiming to cure a host of female ailments, the firm pleaded *nolo contendere* and paid a $50 fine. This was only one of several challenges over the years from various government agencies that questioned the veracity of the company's testimonials from satisfied users. It is all in the National Archives, along with a box of Lydia's amazing chocolate-coated pills.

Obviously, the items mentioned above provide only a sample of the federal government's involvement in the health and welfare of its people. Also documented in the National Archives are the later involvements of the federal government in the lives of its constituents, especially during the New Deal of the 1930s and the Great Society of the 1960s: Social Security, Unemployment Insurance, Medicare and Medicaid, Food Stamps, Student Aid. The programs have proliferated over the years. Some are here to stay; others remain controversial.

Change in community life is also well documented in the National Archives. The Civil War marked a watershed in the transition from a rural to an urban society. Already large-scale immigration had begun to swell the population of modern cities, a phenomenon that grew dramatically until cut off by anti-immigration laws in the 1920s. Despite the availability of cheap land, new arrivals often preferred the large industrial cities where enclaves of immigrants with the same ethnic background could continue to practice their religion, language, and customs. As a result, urban areas grew twice as fast as the total population between 1860 and 1900. Chicago, which had been a frontier town of 30,000 in 1850, doubled its population every ten years until it became a megalopolis of nearly two million; New York became the world's second largest city. In 1900, American industrial production was seven times greater than it had been in 1865, and the nation rose from fourth place among industrial nations to first. The day Thomas Jefferson had dreaded, when Americans would abandon farms in

favor of crowded cities, arrived.

Although the rise of the modern city offered many people a higher standard of living, it also confronted them with a novel and often unattractive environment. Dangerous thoroughfares, monotonous masses of pavement, crime, pollution, and overcrowding were common. Parks, playgrounds, and other recreation areas were often scarce. To combat the problems of the city, the federal government responded with new agencies and new ideas.

One of these ideas was the greenbelt town, a New Deal experiment in urban living which followed a concept developed originally in 1929 for Radburn, New Jersey, "the town for the motor age." Greenbelt towns featured large, park-like open areas with limited access for motorized vehicles. It was the parkland around the perimeter of the greenbelt towns that gave them their distinctive names. Although their construction was part of the federal program to alleviate unemployment, they were planned and developed to help families with modest incomes escape the crowded city and live in carefully designed neighborhoods with controlled land ownership.

Three greenbelt towns were built—Greenbelt, Maryland; Greendale, Wisconsin; Greenhills, Ohio—before the onset of World War II in Europe changed our national priorities. The idea of planned communities was not lost, however. Defense housing programs in the states and the war housing programs of the National Housing Administration, set up in 1942, sponsored numerous projects to house workers in war production centers. A few of these remain viable communities today. After the war, slum clearance and urban planning were recognized by Congress as legitimate concerns of the federal government in 1949 legislation which established the Housing and Home Finance Administration. This umbrella organization embraced home financing, public housing, urban renewal and other related activities. By 1965 its functions were considered of cabinet level importance; the Department of Housing and Urban Development was created. Meanwhile, during the 1950s and 60s, private industry became interested in planned communities. A number of "new towns," such as Reston, Virginia, and Columbia, Maryland, were built by large corporations. Our

After leaving Nazi Germany in the 1930s, Albert Einstein immigrated to the United States. Taking the oath of citizenship with him on October 1, 1940, are his secretary, Helen Dukas, and his daughter, Margot Einstein.

nation is now experiencing renewed interest in planned communities as a means of controlling urban growth. Consequently, the records that tell the story of the innovative greenbelt towns—the records of the Resettlement Administration which built them and the records of the Public Housing Administration which sold them—have also experienced renewed interest.

Communications are a binding force in American communities, and an area in which the federal government has initiated change. The Post Office system, for instance, providing the means for social as well as commercial correspondence, had its small beginnings in the Colonies. As early as 1672, a post road linked Boston and New York. Among the tasks allotted to the new Congress in the Constitution in 1787 was "to establish post offices and post roads." The responsibility rested with the Treasury from 1789 until Congress set up a Post Office Department in 1792.

From the beginning the Post Office preferred to move the mails by contract. In 1791 John K. Inskeep was paid $1,233.13 for delivering the mail five times a week between New York and Philadelphia. In later years the Department's contracts subsidized railroads, airlines, and the trucking industry.

Alexander Hamilton, first Secretary of the Treasury, in 1790 feared that the postal service would prove to be a drain on the nation's economy. In fact, as he reported to Congress, during the fourth quarter of 1789, the service had produced a deficit of $34.84. Hamilton's fears proved to be prophetic. Decade after decade, Post Office deficits and subsidies rose until the Post Office Department was abolished in 1970. In its stead, Congress established the U.S. Postal Service, an independent agency which, Congress hoped, would pay its own way.

Some of the most entertaining stories relate to the Air Mail Service, which began on May 15, 1918. Congress had appropriated $100,000 for the experiment, and the War Department furnished planes and pilots. According to the newspapers, a host of notables gathered at Washington's Polo Grounds that day to celebrate the first flight from Washington to Philadelphia. On hand were President and Mrs. Woodrow Wilson, Alexander

Above, left: Immigrants at the Angel Island hospital waiting for physical examinations in 1923.

Above, right: Ideally located next to the Federal Building in New York City, this shop, which caught the eye of a National Youth Administration photographer in 1939, probably did a brisk business during the height of the European migration to America following World War I.

Opposite: For Oriental immigrants, the usual port of entry was Angel Island near San Francisco. Because of Oriental exclusion laws, the San Francisco field office of the Immigration and Naturalization Service was kept busy investigating cases of illegal entry into the United States. These documents and photographs, including one of Angel Island, are from its files.

271

Among the original architectural drawings in the National Archives is this cabinet sketch of the Post Office in Fargo, North Dakota, found in the records of the Public Building Service.

Graham Bell, arctic explorer Admiral Robert Peary, and a young Assistant Secretary of the Navy, Franklin D. Roosevelt. What they witnessed was a fiasco. The pilot could not start his motor because the plane had no fuel. After gasoline was drained from other planes parked nearby, he took off only to land twenty-five miles away in a plowed field; he had lost his bearings and had flown south instead of north. Fortunately, other first-day flights were more successful. Mail was carried without mishap from New York to Philadelphia, Philadelphia to Washington, and Philadelphia to New York.

Within three years air mail service had been extended to San Francisco. Even flying only by daylight, air mail planes were able to beat the best times of the railroads by twenty-two hours. But it was night flying that enabled the air mail service to come of age.

The U.S. Post Office operated its own air mail system for ten years. During that time, it suffered forty-three fatalities. Most were pilots, but some were members of the ground crews.

Since many of the pilots experienced hair-breadth escapes during their careers, their flight reports make good reading. One of the briefest is by Pilot Dean Smith, whose engine went dead as he tried to land at the Iowa City airport in May 1923: "Dead sticked flying low—only place available [to

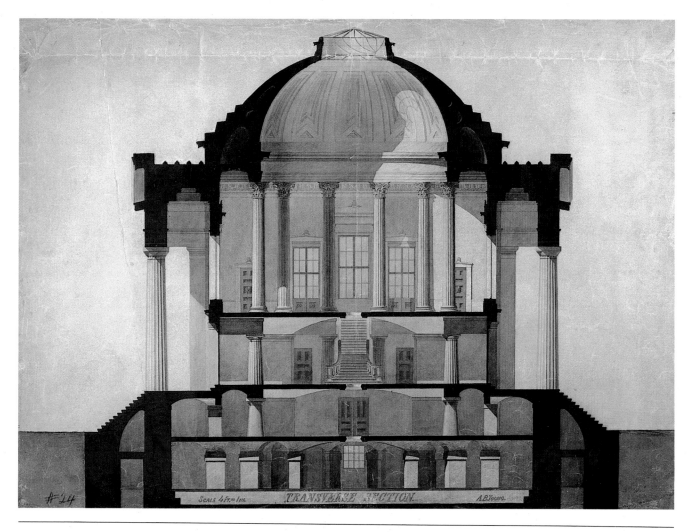

A transverse section of the Boston Customs House, designed by Ammi B. Young and built in 1835.

land] on cow. Killed cow—wrecked plane—scared me." The Post Office paid the farmer seventy-five dollars for his cow.

Pilot Tex Marshall, a former barnstormer, almost hit a tower as he landed at Omaha. He slipped sideways past the tower, ground-looped another one, then hopped over a steep embankment followed by an even higher bluff only to find a hangar in his path. He missed it by inches after a skidding, ground-looping stop that left him facing the direction from which he had approached the airport. The airport manager rushed over, his hand extended in welcome. "Mr. Marshall," he declared, "my name is Votaw and I want to tell you I have never seen anyone come so near hitting so many different things in such a short space of time and miss them all. I want to congratulate or sympathize with you. I do not know which."

The Post Office stopped flying its own planes in 1927. Thereafter, commercial airlines carried the mail under contract with the Department.

The transportation needs of the Post Office had in earlier days stimulated road building. President Thomas Jefferson took a personal interest in plans to construct a post road from Washington to New Orleans. At about the same time the rapid expansion of the population across the Appalachian Mountains created a demand for a National Road. Planned in 1800, this was finally built, after many false starts, from the head of the

273

C. and O. Canal, at Cumberland, Maryland, to Ohio and eventually as far as St. Louis. By the time it was completed, however, railroads and rivers offered easier and less expensive means to travel to the West. With the advent of the railroad, the idea of a national road system took a back seat for almost a century.

In 1893, prompted by increasing public demand for better roads, the Secretary of Agriculture created the Office of Road Inquiry. Its function was simply to collect and disseminate information on road building. Beginning with an initial budget of $10,000, this small office grew into the Bureau of Public Roads and its successor agencies, which have spent billions on constructing and maintaining our national highways.

Two reasons for renewed interest in good roads were the invention of the automobile and the need of farmers to get produce to urban markets. These, plus the realization during World War I that railroads were incapable of dealing with America's short haul needs, launched the nation on a massive road-building campaign. This frightened the railroads, which foresaw a threat to their own prosperity. As late as the 1930s, they tried to legislate a twenty-five-mile limit for cargo-carrying trucks. The railroads lost the battle and the trucking industry and the airlines came close to putting them out of business.

Finally, Congress concluded separate government agencies could not solve the problems created by the three-way competition between railroads, airlines, and trucks. In 1966, it set up the Department of Transportation to oversee all forms of transport of persons and goods around the country.

The federal government's role as a builder in American communities has included more than roads and post offices as the architectural holdings of the National Archives can testify. Rich in research value and visual appeal, they include complete sets of original presentation sketches and working drawings for all kinds of federal structures in small towns and large cities across the country: airports, bridges, customs houses, post office buildings, military fortifications and veterans' hospitals, as well as the major federal buildings in the city of Washington. Most of the original architectural

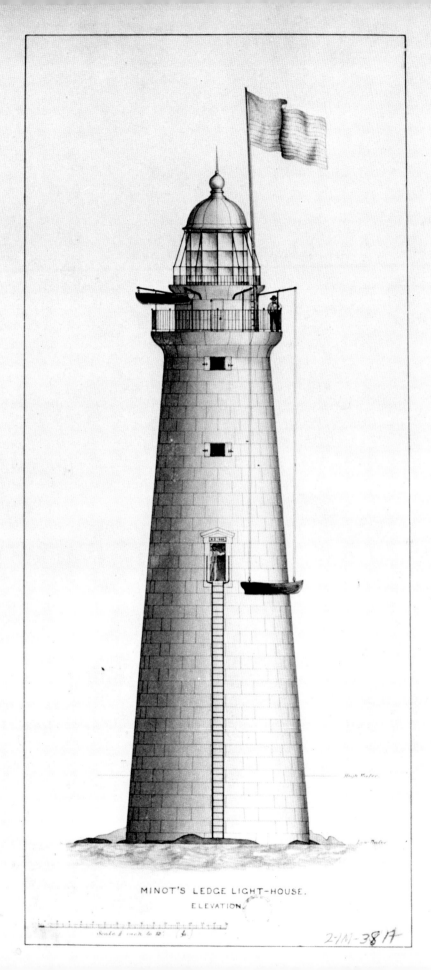

MINOT'S LEDGE LIGHT-HOUSE.

ELEVATION.

A sketch showing the method used to bring stone to the construction site of Minot's Ledge Light House.

Opposite: The plan of Minot's Ledge in Boston Harbor, from a survey made by the Corps of Engineers in June 1854.

drawings and engineering plans date from the 1800s because early in the twentieth century Congress decided to save space by disposing of the often oversized original drawings and keeping photographic copies instead. Superb watercolor renderings and pen-and-ink drawings survive, however. The distinguished architects and draughtsmen whose work is represented include Benjamin Latrobe, William Strickland, Robert Mills, Frederick Law Olmstead, and Andrew Jackson Downing, landscape architect of the White House and Capitol grounds.

The architectural drawings are more than visual delights; they also reveal much about our nation's architectural history.

Consider the customs house, where the eighteenth-century founders of the government expected that the major part of the national income would be collected. Dominating the waterfront skyline in each major seaport, the

Plan of outer rock of the Minot Ledge

from survey made under the direction of
Major C. A. Ogden, Corps of Engineers.
June 1854.

Note

The highest part of the rock is taken as the point of reference, and horizontal
curves are shown every 3 inches below this point.
The surface of the rock above the 1 foot curve is represented in yellow.
That between the 1 & 2 feet curves in red.
That   "   2 & 3   "   green.
That   "   3 & 3½   "   brown.
That below the 3½ feet curve in blue.
The large black circular spots represent the wrought iron piles, that
supported the light house which was destroyed by a violent gale a
few years ago. The smaller black spots are iron bolts that were
used in the construction of the work.
The brown lines represent fissures in the rock.
The blue line, or 3½ feet curve, represents mean low water, during the survey.
Extreme low water is about 2½ feet below this.

Scale, 1 inch to 2 feet

2-1M-A23

Within the image:

SUPERVISING ARCHITECT
TREASURY DEPARTMEN

— U S GOVERNMENT BUILDING —
— WORLD'S COLUMBIAN EXPOSITION. —

A perspective of the Government Building at the Columbian Exposition, Chicago, 1893.

customs house with unmistakeable shapes of dignity and grandeur was meant to express local pride and federal presence to the overseas visitor arriving in port.

Typical was the Boston Customs House, designed and built by Ammi B. Young between 1837 and 1847 of gray, fine-grained Quincy granite from the local quarries. The building was crowned with the first stone dome erected in the United States. Young's petition to travel to Europe to study dome building had been turned down; nevertheless, his drawings in the Archives show the overlapping of thin granite slabs covering the arching granite ribs of the dome in a method not used before in American buildings. The design Young created probably was responsible for his being named later as Supervising Architect of the Treasury Department.

The lighthouse is another federal structure important to seaport communities. These too, like the one constructed at Minot's Ledge, Massachusetts, could challenge the skills of the most competent federal engineers.

Minot's Ledge is the outermost of the Cohasset Rocks near the southeast entrance to Boston Harbor. Visible only at low tide in a calm sea, it claimed forty ships and forty lives between 1832 and 1841 alone. In 1843 the Lighthouse Service decided to place a light on the ledge. Instead of erecting a stone tower, however, the U.S. Topographical Bureau recommended plac-

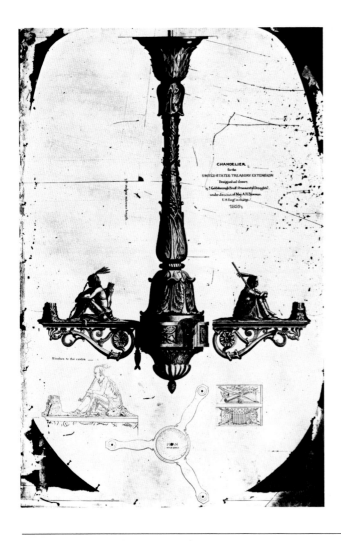

A full-size drawing for a cast metal chandelier installed in the Treasury Building.

ing the light on iron pilings, thinking that these would offer less resistance to the crashing seas. It was not a wise decision. As the first keeper, Isaac Dunham, noted in his log, rough seas made the lighthouse "reel like a Drunken sailor." After weathering a severe storm, he claimed the experience "would have frightened Daniel Webster." When his superiors ignored his warnings to strengthen the tower's braces, he resigned, effective October 7, 1843. Six months later a ferocious storm tore the lighthouse from its supports and cast it into the sea; the two assistant keepers on duty lost their lives.

The government rebuilt the tower, this time using stone. It was a remarkable feat of engineering since the foundation work could be done only in a dead calm sea during spring tides. Although work on the new tower began in 1855, it was two years before the first granite stone was laid. Altogether, construction required five years minus one day. But since its completion, the tower has withstood every assault from the sea. Even waves that sweep completely over the 114-foot tower cause little more than a strong vibration. Whatever threats the sea may offer, they pose no terror to station keepers because the tower has been unmanned since 1947. Perhaps "unmanned" is not quite accurate. Local watermen insist that the ghosts of the two assistant keepers have never left the Minot's Ledge Light.

B $2750.00

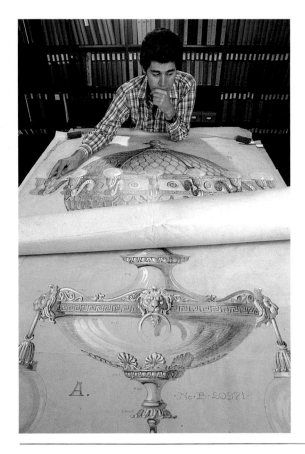

Not all federal buildings were granite monuments, of course. Those constructed for world's fairs and expositions often featured advanced designs, but were usually put together of plaster and board to facilitate demolition when the fairs closed. The Columbian Exposition of 1893 in Chicago, designed by Daniel H. Burnham and landscape architect Frederick Law Olmstead, was dubbed the "White City" because of its classically designed plaster facades, and also because it was lighted at night by electricity, still a wonder to many Americans of the time.

The fair demonstrated the great growth of the federal government and its "adaptations to the wants of the people." It took 368 freight cars to transport the government's exhibits. The Navy produced—in cement and brick—a full-sized replica of a battleship anchored in Lake Michigan. The Mint operated a press that stamped out commemorative medals. Visitors could send cards to the folks back home from a post office that also displayed methods of transporting the mail "now in use upon the frontier." The Lighthouse Board erected a hyper-radiant lens (112 people could stand in it) that was later placed in the Cape Hatteras Light.

As the records in the National Archives reveal, federal architecture was not necessarily plain and utilitarian. Richard von Ezdorf, an Austrian designer, brought to this country a number of talented artisans trained in Stuttgart who were employed on the decorating of the interior of the Old Executive Office Building, called "the wedding cake next to the White House." Built between 1871 and 1883, it once housed the State, War, and Navy Departments in their entirety. Its occupants now are members of the

A researcher examining a full-size drawing for a cast metal chandelier installed in the Denver Mint in 1904.

Opposite: The architectural records include detail drawings like this one, showing the design for the marble mosaic in the portico of the Executive Mansion (now called the White House).

White House staff.

Alfred B. Mullett, its architect and Supervising Architect of the Treasury Department at the time of its planning, believed that public buildings should have appropriate grandeur. The French Renaissance style, with its high ceilings and mansard roofs, appealed to his sense of monumentality. Von Ezdorf and his assistants provided the interior mural paintings, carved mantles, and beautiful hardware that gave the structure its elegant finish.

The National Archives Building itself, as mentioned earlier, was part of an ambitious construction project after World War I. In 1926 President Coolidge signed the act authorizing the planning and building of the Federal Triangle, a complex of twelve impressive structures which were to combine modern techniques with classic design, between Constitution and Pennsylvania Avenues in Washington, D.C. President Roosevelt expanded the federal building program during the Great Depression into the Public Works Administration, which helped communities build needed schools, hospitals, all kinds of facilities. The Works Progress Administration, considered primarily a jobs program, constructed badly needed highways, streets, bridges, and airports. It also hired artists and writers. The W.P.A. Arts Project put murals and sculptures in post offices and courthouses across the nation. Beside the P.W.A. and W.P.A., other "alphabet-soup" agencies, created to meet specific social needs, paid dividends in public works benefits. The C.C.C. (Civilian Conservation Corps) put nearly three million young men to work in reforestation and fire prevention. The T.V.A. (Tennessee Valley Authority) produced electric power and developed a flood control system for a large area of the Southeast.

Public programs did not stop with the New Deal, of course. Later administrations, both Democratic and Republican, have brought into being new approaches and agencies to serve the public welfare. There has been opposition, too, as we all know. Newly enacted services build bureaucracies, capture clients, generate opponents, wax and wane. In every case their fate can be traced at the National Archives and Presidential Libraries.

ACKNOWLEDGMENTS

The only treasures of the National Archives left unmentioned are the staff and docents who made this book possible. It was a team effort, and what a team!

My greatest debt goes to Pat Eames, the docent coordinator at the National Archives. Not only did she work closely with the volunteers, staff, and photographer, keeping everyone busy including me, but she also found time to research and pull together much of the material relating to the land, cartographic, and architectural records.

Another docent to whom I am indebted is Ann Von Storch, who took my very rough drafts and produced sensible text and captions. She discovered the existence of Thaddeus, the Archives ghost, and contributed greatly to the organization and ideas in several sections of the book, notably the Prologue and General Welfare chapters.

Special thanks go to Ruth Rose, who suggested to me that the docents would be eager and able assistants in this herculean effort and who contributed material on the Perry Expedition to Japan.

I am also very grateful to these docents who contributed their time, talents, and energy to the project: Kay Ingalls, genealogy; June Robinson, Port Angeles and John S. Mosby; Howard Oiseth, diplomatic and military records, particularly the stories about the sea letters, the Great Seal, famous authors, and the Battle of Belleau Wood, and captions; Howard Bennett, postal records; Ken Baker, shipping, Minot's Ledge Light House, and Coast Guard records; Christine Urban, the Constitutional Convention, woman suffrage, and Black families in Kansas; Jean Preer and Linda Simmons, Black history and women's history; Malcolm Smith, the presidency; Al Davidson, Lew Wallace; Rosemary Kayser, motion picture collections; Caroline Flaccus, research assistance; Mimi Cullison, the Navy and Coast Guard records and anything else that needed doing; Cynda Wilcox, letters of credence and the history of the National Archives; Lynn Murphy, the War of 1812; Renee Cooper, genealogy. Manes Specter found the story about the Seminoles and the Shakespearean company; Bill Eames provided the material on Idaho in the territorial period; Kristin Eames did research on Lt. Reilly's ring.

National Archives staff members who assisted me in this project include Stacy Bredhoff, Robert Brookhart, Roger A. Bruns, John F. Butler, Stuart L. Butler, James B. Byers, John E. Byrne, George C. Chalou, Jerry L. Clark, Richard C. Crawford, John A. Dwyer III, Elaine C. Everly, Jeanne C. Elderkin, John Fawcett, Robert H. Fowler, Sharon L. Gibbs, Daniel T. Goggin, Milton O. Gustafson, Kenneth R. Hall, Janet L. Hargett, Kenneth Harris, Dane J. Hartgrove, Renee M. Jaussaud, Lee R. Johnson, Sara D. Jackson, Robert M. Kvasnicka, Jane Lange, William E. Lind, Clarence F. Lyons, Nancy Malan, Caryl Marsh, Robert B. Matchette, Teresa F. Matchette, R. Michael McReynolds, John Mendelsohn, Jill Merrill, James W. Moore, William T. Murphy, Michael P. Musick, Richard F. Myers, Timothy K. Nenninger, Trudy H. Peterson, Geraldine Phillips, Dorothy S. Provine, Virginia C. Purdy, Leonard Rapport, Robert E. Richardson, George N. Scaboo, Aloha South, Charles South, Emily Soapes, Ronald E. Swerczek, Charles E. Taylor, Joe Thomas, David S. Van Tassel, Timothy Vitale, Robert M. Warner, Howard H. Wehmann, Edward Weldon, Alison Wilson, and Mary A. Zimmerman.

I am also grateful to the following students in the School of Library Science who did research on specific topics: Jutsie Carter, Sharon D. Galperin, Philip George, Paulette A. Jew, Elizabeth Kirwin, Nancy Mason, Alyce Mears, Kathy Moignard, Mary Catherine Schall, Marianne M. Withers.

The work of providing the illustrations for this book also required the assistance of many people. Jon Wallen took more than 150 original color and black-and-white photographs, often under severe constraints that tested his ingenuity and creativity. He was assisted by Shawn Brunton, Kimberly Passarella, and Paul F. Viola. The remaining photographs were made from existing negatives in the custody of the National Archives. What could have been a logistical nightmare went without a hitch thanks to the wonderful cooperation of picture archivist Ed McCarter and the concern of Bobbye C. West, whose technicians in the photo lab consistently provided prints of remarkable clarity and excellent quality.

Thanks are also due to Jan S. Danis, who helped edit the manuscript; to Ralph E. Ehrenberg and Ron Grim, who generously shared with me their extensive knowledge of the cartographic holdings of the National Archives; and to David McCullough, for his kind Introduction.

Working with the staff of Abrams was a real pleasure. I was especially fortunate to have the friendship and guidance of Senior Editor Edith Pavese, while the book itself is a testament to the design skills of Patrick Cunningham.

Finally, I wish to thank my wife, Susan, and my sons, Joe, Paul, and Peter, who encouraged me to tackle this massive project.

BIBLIOGRAPHY

Important as the records in the National Archives are to writing of American history, they very seldom tell the complete story. Therefore, it is necessary to use a variety of sources not to be found in federal records, such as newspapers, diaries, personal correspondence, as well as published books on a topic. In writing this book about the National Archives, I have had to rely on a number of secondary sources. The most useful are listed below.

PUBLISHED

Armstrong, Ellis L., ed. *History of Public Works in the United States, 1776–1976.* Chicago, 1976.

Bahmer, Robert H. "The National Archives After 20 Years." *The American Archivist,* XVIII, July 1955, 195–205.

Bailey, Thomas A. *Presidential Greatness: The Image and the Man from George Washington to the Present.* New York, 1966.

Bloom, John P., ed. *The American Territorial System.* Washington, D.C., 1969.

Brown, Joan Sayers. "Skippets." *Antiques* (July 1978).

[Bruns, Roger]. *A More Perfect Union: The Creation of the United States Constitution.* Washington, D.C., 1978.

Carroll, Kieran J. "Sources for Genealogical Research in State Department Records." *National Genealogical Quarterly* (Dec. 1964), Vol. 52, No. 4, 189–198.

Conant, James B. *My Several Lives: Memoirs of a Social Inventor.* New York.

Cunningham, Isabel. *Frank N. Meyer: Plant Hunter in Asia.* Ames, 1984.

Dollar, Charles M. "Computers, the National Archives, and Reseachers." *Prologue* (Spring 1976), 29–34.

Ehrenberg, Ralph E. "Cartographic Records in the National Archives." *National Genealogical Quarterly* (June 1976), 64: 83–111.

———. "Taking the Measure of the Land." *Prologue* (Fall 1977), IX, 128–150.

Farrand, Max. *The Framing of the Constitution of the United States.* New Haven, 1913.

Ferris, Robert G., ed. *The Presidents from the Inauguration of George Washington to the Inauguration of Jimmy Carter: Historic Places Commemorating the Chief Executives of the United States.* Vol. 20, *National Survey of Historic Sites and Buildings.* Washington, D.C., 1977.

Foster, John. *American Diplomacy in the Orient.* Boston, 1903.

Groueff, Stephane. *Manhattan Project: The Untold Story of the Making of the Atomic Bomb.* Boston, 1967.

Gustafson, Milton O. "The Empty Shrine: The Transfer of the Declaration of Independence and the Constitution to the National Archives." *The American Archivist,* Vol. 39, No. 3, July 1976, 271–285.

Holland, Francis Ross, Jr. *America's Lighthouses: Their Illustrated History Since 1716.* Brattleboro, Vt., 1972.

Holland, Rupert Sargent. *Historic Ships.* Philadelphia, 1926.

MacCann, Richard Dyer. *The People's Films: A Political History of U.S. Government Motion Pictures.* New York, 1973.

Murphy, William T. "The Method of *Why We Fight.*" *The Journal of Popular Film,* 1:3 (Summer 1972), 185–196.

———. "John Ford and the Wartime Documentary." *Film & History,* VI:1 (February 1976), 1–8.

[National Archives]. *The Declaration of Independence: The Adventures of a Document.* Washington, D.C., 1976.

Nenninger, Timothy K. "The National Archives as a Source for Aviation History." Aviation History Writers Conference, Dayton, Ohio. October 9, 1982.

O'Neill, James E. "Will Success Spoil the Presidential Libraries?" *The American Archivist,* July 1973, 351.

Patterson, Richard S. "The Old Treaty Seal of the United States." *The American Foreign Service Journal.* Vol. 26, No. 3, March 1949, 4–16, 44.

Purdy, Virginia Cardwell. "The Arts of Diplomacy." *American Heritage: The Magazine of History,* XXV, Feb. 1974, No. 2, 25–31, 89–91.

Reingold, Nathan. "The National Archives and the History of Science in America." *ISIS,* Vol. 46, Part 1. No. 143, March 1955, 22–28.

Rhoads, James B. "The Fort Snelling Area in 1835, A Contemporary Map." *Minnesota History.* March 1956, 22–29.

[Schwartz, Eleanor]. *The United States Passport: Past, Present, Future.* Passport Office, Department of State, 1976.

Schwartz, Seymour I., and Ehrenberg, Ralph E. *The Mapping of America.* New York, 1980.

Shelley, Fred. "Jameson in the National Archives: 1908–1934." *American Archivist.*

Smith, Jane F. "The Use of Federal Records in Writing Local History: A Case Study." *Prologue* (Spring 1969), I, 29–52.

Snyder, Robert L. *Pare Lorentz and the Documentary Film.* Norman, 1968.

Stewart, William J., and Pollard, Charyl C. "Franklin D. Roosevelt, Collector." *Prologue* (Winter 1969) I, 13–28.

Stuart, Graham. *American Diplomatic and Consular Practice.* New York, 1936.

U.S. Department of Commerce, U.S. Patent and Trade Mark Office. *The Story of the U.S. Patent and Trade Mark Office.* Washington, 1981.

U.S. Department of Interior. *Franklin D. Roosevelt and Hyde Park: Personal Recollections of Eleanor Roosevelt.* n.d., Washington, D.C.

U.S. Department of State, *A Short History of the U.S. Department of State, 1781–1981.* Washington, D.C., 1981.

Wehman, Howard H., and Fabian, Monroe H. "Pennsylvania German Fraktur: Folk Art in the National Archives." *Prologue* (Fall 1970), 2:96–97.

SEMINAR PAPERS

Papers prepared under the direction of the author for graduate seminar, "Research Seminar in the Use of Archival Resources," School of Library Science, The Catholic University of America.

Carter, Jutsie. "A Woman's War, A Woman's Fight." 1981.

Cullison, Mimi. "Revenue Cutter to the Rescue." 1982.

Eames, Pat. "Lucy's Chimney Sweep: The Pattern of a New England Town." 1982.

Galperin, Sharon D. "Listen. It's Still Ringing!" 1981.

George, Philip. "Uncle Sam Wants You! Artists Enlisted for Two World Wars." 1981.

Ingalls, Kay. "Culture Clash: A Utah Episode." 1982.

Jew, Paulette A. "Ben Shahn and the Bronx Central Station Mural." 1982.

Kirwin, Elizabeth. "The Public Works of Art Project in New York City: Problems and Protests." 1982.

Mason, Nancy. "The United War Work Campaign: An Exercise in Ecumenical Cooperation." 1982.

Mears, Alyce. "An American Hero." 1981.

Moignard, Kathy. "Operations of the Office of War Information in Australia." 1982.

Robinson, June. "John S. Mosby: A Confederate Ranger on the China Coast." 1982.

Schall, Mary Catherine. "The Alaskan Gold Rush of 1898." 1981.

Withers, Marianne M. "Arrangement and Description in the National Archives: RG 78, Records of the Naval Observatory." 1981.

Index

Photo Sources

The following citations are to the maps, patent drawings, and architectural drawings that are illustrated in this book as well as those photographs for which the National Archives has copy negatives. Anyone interested in purchasing reproductions of any of these illustrations should write to the National Archives and Records Service, Special Archives Division (NNS), Washington, D.C. 20408. The other illustrations were prepared by the publisher and are the property of Harry N. Abrams, Inc., Publishers, 100 Fifth Avenue, New York, N.Y. 10011. Inquiries about documents reproduced as illustrations should be directed to the National Archives and Records Service, Reference Service Branch (NNIR), Washington, D.C. 20408.

P. 29, 64-NA-76; P. 31, 79-JAG-9; P. 33; *left,* 121-BD-54M, *right,* 121-BC-9A; P. 40, 64-NAD-48; P. 41, *above left,* 64-NAD-133, *right,* 64-NAD-63; P. 42, *left,* 64-NA-1472; *right,* RG 42: NA Bldg. (Pope); P. 43, 83-G-3138A; P. 44, RG 42: NA Bldg., Lobby; P. 45, 121-BCP-111C-95; P. 48, 64-NAC-207; P. 49, *left,* 121-BC-111A-86; *right,* 121-BCP112A-4; P. 52, 64-NA-399; P. 74, 64-NA-1-434; P. 78, Droodles, Kennedy Library; P. 79, 111-B-3488; P. 83, 111-B-3658; P. 84, 64-NA-6177; P. 85, 165-SB-23; P. 86, 111-B-4669; P. 88, NPX48-22:79; Roosevelt Library; P. 89, Truman and MacArthur, 67-435, Truman Library; P. 91, NPX73-36(1), Roosevelt Library; P. 94, *above left,* 165-WW-44-7B-10; *above right,* 111-SC-91405; *below,* 111-B-4823; P. 95, *left,* Kennedy Library, *right,* NPX56-577, Roosevelt Library; P. 98, 306-PS-61-12992; P. 104, Lawmen, 111-SC-94129; P. 105, 111-SC-93343; P. 110, 111-BA-1084; P. 116, 19-N-9885; P. 120, 111-BA-1515; P. 121, Hawthorne, 111-B-6207; P. 124, Lowell, 111-BA-1077; Irving, 111-B-4144; P. 126, 57-HS-692; P. 128, RG 75: Map 540; P. 129, *left,* 111-B-5865, *right,* RG 75: Map 821; P. 132, 111-SC-95986; P. 133, 49-AR-32; P. 134, RG 49: Seven Ranges, T5, R2; P. 135, RG 49: Disenos, v 1, P. 32; P. 136, 111-AGD-44; P. 137; *left,* 48-RST-7B-34, *right,* 48-RST-7B-28; P. 138, 69-N-13606C, 69-N-195-19C; P. 139, RG 76: Alden Sketches *(above)* 55, *(below)* 15; P. 140, 57-HS-52; P. 141, 57-HS-134; P. 142, *above,* RG 77: Misc. 120, no. 5; *below,* RG 76: Series 11; P. 144, 115-JAF-604; P. 145, 115-JAF-401; P. 146, RG 76: Series 11; P. 148, 115-JAF-384; P. 149, 115-JAA-2168; P. 160, RG 77: F 63; P. 161, 165-SB-94; P. 163, RG 49: ALA, Huntsville Mer, T5E, R4S; P. 164, RG 46: 26A-F6; P. 178, 208-EX-206(3); P. 182, 79-AAT-23; P. 183, 79-AAQ-1; P. 184, 79-HPA-106; P. 185, 245-MS-1942L; P. 186, 208-EX-206(33); P. 187, 208-EX-206(30); P. 188, *above,* 208-EX-206(2), *below,* 208-EX-206(52); P. 189, 208-EX-206(50); P. 190, 111-B-1769; P. 191, 65-327-2, Eisenhower Library; P. 194, 181-WM-1A-1019; P. 195, 208-PP-15M-1; P. 196, RG 77: US 529; P. 197, RG 76: Series 29; P. 200, RG 121: Scranton, PA, Coal Mine no. 2000; P. 203, RG 23: Spec. Whistler Drawing; P. 204, RG 241: 72X; P. 207, RG 241: 5834-X; P. 208, RG 241: 6490X; P. 210, RG 241: 657X; P. 211, RG 24: 1963X; P. 212, Clemens, 200S-FL-6; P. 222, 111-SC-19571; P. 223, Class, 111-SC-11499; P. 231, *above,* 165-SC-40; *below,* 165-SB-41; P. 235, 111-B-2078; P. 236, RG 77: Q288-3; P. 238, 111-SC-2112; P. 240, Marinettes, 165-WW-600C-3; P. 241, 165-WW-600D-5; P. 242, 94-X-Z; P. 244, *left,* 80-G-390608, *right,* 80-G-470985; P. 248, *left,* 44PA188, *right,* 44PA99; P. 249, *left,* 44PA1514, *right,* 44PA2244; P. 251, 19-N-13360; P. 257, 210-G2-A6; P. 260, 165-WW-600A-Z; P. 261, Letter, 64-NA-7207, volunteers, 165-WW-600A-1, suffragettes 165-WW-600A-3; P. 262, *left,* 306-NT-167452C, *right,* RG 241: D-2325; P. 263, Simon Crow, RG 24: D-1897; P. 264, 102-LH-1780; P. 265, 102-LH-488; 102-LH-1756; 102-LH-358; P. 269, 208-PV-58G-1; P. 271, *left,* 90-G-124-10, *right,* 119-C-82M-5; P. 272, RG 121: Fargo, N.D., P.O.; P. 273, RG 121: Massachusetts, Boston Customs House; P. 275, RG 26: Dist. 2, 20-48; P. 276, RG 26: Dist. 2, 20-7; P. 277, RG 26: Dist. 2, 20-69; P. 279, 121-BC-13D; P. 280, RG 79: 14.1-142.

Thursday 26

Latt 5 19 N cro...

& large
...3.09 by
of whales going west

Friday y 27

Latt 5 N 27 cr...